My Culture, My Color, My Self

Toby S. Jenkins

My Culture, My Color, My Self

Heritage, Resilience, and Community
in the Lives of Young Adults

TEMPLE UNIVERSITY PRESS
PHILADELPHIA

TEMPLE UNIVERSITY PRESS
Philadelphia, Pennsylvania 19122
www.temple.edu/tempress

Library of Congress Cataloging-in-Publication Data

Jenkins, Toby S. (Toby Susann), 1975–
  My culture, my color, my self : heritage, resilience, and community in
the lives of young adults / Toby S. Jenkins.
      p. cm.
  Includes bibliographical references and index.
  ISBN 978-1-4399-0829-7 (cloth : alk. paper) — ISBN 978-1-4399-0830-3
(pbk. : alk. paper) — ISBN 978-1-4399-0831-0 (e-book) 1. African
American youth—History. 2. African Americans—History. I. Title.
  E185.86.J46 2013
  305.896'0730842—dc23
                                                              2012025883

♾ The paper used in this publication meets the requirements of the
American National Standard for Information Sciences—Permanence of
Paper for Printed Library Materials, ANSI Z39.48-1992

Printed in the United States of America

2 4 6 8 9 7 5 3 1

To my mother and father

for building a beautiful and rich cultural world for us

Contents

Acknowledgments

What is most special about my professional journey and appreciation of culture is that both were motivated by the imaginative talents of my ancestors—storytellers whose creativity saw neither pen nor paper and whose wonderful cultural talents never entered the doors of a bookstore or the halls of the academy. Instead, they fed generations of young children in our family. My grandpa Joe was a wonderful storyteller and poet. He traveled to churches around the state of South Carolina speaking to congregations through story. His daughter, my mother, inherited this literary creativity, writing poems and telling her children and grandchildren the most imaginative stories. My mother has always desired to write and to publish. For this reason my professional work embodies the spirit of Alice Walker's great insight in her legendary text "In Search of Our Mothers' Gardens." Walker discusses how the immense artistic and literary talents of many black women were repressed through the years by relegating the women to domestic labor and support roles. According to Walker, many of these women chose as their canvas the only mediums they had available to them—gardens, quilts, dinner tables, and clothes. My mother is an incredible gardener and sewer. My grandma Sue was a chef in her own right—we preferred her food to that of any fancy restaurant. I am my great-grandmother Suzanna's namesake. I will always write my name with my middle initial in memory of her spirit. She was an amazing baker. These women made magic and beauty out of dirt, cloth, and grains. But deep inside they were all artists—painters, writers, and singers. This book, and everything that I have done in my work as an educator, is more than research and professional production. I have found all of my mothers' gardens. My family was a modest one, unable to leave a significant financial inheritance. But what my ancestors have passed down through the years is an inherited creativity that I am so pleased to share with the world. I write because they taught me how to make words dance. Through this work, I remember all of those who made me—known and unknown. I thank them for both their brilliance and their tenacity for survival. Through me, they are free.

I thank all of my family and friends for their continued support in everything that I do in my life—especially my immediate family, which includes my sister, Greta (who has always been my biggest cheerleader); my nieces, Breanna and Britney; my nephew, Jaden; my brother-in-law, Billy; my aunt, Susan; and most of all my parents, Joyce and Bennie. In addition, I owe much gratitude to Dr. Dana Mitra, Dr. Gerald LeTendra, Dr. Shaun Harper, and Dr. Peggy Lorah for serving as supportive and joyful guides. Thanks go to my friends for their constant words of encouragement, for simply asking at times how the writing was going, for "liking" my comments on Facebook whenever I talked about this project, and for coming to all of my dinner parties, which fed into many of the insights in this book—all of which kept me writing: LaQuetta Ruston, Jennifer Dunlap, Crystal Endsley, Tony Keith, Marla Jaksch, Erlisa King, Christine Lawrence, Karen James, Nicole Jackson, Michelle Armstead, Peggy Rose, Jin Grant, Will Johnson, Sandy Frank, and William Henry. I also want to reach far back into my past and thank those incredible teachers who have made this career possible for me, since we often acknowledge those who surround us in the present and forget those who started us on our journey. My high school English teacher, Mr. Robbie Grice, made us write extemporaneously every day for thirty minutes. He would just throw out a topic, and we had to write—and write well. He was training us for the Advanced Placement English exam, but in the process he cultivated some pretty incredible writers. He taught us how to write with creativity and without hesitation. I think all of us placed out of freshman English because of him. In college, I took a creative writing class for which I chose to write a paper that compared three lives: my mother's, my grandmother's, and my own. That paper has stayed with me throughout my life. It found its way into my graduate courses, and it was the foundation for the Prologue to this book. This is the model of personally meaningful and transformative education that I strive to create for the students I now teach—to give students experiences at age eighteen that still remain with them at age thirty-six.

I have used the names of some of my dear friends and family members throughout this book in place of the actual names of some of the students who participated in this study. I should note, therefore, that where I have used my friends' names, the accompanying text is not their lives, their words, or their stories.

Prologue

My Culture, My Color, My Self

Nineteen years ago, as a young African American college woman, I began what was to become a significant cultural journey. College came to serve as an extension of a life filled with cultural growth and learning. It was almost impossible to imagine life without the rituals, activities, and values that had come to frame my existence from a very young age. But what was different about my cultural experiences in college was that, for the first time, they were coupled with deep intellectual engagement. I was not only being exposed to information about my culture; I was also being asked to write about it, reflect on it, and recreate it for my college peers. As is the case for many current college students of color, the college experience became an innate part of my personal story—one chapter in my journey of cultural growth that served to shape and influence the person I was to become. But this journey began with my family.

My family is made of three generations of black people, all shaped by the era in which they lived: colored, Negro, and African American. I do not mean something as simple as what we call ourselves. No one in my family has ever referred to himself or herself as "colored" or "Negro." What I am talking about is a mindset, a social outlook on the world that is influenced and shaped by certain time periods in our nation's history. The bottom line is that the three living generations of my family came of age in very different worlds. And we all continue to live in our own era. My grandmother continues to live in a colored past—though, at ninety, she has survived to see a new millennium. Her beliefs are the same, her house remains the same, and even her meals resist today's fast-food form of dining. Similarly, my mother still holds on to beliefs born in a past of perceptions of racial inferiority; evidence of her beliefs appears when her voice changes while talking to a white person or, in many cases, even to an educated black person. I have never lived the life of a colored girl or a Negro one, but because my mother and grandmother still hold on to those times, I have always been exposed to the culture of a "colored" or "Negro" yesterday.

At some point in my childhood, I started going to my grandmother's house during the day. Her house was my six-hour entrance into a colored world. The morning actually started with the rooster's call at daybreak. Soon after the ring of nature's alarm clock, Grandma's kitchen was filled with the peppery scents of fried liver pudding and grits. In her neighborhood, we did not play with any white children; in fact, we never saw children of other races. This was a common community experience among black folks of modest means in South Carolina. Their lives were, literally, full of color, and there was a sense of both physical and psychological safety in that fact. Rather than involving being bruised by the blows of racism or becoming frustrated and tired by the stresses of knocking down walls and breaking glass ceilings, having a "colored" existence meant largely appreciating the loveliness and bountifulness of blackness. Though this type of passive acceptance is unimaginable in a contemporary world, I still appreciate the bits of value that I have extracted from our "colored" past.

When we were at Grandma's, my cousin Pedro and I played in the old tool shed, or sometimes we would dare to go mess with the dirty, screaming chickens. Then we made our way back to the house to eat dinner with the family. Many days Aunt Susan, Aunt Elsie, or Uncle Jerome would join us. And what was cooking? Stewed chicken, mashed potatoes, fried onions, June peas, and gravy to pour over it all. Afterward, the adults would sit and talk in the dimly lit "back room" or out on the screened-in porch. I don't remember what they talked about; all I know is that they had good times, and it seemed like it always ended in a prayer meeting. I'm sure this wasn't a daily routine, but this is how the memories of my childhood come together to form a story of my past. Those early morning breakfasts, playtime with the old farming tools, southern dinners, hearty laughter and conversation, and strong religious practices provided my first insight into "colored' culture, which provided the foundation upon which I could build my life with confidence.

Just as my grandparents' "colored" faith serves as the frame for my confidence, my parents' "Negro" determination supports my motivation to succeed. Being Negro meant working hard and wanting more. My father worked three jobs for more than thirty years. Many days he would leave at 4:00 P.M. and work continuously until 7:00 the next morning. As I reflect on my life, I realize that I was taught my work ethic not by a school or an employer but by the professional model that my father provided. How can I refrain from working hard when my father has worked three times as hard to provide the opportunities that I have today? My parents and their siblings worked to advance the family both socially and economically. They all moved away from a largely rural life environment into cities near and far. Despite coming of age in a separate and unequal experience, they all advanced the family's educational and professional achievement. They graduated from high school, worked the jobs that were available, bought homes, and saved. But they still wanted more for their children. And they got it.

The major difference between my parents' education and my own is that I have always been told that I was superior, whereas the members of my parents' generation were constantly told that they were inferior. Though, within my familial community, loving black peers and elders surrounded me, my educational experiences have been largely white and my professional experiences significantly multicultural. For as long as I can remember, I have been labeled "academically advanced" and have been thrown like a dark pebble into crystal clear waters. When I began kindergarten, I took reading and writing classes with the first grade. After a few months, the school suggested that I skip kindergarten altogether. Skipping a grade in school was probably my first achievement. From there I went on to academically advanced classes and all A's at each report period. Each year, when we took the CTBS and BSAP standardized tests (the Comprehensive Tests of Basic Skills and the Basic Skills Assessment Program Exit Examinations), I scored in the 99th percentile, or higher than 99 percent of students throughout the country. The first time I took the SATs was in the sixth grade; my scores qualified me for college. When I eventually entered the university, I spent all four years in the Honors College. I have no personal experience of what it's like to be treated as if I were not capable. After sixteen years of being told I was smart, my intellectual self-confidence was pretty strong. But I am aware that in both our past and present society too many black children know that feeling of educational exclusion all too well. For my parents, who graduated from a segregated school system, my educational experience seemed amazing. They were always encouraging me. Their pride was apparent as they sat at the open house nights side by side with white parents, whom they would not have been permitted to even look at or talk to twenty-five years earlier. They were finally equal. As a young black child, I understood very early the meaning of my achievements. When I won the spelling bee, scored in the 99th percentile, made the principal's list, or started receiving recruitment letters from Ivy League colleges in the seventh grade, I knew that I was spelling, testing, studying, and achieving for my Negro parents, who had not had that chance. And so I fully embrace and take advantage of all that being a free and educated person involves. Why shouldn't I? My family has already paid for it in so many ways.

School-based education comes easily for me, and so I see it as simply a foundation. I appreciate my formal education. I just don't privilege it. My more broad, deep, and meaningful learning has been a result of self-education—reading books, watching documentaries, traveling for educational purposes to more than thirty countries, learning from community leaders and activists, hearing the stories of people's lives, and consuming some incredible forms of art. This comment reminds me of a statement that Carter G. Woodson once made about education: "Philosophers have long conceded . . . that every man has two educations: that which is given to him, and that which he gives himself. Of the two kinds the latter is by far the more desirable. Indeed all that is most worthy in man he must work out and conquer for himself. It is that which constitutes our real and best nourishment. What we are merely taught seldom nourishes the mind like that which we teach ourselves" (1977, 126).

Yes, indeed. There are some things about the past that I will never understand. I cannot imagine taking a bath in a tin tub in the middle of the floor as my mother did growing up. Nor can I imagine living without my own television as my grandmother did. Whereas both my mother and grandmother grew up in houses where only gospel music was allowed, I have always been permitted to play the music of my choice. Hip-hop music would never have been tolerated in Grandma's house, and yet it frames much of my self-identity. In a lot of ways, my generation is now above living the humble lives of our grandparents. We are removed from the days of outhouses and entertainment from radio stories and family talent shows. Some of us have forgotten the importance of spending time with one another, breaking bread together, and the simple joys that come from activities like family conversation and storytelling. Many uneducated black grandmothers and grandfathers taught us to tell a good story on a porch or a stoop. They served as the catalyst for great writers like Richard Wright, Zora Neale Hurston, and Toni Morrison.

Colored traditions have followed me throughout my life. Through God, colored people found the acceptance that they were not given by the world. Though I am now much more spiritual than religious, I would still experience this strong faith in my grandmother's fifteen-minute grace or whenever she brought out the small brown bottle of anointment oil and painted a greasy cross on my forehead before she let me leave. The strong whispers of "Amen" and "Yes, Jesus," "Thank you, Lord" and "Hallelujah" have always arisen from the circle that my family forms as they pray. In my parents' home, we must pray together before going on trips, taking exams, and applying for jobs. Every time I drive out of my mother's yard, I see her standing in the kitchen window waving her right hand in the air as she asks the Lord to watch over me.

I cannot help but appreciate all these experiences. Although I would not feel right saying, "Hush yo' mout'," or laughing those big, healthy laughs that have always filled my parents' home, my mother probably would not feel comfortable holding them in. I can feel the passion in those laughs and the richness of those expressions, but my educational experience took me away from their use. Those laughs and conversations make me feel at home. When I am home and I hear my mother and her friends talking and laughing as loud as loud gets, I know that this is where I belong. Even now, when I come to work at the university and hear my students laughing and talking hard and loud, I remember home. All of the elements that made my grandmother colored and my mother Negro make me African American. Only powerful feelings could allow me to perceive the defiance of the Afro that I never wore. In our "colored" past, our pride kept us from even wanting to go where we were not welcome. Still, our "Negro" era was marked by a stubborn determination not to be denied what we knew we deserved. One of the most important gifts my mother brought from her Negro past was a satisfaction with and an appreciation of our culture. To her, our culture is not lacking—it is more than enough. In fact, it is all we really need. She has taught me that being African American is not a title—it is not merely what you are called; it is what you are. Whether the accepted term in society is "colored," "Negro," or "African American," we should feel comfort and pride in the African culture and history that it includes.

Thanks to my parents' Negro beliefs, I am strongly committed to making an effort to learn those aspects of myself that have been denied in my education. How can a people with no connection to their past, who cannot trace their point of origin, feel stable in a society that gives them a new label every few decades? The quintessential question of a young African American is "Who am I?" I have traveled to several African countries, and I have been treated and have felt like a foreigner, more American than African. Africa is undoubtedly deep in our blood and, for many of us, in our hearts and spirits. As an African American community we hold fast to our roots, which are planted in the African soil that many of us can't even afford to touch. And for those who do make the sojourn, the economic realities of colonialism's lasting oppressive hold on many African communities makes the dollar that we represent much more meaningful than our black skin, even if we are called "cousin" when we are approached for money. And within some, not all, privileged communities in Africa, it is the distorted and stereotypical media images of African Americans that our country sells to the world that frame the lack of respect that can be seen in the eyes of Africans. But, yes, we have much to share and much to learn about one another—we are both distant and foreign cousins, partial and perfect strangers. And that is the truth, regardless of how hard and unromantic it is to hear. The question "Who am I" for the African American is a hard one; in many ways, we are on the outskirts of both societies—African and American—that we claim in our name. Learning my family's history changed me in some way. The more I clearly visualized the struggles of not just the race but also my own mothers and grandmothers, fathers and uncles, the more I was able to find my place in moving that foundation forward.

I have, through the years, absorbed books and learned about the historical, political, and socioeconomic events that affect populations of people throughout the world. I think the family rituals of watching *Eyes on the Prize*, *Roots*, and Black History Month PBS specials as a child motivated this knowledge in some way. I have, in my career, picked up in learning about my culture where my family's storytelling left off. And I know that I am where I am right now because I believe in my mother's idea that something was lost in desegregation—something that you can't get from any white restaurant or store and something that many educational institutions continue to struggle with today. It is a spirit, a pride, and an ethic of love that can be given only through cultural heritage. And giving this gift to my community through education is what I have vowed to do with my life.

As my community's daughter, my sense of cultural responsibility is strong. It resonates in all that I have become and in all that I do. It flows through every form of expression, including my poetry:

The needy
Aren't some distant image
A black and white snapshot,
A 30 second media spot
They are my community . . . some are in my own family
I don't need to search to find the poor; they come through my back door
For every family gathering . . .
Serving for me isn't always about helping someone else . . .
My family needs help . . . my people need some self
Motivation—economic elevation—judicial representation . . .
I need to take my education and feed the foundation
Of my little block . . . I need to push so hard my ideas stir and rock
The soul of the neighborhood . . .
I need to transform it and make suburbanites wish they could
Live the same . . .
Make my students reexamine their professional aims
It's not okay to search for a success that looks like anything opposite of from
    whence you came . . .
Being so pressed to get away that you'll change
Address, phone and name . . . to get on the first plane . . .
The hell out of the hood
If we don't care about our own block, please tell me who should?
Who should work harder than me? Who should be the constant gardener
    but me?
Planting the seeds of change . . . pulling the weeds of pain
Giving it light and water
through cash flow, education and improved bricks and mortar . . .
Assuming my role as the community's daughter . . .

I am armed with the choices and the confidence that make me African American because I carry inside the colored pride and the Negro will that is the *essence* of my culture.

What Culture Means to Me

For me, culture has always been much more of a life foundation than a collection of rituals, symbolic practices, and artistic expression. Culture is the mental strength and confidence that allows me to look in the mirror and love my black skin. My healthy and positive sense of self is undoubtedly an appreciation for the culture that I represent—I love being an African American woman.

I am energized by the audacity, strength, sassiness, humility, and diligence that being an African American woman embodies.

Through traveling, learning, and worshipping in many houses of God, I know that the soulful and deeply spiritual belief in a higher being is cultural. I have felt as much at home in mosques in Turkey, Orisha Yards in Trinidad, temples in Egypt, and Hindu shrines as I felt at Brown Chapel, our family's small Christian church in South Carolina. And, yes, I guess culture does involve music and art in some ways for me. Hip-hop culture, as I mentioned, has framed much of my cultural identity because I reached my teen years in the mid-1980s. At the same time that I was beginning to grow as a young woman and form a real identity, so was hip-hop. I align hip-hop with my cultural identity because it is an art form that respects, appreciates, and borrows from other genres of music. Hip-hop has always been eclectic—it's a love of blues, R&B, funk, soul, disco, jazz, rock, and folk. It represents those of us who refuse to live our lives in boxes and seek to bring all of ourselves into the work that we do. But it is not just the music. It is the essence of hip-hop culture that tells a true story about my generation.

Hip-hop culture is about unapologetically speaking the truth. Regardless of how hard it is to hear or how raw it comes out, it is a dedication to being real and true. So, unlike other generations in my own family, I refuse to be anything other than myself. And if others cannot handle that, whether they are friends, colleagues, or employers, I now live in a world that allows me the freedom not to care. If I cannot be true to myself, it will not be possible to serve and represent my community in an authentic way. At a more basic and simplistic level, this boldness and audacity that are so much a part of my culture even manifest themselves in dress. I laughed to myself one day as I looked around a conference room to see most of my older colleagues dressed in suits and "business attire" while I was sitting at the table wearing a Kangol. I am who I am—that's hip-hop. And I have carved out a career that allows me to be me—that's also hip-hop. As the hip-hop group Outkast suggested, we must make and bake our own piece of the American pie. I'm not waiting for it to be served to me, and I refuse to accept someone else's recipe. As a Gen-X woman, I've found that this ideology serves as the foundation of my culture in many ways. But I know that I can see my purpose in life clearly because of the sacrifices that my family made to wipe life's window clean for me.

Laying Down a Cultural Legacy

Because my family laid the foundation, culture has always been tied to family. So I think of culture when I reflect on my belief that it is the responsibility of our entire family to help raise my sister and brother-in-law's three children. They aren't just *their* children—they are also *ours*. We are all responsible. What I know for sure is that I have inherited a value for motherhood, family, and culture from the mothers who raised me. Our lives were starkly different. My grandmother was a wife in her midteenage years, my mother was wed at age nineteen, and I am still unmarried. By twenty-eight my grandmother had five children, by thirty my mother had two, and at thirty-six I still have none. My grandmother worked domestically, making as her career the cultivation of five lives; my mother has been a stay-at-home mom and has also worked as a housekeeper, as a factory worker, and as a teacher's aide. I have worked my entire adult life, have earned a Ph.D., and have made my professional home the university—an environment that neither of my mothers ever knew. Each generation of women in my family has known a different experience inside and outside the home. But I have made a firm commitment not to choose between the life that I have created for myself and the cultural legacy that I have inherited from these incredible women. As a professional, educated woman, I value domesticity. I value the importance of a clean home and a healthy environment in which to live. So I am also domestic. I value the meaning behind cooking a good meal—the reward that we feel when we (literally) nourish our loved ones and they enjoy it. I appreciate the peace that I feel in preparing the meal and the rush I experience from unleashing my creativity right there in my home. So I cook, and I do it well. But most important, I understand deeply the incredible genius, sacrifice, humility, selflessness, and discipline that it takes to shoulder the responsibility for another person's life. This sense of commitment to family is cultural for me.

The women in my family have set an incredible bar—they have in many ways sacrificed their own lives, deferred their own dreams, and worked themselves into a lifetime of exhaustion just so that I could achieve my goals and live my life fully. They have taught me that love is not a sentiment; it is an action—every lesson taught, every room cleaned, every meal prepared, every disciplinary action made, every value imparted was an act of love. The responsibility of sculpting and molding another soul is quite intimidating. Though I have three degrees, the only education that I have received on motherhood has been the model set by the women in my family. In many ways the role they have played as educators in our family has been an important one—they educated us about how to *be* a family, how to create what family is. Our families teach us valuable lessons from the day we are born. On our day of birth, the first lesson is unconditional love and self-sacrifice—only sheer love can drive the will to tear one's body apart to bring a child into the world. I want to build on the foundation set by my mother and grandmother. I want to lay down an even greater legacy for my children and my community to inherit. And so I wait. I wait until I am humble enough, selfless enough, and wise enough to be the mother that my mother was to me. I wait to find a partner who embodies what I will need not just to be happy (only I can create true happiness in my life) but also to create a legacy. Years of being single have probably made me much more certain of what I want in a life partner than my mother and grandmother were as very young women. But, at the most basic level, we all just wanted good men. I learned from my mothers to love laboring men and from experience to love educated ones—I'm truly happy with either, and I actually prefer a man who is both. My goal is to be able to build a foundation together—to make the world a better place as a result of our partnership. I read somewhere that this is the true meaning of a soul mate. I am looking beyond someone with whom to simply plant the seed and toward someone with whom to sow and grow the state of our cultural pedigree.

And I think that goal is at the core of what is really important to me. I do want to conceive. But what I hope to conceive is a cultural ethic of love, as a wife, as a mother, and as an educator. I don't want to just be married—I want to conceive synergy. I don't want to just have a baby—I want to conceive a family legacy. I don't want to just gain professional status—I want my success to be inextricably bound to the success of my community. And I don't want to just "give back" to my culture—I want to raise up the community that raised me. I want to be the woman, the mother, the wife, the sister, the social servant, the teacher, the activist, and the nurturer that my mother taught me to be—not through her words, but through the loving act of raising me.

Introduction

Cultural Leadership:
The Audacity in the Ordinary

> A hero is an ordinary individual who finds the strength to persevere and endure in spite of overwhelming obstacles. —**Christopher Reeve**

The Precipice

Lloyd, an African American student who participated in the study that informed this book, saw his culture in the broad sense of a local and national community. He wrote, "It is my hope that I will one day be in a position to further dispel the negative notions by reaching back into my cultural community to pass on cultural lessons and provide an alternative future for those who come after me." For Lloyd, cultural heritage can be used to save lives and change futures. Ultimately, what he is referring to is cultural leadership. By gaining a deeper, more critical understanding of their cultural heritage and history, individuals can be motivated to take agency and to create cultural change within their communities. Heritage inspires more than pride; it inspires leadership. Cultural leadership compels us to revive and appreciate a culturally driven life ethic—a sense of community, a drive to create and imagine, and a value for making time to tell the story. When we couple cultural heritage with our commitment to serve, it expands and adds depth, texture, and spirit to our leadership proxy.

Having a solid cultural foundation causes us to look at the world more critically and to experience our sense of responsibility more deeply. Why? It is simply because cultural heritage (the act of passing on culture) causes us to remember and acknowledge the struggles of our parents and grandparents. Cultural heritage helps us to paint a complete and endearing portrait of our culture—one that causes us to step back, observe, and comment on its beautiful complexity. The moment when a young person first comes to see her role in her culture clearly, to appreciate and face her culture openly brings to mind the idea of a precipice—the moment in time when a person is drawn to the edge and either stands still or jumps. We have seen such scenes in the movies, where the good character, who is being chased by the bad character, runs right up to the edge of a cliff or rooftop and stops just in time to think through the situation. If he goes backward, he will confront the same evil that he was running from. If he moves forward, he will jump into the unknown, with only the hope that he will survive. Most often he chooses to jump, and most often he makes it. This is the situation we face as leaders within our families, our communities, and society at large. We reach a point in our lives where we must decide the following: Will I continue the dysfunctionality, or will I change it? Will I sit still and watch the oppression, or will I jump headfirst into social action? Ultimately, strong cultural efficacy motivates us to jump in and to look at our communities with hope rather than with disdain.

Activism and Resistance

Oppression is a running theme throughout this book. Oppression is not simply about others being unable to achieve what you have because they do not have the same privileges. The larger issue concerns the social systems that create a situation in which a person does not have access to privilege, opportunity, or a sense of inclusion. These issues include significant inequalities in the education system, the ways that urban poverty is geographically mapped and planned, inequities in the criminal justice system, a lack of economic infrastructure in poor communities, dysfunctional administrative policies in social agencies, and inadequate access to health care and health education. As Marilyn Frye reminds us in her classic essay on oppression, a commitment to social justice requires a macroscopic rather than a microscopic approach:

> The root of the word "oppression" is the element "press" . . . *to press a pair of pants; printing press; press the button*. Presses are used to mold things or flatten them or reduce them in bulk. . . . Something pressed is something caught between or among forces and barriers, which are so related to each other that jointly they restrain, restrict or prevent the thing's motion or mobility. Mold. Immobilize. Reduce. . . . It is the experience of being caged in. . . . Consider a birdcage. If you look very closely at just one wire in the cage, you cannot see the other wires. If your conception of what is before you is determined by this myopic focus, you could look at that one wire, up and down the length of it, and be unable to see why a bird would not just fly around the wire any time it wanted to go somewhere. . . . It is only when you step back, stop looking at the wires one by one, microscopically, and take a macroscopic view of the whole cage, that you can see why the bird does not go anywhere; and then you will see it in a moment. . . . It is perfectly obvious that the bird is surrounded by a network of systemati-

cally related barriers, no one of which would be the least hindrance to its flight, but which, by their relations to each other, are as confining as the solid walls of a dungeon.[1]

When viewing oppression from this macroscopic standpoint, it might seem much too big a monster to tackle. To create this type of major change, you must be a powerful leader. We often see a leader as a person of great power and influence, a person in a significant position—a president, a politician, or an executive. But leadership is about much more than position; in fact, it has nothing to do with position.[2] Leadership is about purpose. Authentic leaders have a profound impact on people's lives—they transform communities and organizations, and they inspire and model ethical living. Dynamic leaders are critical challengers of the status quo. They speak as bold voices of resistance to oppression and inequality. True leaders make our world better—whether that world is a country, a city, a block, or a home. And so, in this book, I explore the audacity in the ordinary—the ways in which everyday people living their daily lives boldly exhibit cultural leadership, resistance, and activism. Culture and leadership lived in towns, villages, shacks, and shanties long before they lived in books, retreats, training programs, and conferences. To learn about how culture intersects with leadership requires us to look beyond textbooks and classrooms and to reconsider our understanding of what leadership should entail. As Juana Bordas asserts, "Within this kaleidoscope of diversity, mainstream American leadership has not integrated the rich practices of communities of color. Until a more inclusive form of leadership embodies our diverse society, a truly multicultural society will not be attained."[3]

The Study

This book explores issues of culture, leadership, activism, and resistance by engaging three important perspectives on inquiry. First, the book is primarily a critical discussion of various perspectives and relevant literature on culture and contemporary social issues. Second, critical race theory frames the use of the counternarratives of people of color. Third, in its effort to explore the intersection of race, class, and gender as factors that influence leadership proxy and resistance to oppression, this book is grounded in transnational feminism.

A. Montuori describes the literature review as a creative process: "The process of the literature review is framed as a participation in a community, a dialogue with those who are part of the community now and with one's 'ancestors.' The literature review can also explore the deeper underlying assumptions of the larger community beyond scholars and academics."[4] He describes the literature review itself as a "survey of the land" and an acknowledgment of the important "landmarks such as key players and theoretical movements."[5] But most important, in his work, he acknowledges the sensitive issues of knowledge production and cultural difference—whose understanding is included in the literature review and illustrates whom we view as valuable members of the educational community. This is the ethic that has engaged the review of literature within each critical essay. It causes me to wrestle with the inclusion of nonacademic voices in my search for meaning and theory. By offering a broad portrait of various perspectives, theories, and lived experiences, I hope to paint a clearer picture of what we encounter at the intersections of culture and leadership.

This book shares thoughts and perspectives on culture in the voices of college students. Ultimately, the book is about grooming a sense of cultural leadership in younger generations. Over the past five years, I have engaged in a research project based on the cultural life stories of these young people. At the start of the original study, I collected data at two large, predominantly white public universities. Considering the issues presented in the literature that concern the experiences of students of color at predominantly white universities, I sought to understand what culture meant to this group. One university was located in a largely rural environment; the other was situated in an urban community. After the onset of the study, an additional school located in a metropolitan city was added. With the exception of students who requested otherwise, the names of the study participants have been changed to protect their identities.

A sample of 18 students of color participated in the original study; in the five years since its completion, more than 100 young adults came to participate in the larger study, bringing the total to 118 cultural self-portraits examined for this book. Students ranged from freshmen through seniors. The study included 30 white students; 20 Asian American students; 42 African American, West Indian, or African students; and 26 Latino students. This book concerns the viewpoints of the students of color. The cultural worldviews of the white students are the subject of a forthcoming project.

The Art of Storytelling

Storytelling was a major focus of this study. J. Featherstone has noted how storytelling can inform such research. He describes not only the richness and complexity of the information gained through story but also the significant responsibility of the researcher:

> The telling of stories can be a profound form of scholarship moving serious study close to the frontiers of art in the capacity to express complex truth and moral context in intelligible ways. . . . The methodologies are inseparable from the vision. Historians have used narrative as a way in which to make sense of lives and institutions over time, but over years they have grown abashed by its lack of scientific rigor. Now, as we look for ways to explore context and describe the thick textures of lives over time in institutions with a history, we want to reckon with the

author's own stance and commitment to the people being written about. Storytelling takes on a fresh importance.[6]

Guided by the research methodology of portraiture, I had students write what I have titled "cultural self-portraits." These portraits are essentially the "cultural stories" of their lives. As a research method, portraiture has as one critical component a focus on goodness. A propensity toward goodness does not mean that portraits must focus on only positive aspects of a topic or always present information in only a positive light. Rather, "goodness" refers to the refusal to be driven by past research tendencies to focus on failure and deficiency. Much of the research on cultural diversity in higher education is dominated by pathology: What are the problems? What practices fail to work? What alienates students? Why do students leave? Many of the broader social narratives about "people of color" have also followed this path of negative imaging. But in its natural habitat—in communities and homes—culture is not created in reaction to negativity; it is a tool to sustain positive life practices. So portaiture shifts this focus to a discovery of the inherent good in the people, institutions, or concepts studied. And most important, it focuses on how the people who experience the phenomenon define or interpret *goodness*.

In this project, the pure voice came through the student-authored cultural self-portrait. Rather than seek to understand the meaning of culture by having students react to existing definitions of and theories about culture, I began with a blank canvas on which they could paint a cultural self-portrait. Their stories provided an authentic articulation of the structures, layers, and practices that constitute what they perceive as culture. The value of creating the space for voices of underrepresented communities to be heard is underscored by critical race theory.[7] Critical race theory was originally developed within the field of legal studies, but it has since been adapted within educational environments to study the experiences of underrepresented racial groups. A component of critical race theory particularly salient to this study is the concept of cultural nationalism. Cultural nationalism places an inherit value on self-created cultural structures that allow people of color to continue the tradition of raising, teaching, and empowering the cultural orientation of their youth. R. Barnes offers an important explanation of the relevance of this theory: "Minority perspectives make explicit the need for fundamental change in the ways we think and construct knowledge. . . . Exposing how minority cultural viewpoints differ from white cultural viewpoints requires a delineation of the complex set of social interactions through which minority consciousness has developed. Distinguishing the consciousness of racial minorities requires acknowledgement of the feelings and intangible modes of perception unique to those who have historically been socially, structurally, and intellectually marginalized in the United States."[8]

A crucial component of acknowledging such feelings and modes of perception includes hearing the authentic stories of the cultural experience. As

R. Delgado (1990) argues, people of color may speak from a very different experience. Thus the concepts of authentic voice, story exchange, and naming one's own reality are essential to the critical race theorist.[9] M. Marable (2005) explains that such story sharing has been central to the act of cultural protection engaged in by many past leaders and intellectuals of color. He relates how public intellectuals such as Malcolm X (through raw and uninhibited oral story sharing), James Weldon Johnson (through creative and artistic story sharing), and W.E.B. Du Bois (through ethnographic story sharing) have contested dominant cultural narratives. Through the authentic telling and thus documenting of their cultural histories, these men validated the importance of the cultural experience.

Cultural Hegemony

We cannot explore the ways in which culture influences leadership and resistance without considering factors such as race, class, and gender. The traditional view of powerful leaders and influential communities has often been white, male, and/or upper class. Understanding how cultural hegemony impedes the healthy growth and appreciation of cultures that have been placed on the margins of society helps us to visualize the type of leadership ethic that is needed to resist cultural hegemony. Because cultural hegemony involves devaluing nondominant cultures, the bold and visionary work of many members of these communities is overlooked and excluded from traditional ideologies of citizenship, leadership, and politics. Often the oppressed are not viewed as leaders, experts, or knowledge producers even though they are leaders within their cultural circles and experts of their own experience. Transnational feminism is a feminist approach that wrestles with the interplay of politics, economics, gender, and race in an effort to deconstruct systems of cultural imperialism. L. Surhone, M. Timpledon, and S. Marseken explain the concept: "As a feminist approach, it can be said that transnational feminism is generally attentive to intersections among nationhood, race, gender, sexuality and economic exploitation on a world scale. . . . Transnational feminists inquire into the social, political and economic conditions comprising imperialism; their connections to colonialism and nationalism; the role of gender, the state, race, class, and sexuality in the organization of resistance to hegemonies in the making and unmaking of nation and nation-state."[10]

Hegemony and cultural imperialism concern the domination of power—one social class or entity has power over the other. Beyond the ways that this power of dominion provides the dominant group access to resources, wealth, and opportunity, the group's values, behaviors, beliefs, and ways of knowing and being become the norm.

> In twentieth-century political science, the concept of hegemony is central to *cultural hegemony*, a philosophic and sociologic explanation of

how, by the manipulation of the societal value system, one social class dominates the other social classes of a society, with a world view justifying the *status quo*. . . . One of the reasons often given for opposing any form of cultural imperialism, voluntary or otherwise, is the preservation of cultural diversity, a goal seen by some as analogous to the preservation of ecological diversity. Proponents of this idea argue either that such diversity is valuable in itself, to preserve human historical heritage and knowledge, or instrumentally valuable because it makes available more ways of solving problems and responding to catastrophes, natural or otherwise.[11]

And so, in many ways, an approach to life that is centered in culture and based on resistance engages creative strategies to privilege the marginalized. It uses culture itself—family, community, art, heritage, and folkways—as a tool of resistance. It destroys systems of cultural hegemony not by raging against the machine, but by strengthening an ethic of love within oppressed communities. The foundation of this type of leadership is rooted in the idea of ordinary people helping one another. It is a grassroots effort focused on helping underrepresented cultural communities to better appreciate, and recognize the utility in, their culture and to value the amazing potential in what they may initially see as ordinary life and ordinary people.

Because viable social change is often best created from within communities, it is critically important that we pay attention to how college students of color are taught. The firm and positive commitment to the communities that they create in college can have potential long-term effects on not only the students themselves but also the communities that raised them.[12] I see cultural leadership education as a space where students can wrestle with their own sense of their cultural selves and secure their cultural agency and efficacy. Scholarship on cultural leadership must affirm the fact that valuable knowledge has been produced not only within organizations and institutions but also on street corners, at lunch counters, in barbershops, in churches, on porches, on stoops, and in family rooms. It is easier to acknowledge this fact than to give the people a voice with which to incorporate their wisdom into our scholarship on the subject of leadership. Students' comments about the important lessons they have learned from family bring home the importance of incorporating community knowledge. This knowledge, rooted in a cultural tradition, rooted in a community experience, forms the foundation of "cultural leadership." In our efforts to purge our communities, our society, and our world of oppression, we must sweep away the social garbage that causes us to demean the substance in our everyday lives, and we must learn to appreciate the audacity in the ordinary. What this project made unmistakably clear to me is that "culture" is an awe-inspiring and incredible blend of struggle, resilience, and love. And so, in the pages that follow, I share with you the soul, spirit, genius, and audacity of culture in the lives of young people of color.

1

There's No Place like Home

An Ethic of Cultural Love

> There is no greater agony than bearing an
> untold story inside you. —**Maya Angelou**

We often imagine our cultural historians, storytellers, and griots to be elders—those that have lived long lives with deep meaning. But my own, Gen-X story bears witness to the fact that seeds of insight and wisdom do not take very long to grow. Whether the cause is the nurturing sun and rain (family love and encouragement) or toxic pesticides (poverty and oppression), our young flowers grow up fast. And they have incredible stories to tell. The voices and cultural experiences of young adults need to be heard.

However, across many ethnicities today, folks often wonder if younger generations have what it takes to keep culture alive. Culture is not simply an individual experience—there is a strong sense of group ownership and history. And the group is becoming increasingly worried about the sustainability and future outlook of their cultural heritage. The torch is still burning, but many older generations are worried that young people may not have the stamina and training to keep the fire lit. As a scholar-practitioner in higher education, I have worked for almost fifteen years with young adults as they grew personally, intellectually, and socially. I use the term "scholar-practitioner" because I have enjoyed a career working with college students both as a professor in the classroom and as a campus administrator guiding their broader college experience outside the classroom. I have worked with young people as they prepare to enter the university in precollege or orientation programs. I have advised college students as they experience the initial excitement of becoming involved in campus leadership activities. I have guided students as they wrestle with truly understanding sisterhood, brotherhood, community, and service through membership in fraternities and sororities. I have lived with students as they experience the first taste of autonomy and independence. I have traveled all over the world with college students—observing them as they come to know themselves and the world more deeply. In visits to prisons and local public schools, in mentoring programs, at campus cultural events, in community leadership trips that have taken us across the United States, and in college classrooms, I have had an incredible educational journey with my young traveling partners. I have witnessed the process of life transformation and personal growth in young people's lives. There are many things in my life that remain a mystery, but one thing that I know well is college students. I have spent far too much time with them not to understand their hopes, dreams, and fears. And during my time working with these incredible young people, they have often confided in me—sharing bits and pieces of their life experiences, family struggles, and personal challenges. About five years ago, I began engaging students in a more formal reflective writing exercise as part of a research study. My goal was to pen these life stories, which I call "cultural self-portraits" in a more intentional way. Students were asked to tell me their cultural life story—the good and the bad. I originally hoped that by analyzing the elements and experiences included in their stories, I might be able to tease out an understanding—a portrait of how young adults define and value "culture" in a contemporary world. What I found was that young people today not only have ideas and perspectives on culture; they also have lived truly incredible and awe-inspiring lives. Since the first group that participated in this study, I have had more than a hundred students author cultural self-portraits. These students have come from different geographical areas, economic backgrounds, and racial and ethnic groups. What has been almost shocking is that across differences in age, ethnicity, and race, most young adults describe the core foundations of culture in the same ways. For example, family is consistently discussed as a critical component of culture. Across racial and ethnic groups, the specific family experiences, traditions, and rituals differ. But the *idea* of family as an important cultural foundation is shared regardless of race.

The stories about family, poverty, life struggle, commitment to education, and spirituality that young people shared with me were insightful and inspiring. Their stories helped me to understand this generation much better. I have spent many years interacting with older educators and community members who have been disappointed by what they have classified as cultural apathy among younger generations. Many K–16 educators work hard to secure campus or school resources for cultural programs only for those programs to be received by empty seats and a lack of student interest. Some educators are frustrated that when an institution does actually make the effort to create cultural education opportunities, it seems that students do not want to learn about culture. And this frustration does not solely reside on campus. I have been a part of many personal conversations with community leaders, family members, and neighbors who share a frustration and lack of confidence in the cultural grounding of those now coming into adulthood. Though the generations of the Great Depression, Baby Boomers, and Generation X do not seem to agree on many things, one shared belief is that our cultures are gradually being forgotten—families are becoming disconnected, heritage is not being passed on, technology is replacing personal interaction, a sense of community is being lost, and our stories are not being told to our young people. Focusing specifically on the African American community, Harvard Professor Henry Louis Gates Jr. references this idea in his book *Finding Oprah's Roots*. "The very history of the African American people, starting with the newly freed slaves, is a history of the hardheaded determination of a people to overcome their environment. I'm not the only African American of my generation who worries that a younger generation has forgotten this most basic aspect of the Black tradition."[1]

The idea that young adults of color may lack adequate knowledge, understanding, and positive regard for their culture is not new. It is an issue that has been argued by scholars since the turn of the twentieth century and is a driving force behind the idea that educational environments need to be critically evaluated for the role that they play (or fail to play) in building a value for culture among students.[2] One of the foremost scholars on the subject was Carter G. Woodson, who originally wrote *The Mis-education of the Negro* in the early 1900s. Woodson's scholarship placed a firm focus on how African American students were educated and the impact of the cultural perspectives through which education of any kind takes place. Woodson asserted that the Negro, at that time, lacked the faculties of critical thought about her culture as well as the agency to create positive change within her cultural community because of the culturally oppressive lens through which she was educated.[3] bell hooks offered a present-day analysis. According to hooks, in order for African Americans to truly develop agency for positive, loving, and progressive cultural development, the act of decolonizing one's mind must occur. In other words, people of color must recognize, understand, and work to counteract the forms of cultural and racial oppression that Woodson acknowledged years ago.[4] As hooks states, "The practice of self love is difficult for everyone in society, but it is even more difficult for black folks, as we must constantly resist the negative perceptions of blackness we are encouraged to embrace by the dominant culture."[5]

Both historic scholar Woodson and contemporary scholar hooks establish a strong value for culturally dedicated educational spaces. Their comments on negative stereotyping can apply to many underrepresented ethnic groups, particularly regarding the need to have culturally affirming educational environments. In fact, hooks offers a critical reflection on the days of segregation arguing that though educational segregation was legally unacceptable, it did have some culturally beneficial structures for black youth: "Segregation meant that in our black spaces, the institutions which governed our communities—church, school, social club—black folks could fully claim the subjectivity denied us by the larger white world. It was even possible for some clever individuals to live and prosper without encountering the white power structure. As in the case of those escaped slaves (Maroons, renegades) who became insurgent resisters creating their own oppositional freedom culture in hidden locations, powerful individuals in our all-black communities were able to offer us liberatory ways to think about blackness."[6]

This argument is particularly salient when you consider the historical expectation for education to serve as not only an academic opportunity but also a means for cultural engagement and development. Education is about much more than knowing and testing, it is about striving, achieving, uplifting, and understanding—yourself, your community, your culture, and your world. In the past, institutions like colored schools often served as both standard education and cultural education venues. Many communities of color have viewed knowledge of the community's history, rituals, traditions, language, values, and tactics for survival as equal in importance to learning to read and write. In fact, cultural education often teaches young people how to "read" society and navigate their way through poverty, racism, and oppression. Both types of education have been crucial to oppressed communities. However, as schools desegregated, many students found education about their culture either not present or so far in the margins of the curriculum that they might miss it if they blinked (missed a day of school). Allen suggests that there is a conflicting dichotomy within the field of education. "There is a base of existing knowledge that grossly distorts and romanticizes the history of people's origins and accomplishments and then, at the same time, [people of color are] ignored or patronized. The effect is to deny the silenced person's identity and to create disjunction between the values and beliefs about the nature of knowledge, its transmission, assessment and constitution."[7]

We may need to revise the way that we construct and define the idea of "college" through a deeper and more concentrated effort to truly integrate culture and community into the college experience. We may also need to reconsider who we privilege as knowledge producers and cultural scholars beyond the traditional faculty, authors, speakers, and performers that we often bring onto campus.

It's All about Love

> If love is not present in our imaginations, it will not be present in our lives. —**bell hooks**

I was motivated to do this work in order to determine whether young adults of color did in fact suffer from historical and cultural amnesia. Have our parents, sisters, cousins, aunts, and teachers raised a culturally numb generation of adults who will now inherit the world? What makes this a pressing issue is that many community leadership activists and scholars affirm that viable community change most often comes from within the community.[8] This is the ethic that drives my personal interpretation of W.E.B. Du Bois's "Talented Tenth" philosophy.[9] It is much less about the educated being the chosen ones within the racial group, and more about instilling a sense of community responsibility in those that are provided the privilege of a college education. In my opinion, his philosophy holds weight now more than ever. Though our world has indeed become more flat, close, and technologically open, we are living in a much more individualistic state across countless ethnic groups. Education has become much less about community. Many view college as an individual opportunity—the road to a lucrative career or the avenue to "make it out" of poverty. And so we should be concerned about what the young college graduates that have come from any traditionally oppressed community will do with their education. Do they feel a sense of responsibility to use their education to help their culture and their community in any meaningful way? Do they feel an obligation to help raise up the communities that raised them? That is the essence of the talented tenth concept that I hold dear to my heart—Du Bois called us to question the purpose of an education.

> Now the training of men is a difficult and intricate task. Its technique is a matter for educational experts, but its object is for the vision of seers. If we make money the object of . . . training, we shall develop money-makers but not necessarily men; if we make technical skill the object of education, we may possess artisans but not, in nature, men. Men we shall have only as we make manhood the object of the work of the schools—intelligence, broad sympathy, knowledge of the world that was and is, and of the relation of men to it—this is the curriculum of that Higher Education which must underlie true life. On this foundation we may build bread winning, skill of hand and quickness of brain, with never a fear lest the child . . . mistake the means of living for the object of life.[10]

I understand why many of Du Bois's other comments in the larger essay have not been received well by many black people—I also find some of his thoughts disagreeable. And more broadly, even the language of this particular passage is consistent with the era in its exclusion of women. But the point is still important, and critical thinkers know how to apply the ethic behind the idea in a more inclusive way. I acknowledge and understand that Du Bois was arguing for the honor of the educated during a time when education was both valued and mistrusted. Learning has always been and continues to be a complicated process among the oppressed. Families want their children to be educated, but that very education often creates great distance between them. We continue to struggle to find a healthy balance—to make education good enough to elevate a young person out of cycles of oppression but relevant enough that it causes each one to understand, evaluate, and connect to that former experience in new, activist ways. What we choose to teach ultimately directs what our students choose to love. And by love, I mean more than a feeling or emotion. Love is a verb—to love is to act. Our actions demonstrate our loves—our priorities, our values, our cares, and our concerns. The question at hand is truly a question of cultural love. It is not simply a question of "Do you love your culture?" But more importantly, I am suggesting it is a question of "How do you display an ethic of love as a form of cultural engagement . . . as a product of culture itself?" Loving communities back to health is about working hard to put communities back together. When you consider any traditional love relationship like marriage or parenting, veterans in that experience will affirm that love ain't easy—it's hard work. And so, ultimately, as educators we must ask ourselves what type of relationship we are educating students to have with their families, communities, and cultures. How are we preparing students to help create communities of love—healthy, strong, and nurturing neighborhoods? How are we building their capacity to be love-driven leaders—honest, dedicated, selfless, and giving? We want our young people to be driven, but we must be critically concerned with their destination.

Questioning the idea that younger generations are void of an ethic of genuine love . . . for community, for culture, for anything other than themselves . . . truly drove this study. And they answered. I found young people to align culture closely with family connectedness, a value for education, the ability to survive critical social experiences such as drug addiction and poverty, the functional role of religion and artistic expression to serve as community voices, and a form of legacy within the community, in the family, or on the college campus. And ultimately, the major element that culture seemed to boil down to was love. Love is the foundation of culture. Yet, it is an ethic and concept that is rarely discussed as a critical component of racial, social, and even cultural conversations. Most often, studying culture involves issues of ritual, tradition, art, religion, and language. Of course, somewhere in each of these cultural elements is the concept of love; it is just rarely named as the most important foundation of culture. Love is present in ritual and tradition. Love serves as the foundation of most religions. Cultural production through art, music, and speech is often an expression of love, care, and concern. So why do we not discuss love more clearly and directly in cultural scholarship? The young people in my study surely did. The Dalai Lama has written and stated much about the consistent devaluing of love as an important social foundation. In *The Art of Happiness*, the Dalai Lama writes, "If there is love, there is hope that one may have real families, real brotherhood, real equanimity, real peace. If the love within your mind is lost and you see other beings as enemies, then no matter how much knowledge or education or material comfort you have, only suffering and confusion will ensue."[11]

When the young adults in my study discussed their concepts of culture, they actually gave voice to the role of familial and community love, the importance of racial acceptance, the lack of an ethic of care within educational institutions, the daily realities of tired single mothers mustering up enough energy to show their love through teaching valuable life lessons, and the warm embrace of their cultural heritage that has sustained them throughout life. So, when we talk about culture, we are talking about an ethic of love, a politic of survival. The information provided in this book allows readers to explore not only the ways in which a love ethic is manifest throughout many cultures—in families, communities, popular culture, and spirituality—but also the ways in which the next generation interprets, understands, and embraces this ethic of cultural love. As bell hooks points out in her book *Salvation*, "Since our leaders and scholars agree that one measure of the crisis black people are experiencing is lovelessness, it should be evident that we need a body of literature, both sociological and psychological work, addressing the issue of love among black people, its relevance to political struggle, its meaning in our private lives."[12]

Now, more than ever, there is a need and desire to better understand the lived cultural experiences of communities of color. Literature that allows the world an intimate glimpse into the lives of young adults of color contributes to this discourse. This book gives a voice to younger generations, sheds light on their contemporary ways of approaching the world, and challenges mainstream ideologies on culture and cultural heritage in a way that both intersects with and moves beyond traditional views of culture Marable provided an important explanation of why an opportunity to immerse deeply in culture learning can be so critical to the civic and personal development of young adults. He called this "living history":

> Most White Americans, for example, do have a somewhat vague awareness of what the American Civil War was, but no detailed, personal understanding about slavery, abolitionism, and why the conflict came about. Because my great grandmother, Morris Marable, was sold on an auction block in West Point, Georgia, at the age of nine in 1854, I have consequently acquired a very different relationship to those distant events one hundred and fifty years ago. When we feel personally connected with events from the past, they help to shape our actions today—historical amnesia blocks the construction of potentially successful social movements.[13]

Cultural centeredness and exposure can contribute to the growth needed for young adults to become whole persons and productive citizens. In my article "The Color of Service," I describe the moment when this issue first became salient for me as an educator:

> I began to look at my students and see a community of educated individuals who were disconnected from the majority of their community. I began to see more clearly the invisible wall that had been built between the middle-to-upper-class black professionals and the poorer black community at large. Not only were my students completely unaware of the major political and social issues affecting the black population in America, but they were also living a life physically isolated from this population, literally separated by the gates of their majority

white institution. What was even more disheartening was that I realized that many of them were not striving to gain professional stature so they could work for the very communities of people that had raised them. Instead, many saw service to their community as a one shot hour of their life—a car wash, an Adopt-a-Highway morning—rather than a lifetime commitment of their professional talents. And more important, I realized that although such one-time service is needed, someone in the higher education arena must also provide students with an intentional experience that teaches a deeper understanding of civic responsibility and encourages communities of color to see community service through a very different, more meaningful lens. Consider the possible outcomes when college students are encouraged to see how their jobs can be a form of service. What could be the results of encouraging young black and Latino college students to obtain medical degrees so they could open practices in black and Latino neighborhoods and provide more quality health care to communities of color? And what of our future teachers? Outstanding education graduates may be more likely to lend their talents to a high school in an urban community if they are provided with a sense of connection and an understanding of the need for their presence in that community. If the black middle class isn't concerned with our poor and disadvantaged, why should the political and economic elite be?[14]

A contemporary examination of this issue provides valuable insight to gain a better understanding of the emerging generation of young leaders within communities of color in America. The current political environment, which has once again brought issues of race and culture up for national discussion, makes society ripe for exploring topics like this. The experiences of young people of color in America wrestling with their cultural identity can help all people to understand that cultural centeredness may be an important tool in strengthening the soul of our future leaders and citizens.

Why College Students?

From the screams of protest for the creation of cultural resources in the 1960s to the contemporary demands for a more sophisticated understanding of race, ethnicity, sexuality, masculinity, feminism, and oppression, culture as a broad concept continues to be an important form of identity formation and civic capacity building for college students of color.[15] Historically, college students not only have valued culture; they have fought for it. They have demanded that culture surround them in college—in their curriculum, in campus programs and entertainment, in campus buildings and structures, and in the makeup of faculty and staff. College students have breathed cultural life into higher education. But why did they do this? What made them believe that culture was the answer to the challenges that they faced in college? Undoubtedly, culture needs people in order to survive, but it is clear that people also need culture. In a personal letter to his daughters, Henry Louis Gates Jr. tells a story that illustrates how culture often serves as a firm foundation for those living on shaky ground:

> I enjoy the unselfconscious moments of a shared cultural intimacy, whatever form they take, when no one else is watching, when no white people are around. Like Joe Louis's fights, which my father still talks about as part of the fixed repertoire of stories that texture our lives. You've seen his eyes shining as he describes how Louis hit Max Schmeling so many times and so hard, and some reporter asked him, after the fight: "Joe, what would you have done if that last punch hadn't knocked Schmeling out?" And how ole Joe responded, without missing a beat: "I'da run around him to see what was holdin' him up!" Even so, I rebel at the notion that I can't be part of other groups, that I can't construct identities through elective affinity, that race must be the most important thing about me. Is that what I want on my gravestone: Here lies an African American? So I'm divided. I want to be black, to know black, to luxuriate in whatever I might be calling blackness at any particular time—but to do so in order to come out the other side, to experience a humanity that is neither colorless nor reducible to color. Bach and James Brown. Sushi and fried catfish. Part of me admires those people who can say with a straight face that they have transcended any attachment to a particular community or group . . . but I always want to run around behind them to see what holds them up.[16]

Indeed, what may "hold them up" is the strong sense of cultural efficacy that allows them to travel to and through other cultures without feeling a lack of value, jealousy, or defeat. It may be the very attachments to cultural heritage that some seek to move beyond that actually provides them with the tools necessary to keep going and growing. In many ways, developing a strong understanding and appreciation for their culture helps to build cultural capital among young adults of color. Influenced by the notions of physical capital (physical objects), human capital (individual properties), and social capital (social networks and norms), the term "cultural capital" represents cultural beliefs, values, rituals, norms, and experiences that both equip and include people in the life of a society or environment.[17]

In many ways, the structures, rituals, symbols, and traditions of a college campus represent cultural capital for some.[18] Disparities in educational structures for and services to underrepresented students have long been an issue on college campuses around the country. In their examination of the disparities of service within the student affairs division at a large predominantly white institution, Perry and Ting argued that the historical vestiges of privileged, educated, and celebrated majority cultures within the institution were often a key factor in contributing to long-lasting service disparities. "The historical narratives of how oppression becomes institutionalized reveal characters, settings, and resources that ossify power along lines of culture, race, gender and ethnicity."[19] Furthermore, such historical legacies can impact the campus climate and create an institutional culture of exclusion.[20] Thus the demand made by students for universities to increase diversity and evaluate the effectiveness of cultural offerings was an expectation to equalize cultural capital.

Cultural capital can take different forms. Yosso[21] presents six forms of cultural capital, which are centered in the cultural experience of people of color, that are often deemed valuable by the cultural group regardless of their value to the larger society. These include (1) Aspirational Capital, or the ability to achieve hopes and dreams, (2) Linguistic Capital, or multiple language skills, (3) Familial Capital, or family history and memory, (4) Social Capital, or support systems in the form of friendship and community networks, (5) Navigational Capital, or the skill to navigate through various institutions, and (6) Resistant Capital, or the skills developed through behavior that works in opposition to oppression. To understand the rich cultural heritage with which students enter any educational environment is to truly understand the benefits and personal impact of culture. O'Neill and Chatman's[22] study on the educational experiences of students in relation to interpersonal, social, and spatial factors found this to be true among the African American student participants. One student recalled that his educational experiences before college influenced his desire to learn more about African Americans in college: "Ms. Simms encouraged me to understand my potential, but my subjects never taught me anything about being black. Social studies usually had about a paragraph on slavery, and they always talked about how it was a legal practice. I was shocked when I got to college and learned the real historical experiences of my people. I think that school tries to instill American patriotism and integration."[23]

Another student in this study gave voice to the detrimental effects of not having opportunities to learn black history: "I went to the same school from the time I was three until I entered college. I was the only black student and all I learned about being black came from our textbooks. I guess you could say I have learned mostly to be more white than black. This caused me problems because I don't feel accepted by other blacks. This has made it hard to shape my identity as an African American female."[24]

In their book *Balancing Two Worlds: Asian American College Students Tell Their Life Stories*, Garrod and Kilkenny present several autobiographical stories of race, ethnic identity, and education. In the story "Balancing the Hyphen," a young Japanese American woman discusses the challenges that she has faced in balancing her two cultural worlds in school:

> It has been a struggle to bring together the teachings of my parents with the American values of individualism. . . . People often ask me if I have liked my college. . . . Honestly, in retrospect, although it hurts to admit,

I probably would have chosen another school—one where diversity is not quantified by the number of minorities accepted through admissions, but accepted as part of life and a part of the campus. . . . I felt that it was my job to fit in, and if I didn't it was my fault. I think about the facade of diversity I saw on campus and I wonder what life will be like after college. It scares me.[25]

Scholars Alicia Chavez and Florence Guido-Dibrito share their unique personal experiences navigating the conflicting environments of culture and education, home and school:

Alicia, who is Hispano and Native American (Mestiza), was raised both connected to and in her ancestral home in northern New Mexico. The village of Taos is isolated enough that individuals from these ethnic groups hold most educational, governmental, and business positions in the community. In addition, time, relationships, and other daily aspects of culture are primarily normed on a combined Native American and Hispano culture. For Alicia, this meant that even with many childhood years spent away from Taos (attending school), cultural messages within her community were consistent in providing positive, cultural role modeling. Brief time periods in other states with their educational and neighborhood communities provided more than enough negative treatment for an understanding of the low value placed by many in the United States on these two cultures. These forays also provided triggers in her consciousness of ethnic identity and personal sense of otherness.[26]

This last example illustrates how a deeply rooted sense of culture can help to counter the dominant social norms and negative opinions that often oppress the cultural experiences of people of color. Collectively, all of this scholarship illustrates that deep cultural engagement within education plays a vital role in the construction of student identity. Validating student identity and providing students with a stronger sense of self is most closely aligned with the concept of "engaged pedagogy." Engaged pedagogy is a teaching and education practice in which everyone's presence is recognized and valued.[27] Concepts like multicultural education and engaged pedagogy are important to influence change and advance educational practice. But one of the major criticisms of multicultural education in particular is that multicultural education theories and programs are not usually based on actual studies of *underrepresented cultures*. They instead focus on the experience of being an *underrepresented student*.[28] The typical practice to concentrate on the student's interaction with her *school* and not the student's interaction with her *culture* may limit real cultural innovation in educational settings. Transformative practice should be guided by an actual understanding of what culture is to students, how it is experienced in students' lives outside of campus, and how these external cultural experiences can be integrated into higher education to better prepare students to interact with the world.

This book offers meaningful information to help educators, family members, community leaders, mentors, and elders to better understand the very personal and diverse nature of culture in a contemporary world. Through this research, I sought to understand all of the students' cultural experiences, past and present, and to illustrate how these experiences come together to shape a young person's cultural story. Baxter-Magolda's[29] principles on student involvement in research support the intimate involvement of student voice in this study. These principles call for educators to validate students as knowers and to situate learning in the students' lived experience. These practices involve the researcher or educator in relinquishing formal notions of power and inviting the students to inform practice through sharing their life experiences and meaning making.[30] In this case, they both involved allowing college students to tell their cultural stories and construct their own definition of culture.

Culture: What Is It and Why Is It Important?

The term "culture" most often invokes concepts of the imaginative and creative spirit—art, folkways, storytelling, spirituality, and community fellowship. But how do concepts of culture change with each generation? The question that had to be answered was "Is culture dying, or are ideologies about culture changing?" Before moving forward into a new contemporary understanding of how young adults define culture, it is important to briefly discuss existing ideologies on culture. What was my starting point as I approached this project? Offering one core definition of culture is difficult, as debates have occurred throughout several disciplines. Culture is studied in anthropology, sociology, cultural studies, history, and education to name just a few. Culture has larger social influences as well as components that are specific to the individual. Therefore, how culture is described, valued, and interpreted may greatly differ from one person to the next. Since the early 1990s, definitions of culture have generally evolved to view culture as the symbolic vehicles of meaning and experience such as beliefs, ritual practices, artistic expression, traditions, and ceremonies.[31] These critical experiences and interpretations of meaning influence the actions, worldviews, approach to life, and values of cultural group members.

According to Swidler,[32] culture's influence on actions can be seen not as specific and definitive prescriptions of how people should act, but rather as a tool kit of skills, habits, and approaches by which people build strategies of action and move through everyday life. Additionally, Leith Mullings's[33] definition of culture, as a constantly evolving phenomenon, is central to approaching the study of culture among contemporary young adults. "[Culture is] the symbols and values that create the ideological frame of reference through which people attempt to deal with the circumstances in which they find themselves. Culture is not composed of static, discrete traits moved from one locale to another. It is constantly changing and transformed, as new forms are created out of old ones. Thus, culture does not arise out of nothing: it is created and modified by material conditions."[34]

The culture of today's young adult of color has been shaped by past experiences as well as the contemporary circumstances that often change the way traditions and rituals are utilized in daily life. Culture can often be observed in two forms. Objective culture includes the artifacts expressed in a visual form that communicate a group's political and economic systems, collective history, artistic expressions, literature, and special days.[35] Examples of objective culture include food, fashion, festivals, and folklore. Subjective culture involves patterns of behavior as well as learned and shared beliefs.[36] Examples of subjective culture include nationality, regional traditions, religious beliefs, ethnic values, and organizations.

Another relevant definition of culture was provided by Maulana Karenga and focused on underrepresented groups. Karenga's[37] definition includes seven major areas that serve to construct a broad culture. These seven areas include history, spirituality and ethics, social organization, economic organization, political organization, creative production, and ethos. Most of Karenga's components of culture are similar to definitions presented earlier. However, he offers an important addition through the concept of ethos that may be particularly relevant for persons of color. He defines ethos as "a people's self-understanding as well as its self presentation in the world through its thought and practice."[38] Ethos is the *agency* component of culture. Ethos is the very ethic that I referenced earlier when I talked about how our love of our community is manifest through our actions. According to Karenga,[39] culture is not merely about the existence of structures, rituals, and practices; it also involves a responsibility for the individual to know, understand, and share the most important aspects of the culture. In other words, it is not enough to simply appreciate culture; we must embrace it, wrestle with it, and pass it on. He argues that this responsibility is particularly great for communities of color because the act of knowing, understanding, and sharing has been prohibited in the past among underrepresented racial and ethnic groups. And so, the ability for younger generations to value, understand, and move their culture forward in a progressive way is critically important. They hold before them an opportunity of which many of their ancestors only dreamed—the freedom to embrace, engage, and share their cultures. Marable offered the following insight on the central role of culture in the lives of oppressed people: "For the oppressed, the central and overriding question was one of identity: who are we as a people, what is our cultural heritage, what values or ideals can we share with other groups to enrich society as a whole, and what do we have a right to expect from the state and civil society? Within explorations of culture resides the kernel of an oppressed group's consciousness."[40]

Culture is one of the characteristics that make people who and what they are. The cultural experience is an intimate experience for the student, the educator, and the community. The personal nature of this work can best be understood by reflecting on the critical work of the grandmother of African American folklore and storytelling, Zora Neale Hurston. Hurston serves as a strong historic example of a researcher who, through the work, was able to come to terms with her role as a writer, a community daughter, and a cultural group member. Her time listening to, reflecting on, and writing about others' cultural stories helped her achieve a better understanding and appreciation of her culture. And even more meaningful, as a young African American female researcher, she, like me, saw the college years as being the start of her critical understanding of her culture. "[My culture] was fitting me like a tight chemise. I couldn't see it for wearing it. It was only when I was away at college [that I was] . . . able to fully see and appreciate my culture." This was my hope. That students did in fact have a sense of culture, but that it might be so tightly bound to them, so much a part of their daily lives that they sometimes took it for granted.

And so I have spent the past five years talking to young people—sons and daughters who were on the brink of becoming professionals and parents. During the time that I spent inside their lives, I found myself laughing and crying, nodding in agreement, and sitting back in surprise as the students revealed to me their struggles with issues of racism, colorism, poverty, oppression, and the culture that sustained them through it all. I entered the cultural lives of those who participated in this study as a guest, visitor, community cousin, and friend. And as I left the experience, I shut the door gently, glanced at their cultures affectionately, and committed myself to retelling an authentic love story—revealing the true beauty of how culture has evolved in a contemporary America. Through this study, I found "culture" to involve five core components: strong family bonds; strategies for survival; a value for education; spirituality and art that is purposeful, approachable, and functional; and a sense of legacy. Figure 1.1 illustrates these five components.

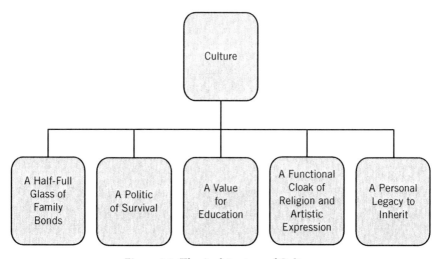

Figure 1.1 The Architecture of Culture

This book shares with the reader the cultural life stories of ten of the young adults interviewed for the project. Their life stories are written as both autobiographical cultural self-portraits and as narrated cultural snapshots. These stories reveal how each person perceives culture and how they use it as a tool to help them navigate issues such as race, poverty, popular culture, education, and spirituality in today's world. Following the portraits and snapshots are reflective essays that offer my critical analysis of the key social issues that come out of these students' lives. In my essays, I present many more stories and introduce other students who have participated in this project over the past five years.

2

A Half-Full Glass of Family Bonds

A Cultural Self-Portrait: D'Leon
(in His Own Words)

This Is Me

Bottled up inside
Are the words I never said
The feelings that I hide
The lies you never read
You see it on my face
Trapped inside are the lies
Of the past I can't replace
Why can't I be happier?
Today's a brand new day!

I hope to be a visionary—someone who is driven by dreams and fueled by faith. My professional interests are not merely monetary or rooted in my own ambitions. Instead, I hope to transform others with the fruit of my lips, labor, and love. I am optimistic in every aspect of life and all avenues that I pursue. I want to make history by just following my calling in life, which is helping others prosper. Knowing that my word is my bond to everyone that I encounter in life, I plan to make a lasting impact on people by being genuine, honest, humble, loyal, and fearless. My interests also include finding ways to appropriately and effectively inspire African American men. I will be a positive example for all African American men, because it is important to counter the impact of the atrocities in our history and culture that have occurred. I would like to think that I'm a good representative of how to create better opportunities for shared experiences within our culture. I have a passion for youth, because many of the underrepresented high achievers are just that, underrepresented especially among young African American males. I am passionate about life and being able to live to the fullest. Family is like breathing to me, and they have always been one of my strongest tools for success. My family is my foundation and reason for living the way I do, for the pursuit of helping others.

My cultural background stems from my upbringing in my grandparents' house. I didn't have the typical childhood living with a mom and dad. I had the privilege of hearing all of Papa's old stories whenever I wanted and got to eat all of Mama's good southern food, especially those cakes and pies. In our family, it's a part of our culture to call my grandparents "Mama and Papa" regardless of age. Mama and Papa's house serves as the root and foundation of my life. It's where I learned the basics: right from wrong, good and bad, and most importantly good morals and leadership. Our home is exceedingly special because of the tradition held in it and legacies that will be left. This place is also special because at one point most of my relatives on my mother's side lived under Mama and Papa's roof. It was Mama (Eula), Papa (Lou), my mom (Deborah), aunt (Donna), uncle (Louis), cousin (Troy), grandma (Lydia), brother (Jerome), and me (D'Leon), of course. It was a packed, but loving, household where many lessons were learned and legacies were started. This is an extraordinary place that is welcoming and where I can let my guard down and always feel protected.

On October 5, 1989, our home burned down, taking all our memories with it, but leaving our traditions in our hearts. When our house burned down, the community was exceedingly helpful, especially our church. This tragedy left my family hurt mentally, financially, and spiritually. But the community stepped in to help my family in this time of need. We had a large family with tons of duties such as school and work. The community helped us get clothing, meals, and transportation. Even though I was young at the time of this event, looking back on it, I noticed how civically engaged the community was with our family, and I can see my family doing the same for others.

This experience made our bond stronger not only with ourselves but also with the community. After our home was restored, my grandmother started to get lots of business for her famous cakes and pies. Also, her sewing business boomed, especially during prom season. My uncle and grandpa's barbershop in the basement was so busy that they were forced to relocate to a central location in the community. From these experiences I learned that though our place was once destroyed, we grew and learned in ways that benefit our family and allow us to better connect with our community.

Home is important to my family. In our family home, there are several places that are known for their rich teaching. The family room was a place in Mama and Papa's house to let loose and relax on the couch, watch the game, and hear Papa's old war stories. The family room was essential, because it's where I learned what was going on in the family, like when our next community outing would be, such as basketball, football, or having a cookout. I can recall listening to Papa's sto-

ries and learning that he wanted his children and grandchildren to achieve great things in life. In the family room, I learned how to be myself, while also representing my family well within the community. The kitchen brought our family together as a whole. I was taught many ethics and morals, such as praying before meals, not talking with food in your mouth, and not putting your elbows on the table. Mama and Papa's kitchen was also a place where everyone was welcome and received a good southern meal. But the living room and dining room were totally off limits. The only times that someone was permitted into these rooms were on special occasions such as Thanksgiving, Christmas, Easter, and so forth. But, even then, access was only granted to adults eighteen and older. In all of these rooms, I learned values, morals, and traditions.

My legacy is something that is still in the making. It is currently stamped "unknown" because I am still living and am still bestowing my gifts and creations on society. When I am dead and gone, my legacy will forever be revealed as a man that stood for what he believes in. I am passionate about life and about living it to the fullest. This is me.

A Cultural Snapshot of Shernã

S hernã is a petite young woman with a very reserved manner. She is a small woman with an even smaller voice. Though her statements are not audibly "big," they always seem to have a large impact. Her words are meaningful and important. She is majoring in journalism and has aspirations of being a writer. For her, this is a very meaningful process. Though she knew what her family valued and how they approached life, she did not necessarily know why. Being asked to tell her cultural story helped her to understand her family. She shared with me that participating in this experience helped her reflect and come to know and appreciate herself even more. Her story captures the essence of why family is important to a young person of color.

Shernã is from Baltimore, Maryland. Although there are parts of Baltimore that are bad, she is often frustrated by the gross stereotypes that many people now hold of her city because of what they view on television shows like *The Wire* or *The Corner*. But she admits that Baltimore has its rough edges—with blades that cut deep. Shernã is a woman who is both proud and bothered by the realities of her city. Her mother was raised on Bonaparte Avenue in Baltimore and still holds fond memories of the neighborhood. But when Shernã looks at the street, she can see only a neighborhood drowning in crime and negativity.

Mommy said it was more of a community. . . . Back in the day people kind of looked out for one another. It's hard for me to imagine people on Bonaparte Avenue looking out for anyone but themselves. Whenever I tag along with Momma or Mommy to visit people in the old neighborhood, I can't resist the temptation to watch over my shoulders. One time, Momma ran into a man on the street that she once babysat as a child. "Little Something" is what she called him. He smiled, gave her a hug, told her his parents were in the house, walked to the nearest curb, and kept right on pushing drugs. The crime rate on Bonaparte Ave. alone could put any ghetto to shame.

But she also has a love for Baltimore—"home" for her is more of the quality places and good memories than the community failures. One good place in Baltimore is her grandmother's "big, yellow, unattached house." Shernā's grandmother worked extremely hard to buy the house—she "saved and saved because she always wanted an unattached house" rather than a row house. Each time Shernā talks about her grandmother's home she describes it as "unattached." At first, I couldn't understand what the big deal was about this unattached home. I am originally from South Carolina where unattached homes and big yards are the norm. But as I sank deeper into her story and thought more critically about the African American urban experience, I got it. There is distinct pride in her family having a lot that is all their own and complete control over their circumstance. There is comfort in not being bound to another's situation—not having to hope that your neighbor acts right, does right, and lives right. Families in urban communities are so used to sharing so much of their lived experience and doing it all within such limited space that an unattached home can be a much-appreciated gift.

It was in this house that Shernā was raised for the first two years of her life. She lived with so many family members in her grandmother's house that she began to confuse titles and called her grandmother "Momma" and her grandfather "Daddy." Her relationships with her extended family members were cemented during those years of living together. She feels a closeness to her grandparents that resembles the relationship of parent and child.

> For two years, though I can't remember exactly, I lived with my maternal grandmother, Annie May Johnson (better known as "Momma") and my grandfather, Willie James Johnson (better known as "Daddy") in their big yellow unattached house with nearly all of my immediate family members: Momma, Daddy, Mommy, Aunt Thomasine, Antoine (my brother), Cousin Q, and I lived together under one roof, and Uncle James would often come visit us. Within those two years of my life, I decided to call my grandfather "Daddy," my grandmother "Momma," and my mother "Mommy." I'm not sure why. I just couldn't distinguish between parents. I heard my mommy calling my grandfather "Daddy," so I did too. Until this day, my grandfather has been the only true father figure in my life. So calling him "Daddy" is explanatory. As for Mommy and Momma, I'd like to think that in my first two years of life I immediately realized our connection. And perhaps that's why their identities are separated by a letter—one letter—one generation of change, an evolution even.

Throughout Shernā's life story are stories of single motherhood. When Shernā's mother was nineteen, she gave birth to Shernā's older brother, and then, seven years later and still a single mother, she gave birth to Shernā. She and her children lived with her parents because of financial need and the challenges that she faced raising two children by herself. On a different note, Shernā's grandmother, though married, was often left to take on household and parental responsibility alone because Shernā's grandfather drank a lot. Like many good men with good intentions, her grandfather worked hard, dealt with racism, came home, and embraced a bottle of alcohol to escape it all. Unfortunately, though he was physically present, he often was not mentally present in the household. It makes sense that when she thinks of culture, she thinks of it as female dominated. "The women in my family run things. . . . When I look at Mommy I see myself in twenty-seven years. I see a strong, self-sufficient woman who has carefully molded me into a replica of her essence." Shernā has never met her father, and her grandfather died ten years ago. She is a student surrounded by beautiful black female role models.

A writer, poet, and singer, throughout her narrative Shernā weaves in song and poem that give texture both to the flow of her writing and to her life story. She comments often that she sees herself, her mother, and her grandmother as one person. Shernā's story challenges the stigma that is often attached to single motherhood. As a child of a single mother, she does not run away from her mother's life choices—she embraces and appreciates them. She is proud of her single mom. Shernā is appreciative of all that her grandparents have done for her, regardless of their struggles, challenges, and imperfections. These family members are models of the resilient and skillful person that she hopes to become—not through having their same experience, but through sharing their same spirit and drive to overcome any situation. Life may have dealt her mom a challenging hand, but she won the pot. Shernā's mom came out of single motherhood with a steady professional job and a healthy extended family foundation for her two children.

Shernā says that every black girl has a song to sing. This song is both philosophical (the song of her life) and literal (a song that re-members her culture, that puts it all together). As Shernā puts it, "Though each generation has a unique song to sing, all are in harmony." This harmony of memory, belonging, and heritage is illustrated through the childhood rhyme songs that Shernā and her two mothers sang as children. For her grandmother the song was sung in the countryside of South Carolina.

Every black girl has a song to sing that lures her to the past. In the 1940s southern black girls played on dirt pathways and sang songs like this:

Little girl had a rooster
She brought her hen a rooster
The old hen died, the old rooster cried
"I couldn't lay an egg like I use to"

Her mother sang her song on a stoop in Baltimore with her friends.

> Yeah, every black girl has a song to sing, but it's not always pretty. In the 1960s southern black women moved to the North, where their little black girls sat on the stoop and sang songs like this:

Miss Mary Mack, mack, mack
All dressed in black, black, black
With silver buttons, buttons, buttons
All down her back, back, back
She asked her mother, mother, mother
For 15 cents, cents, cents,
To see the elephant, elephant, elephant
That jumped the fence, fence, fence . . .

And Shernã sang her song throughout Baltimore City.

> I sang this song at the playground during recess at Cross Country Elementary School, on the stoop at my apartment house in West Baltimore City—I sang this song among childhood friends with sassiness everywhere possible. Thinking of this song brings back childhood memories that I'm now certain Momma and Mommy must share. Yeah, every black girl has a song, but it's not always easy to sing. In the 1990s northern black women raised their citified black girls, who danced in the street to sing songs like this:

We're going to Kentucky
We're going to the fair
To see that sister Rita
With the flowers in her hair
Oh, shake it, sister Rita
Shake it like you can
Shake it like a milkshake
And do the best you can

These songs illustrate both cultural evolution and cultural sustainability. The environment changed, the topic matter evolved from a rural perspective to an urban one, but young black women continued to get together with their friends and sing these creative songs that were a reflection of their experiences. Shernã's story is full of the beautiful reasons why family seems to be so important to students of color. Family is important because the first community to which young people belong is their family. This was most often an extended community and included anyone that cared enough to get involved. Family is important because they were the first people to work tirelessly to offer help and support. Shernã's grandmother working several jobs to buy a large "unattached" home was not a selfish effort. That house sheltered her children and her grandchildren when they had no other place to live. Family is important because it has been the one steady, close, and enduring rock on which they could lean all of their lives. Childhood friends come and go, but family sustains. Shernā may have sung that sassy "Shake it Rita" song with her friends, but her familial song is ongoing and everlasting. Because her family modeled the way, paved the way, and created a way to live, to Shernā family is culture.

> Every black girl has a song to sing, and sometimes it's quite happy. . . . Mommy says that we are all giving people, we like helping people. We are strong and we stick to our ground. I say, "I am who I am because you have showed me the way. I have strength because you are strong. I am content with being alone because you are independent. I value my education because you never took it for granted. I'm a hard worker because you never gave up. I am who I am because of my Momma and Mommy. I love you.

A Half-Full Glass of Family Bonds Critical Essay

First and foremost, the foundation of any family is based on the relationship between the two stewards that create it. This past year, I began to invite friends over for a monthly supper club to break bread over good food and good conversation. Our conversation topics have been many and varied, a mix of deep philosophical debates and simple lighthearted and sometimes silly fun. But the persisting topics of conversation are the relationship between men and women, the challenges with marriage, and the varying perspectives of what it is like to be still single in your thirties or forties. Ultimately, these conversations have explored the first step in family making. Today there are many social influences that impact the building of healthy families. The challenges of trying to do something as basic as form a couple are bolstered by the presence of issues that were not a reality for other young couples in the past. The now generally wide acceptance of divorce and the feeling that there is no longer a required permanency when it comes to marriage can sometimes influence how willing a couple is to stick it out or stay the course and work it out. Divorce and dysfunction have existed for decades—many partners have abandoned the family or drunk themselves into a mental detachment. So I do not suggest that all couples in the past valued commitment more than those today. I am also not suggesting that divorce is not an important choice—sometimes the best thing for a child is not to be raised in a house where the two parents have contempt for or hate each other. Such a situation does not model a healthy and loving image of a relationship for the child, and so sometimes it is best for the couple to love their children separately. But just as things like going to rehab and at some level going to jail have been normalized, have come to be accepted, and are sometimes expected in society, so has the reality of marriage being dispensable.

Forming healthy, loving, and lasting relationships is a key issue that young people today must directly confront. In one of our dinner conversations, a friend commented that the realities of today make relationships different—people date much longer and more widely over the course of their lives, and so the rules of engagement have changed. This is true. Society is different. People are different. The very meaning of dating is different.

But these have not been the only changes to the act of coupling. There is also an ethic of humility that is not present within many contemporary relationships. I shared with my friends the ways that my parents actively demonstrated love and commitment to one another. My mother ran my father's bath every day, and she ironed his clothes, not out of obligation but out of love. Her husband worked three jobs. He would go to work at four o'clock in the afternoon and come home at seven o'clock the next morning, sleep for six hours, then do it all over again. My dad was always tired. So he was not looking for love to take the shape of romantic encounters. He needed love to be an act that simply helped him to get through his day. How do I want you to show love for me? Please iron my clothes because my body is simply worn out after working fifteen hours to support you and our children. I don't need anything big or fancy, just simply a warm bath and work clothes that are pressed and ready. If you love me can you please willingly and simply help me to make it through. But in today's world, men and women seem to be pitted against one another. Simple acts of humble love are often classified as oppressive and sexist expectations that all women should resist. This loving image of my mother—a black woman—caring for her man is almost nonexistent in the social messages and images that we now consume.

Pop culture often has a large and subliminal influence on how we are socialized to form ideas about men, women, gender roles, marriage, and relationships. Repetitive messaging and portrayals of women as gold diggers and manipulators or controlling dictators in relationships make some men believe these things and teach some women that to act in such ways is expected. One of the best examples was a controversial Pepsi commercial shown during the 2011 Super Bowl. The commercial features a black couple in a series of day-to-day situations in which the wife seriously harasses, belittles, and demeans her husband. With each scene we are shown a message that ultimately communicates that black women drain the joy out of a man's life. The commercial ends with the couple sitting on a park bench when a young and seemingly carefree white woman jogs up and sits on the next bench. The husband looks at her with the first lasting expression of joy and happiness that he has shown in the entire commercial (every other time he is about to experience a moment of joy his wife comes in and steals that moment). This other woman is superficially opposite to the African American woman—she is white, she is younger, she is fit (as she jogs while the black woman is sitting drinking soda). And so the message is that she is a refreshing departure from the dry marriage to which he is obligated. The commercial concludes with the black wife throwing her soda can at

him and mistakenly hitting the white woman. And so the last scene is the cul-
mination of the anger and hostility that society believes to be present in black
women—she will control you and harass you, and she is capable of violence.
Many folks laughed at this commercial, and I am not suggesting that this one
commercial is responsible for the high levels of misunderstanding and negative
opinions of men and women of color. But I am firm in my belief that it is just
one of several examples of the ways that we have been socialized to accept and
laugh at negative imaging of ourselves. Mass media surround us, and we now
often pay to receive cable messages that are racist, buy tickets to movies that are
sexist, and pay for admission to social functions that are classist. We have more
access to society than ever before, and the result of that access has not necessarily been all positive. Never before have people so widely invested in their own
oppression. And too often, we do not see how these structures subtly impact
and influence our thoughts, priorities, beliefs, and values. The two young adults
featured at the beginning of this chapter reveal their cultural life experiences
in a black family. I share their stories because across several ethnic groups, the
breakdown of the family structure has been most deeply experienced by the African American community.[1] And so a critical focus on the African American
family is first warranted in this larger conversation about family and culture.
What has happened within the African American community has implications
for oppressed communities of all ethnicities.

If you rely on news articles, policy papers, and research reports to form
your sole impression of the African American family unit, undoubtedly the
outlook is bleak. We are surrounded with information that tells us that families are failing, fathers are not present, parents are not parenting, and the bonds
of family have been broken. The comedian Chris Rock sums it up perfectly: "If
a kid calls his grandmother 'Mommy' and his mother 'Pam,' there's something
wrong."[2] Something is out of order for some, not all, black families. The report
on the black family is often a pathology report. But to understand this issue requires an examination of the larger society in which families are formed, not
just the family itself. The American power structure and the history of oppression that it has created for African Americans have had a devastating effect on
the African American family unit. The issues that we see today are merely links
on a chain of oppression that began a long time ago. Whether forcibly during
slavery or as a voluntary reaction to life pressures, disruption to the immediate
family unit is not new to black families. Frederick Douglass, in his acclaimed
autobiography *The Narrative of the Life of Frederick Douglass* noted that it was
a general practice among slaveholders in the South to immediately separate an
infant from its mother and to charge an elder enslaved woman with raising the
children of the plantation.[3] This practice prevented infants from developing a
strong attachment and allegiance to the mother and the mother from enacting
the role of nurturer, which might distract her from her labor duties.[4] Furthermore, as the practice of slavery grew as a domestic institution, so did the number of slavery-specific laws in America. Enslaved African Americans could not

enter into legal marriage because it was against the law for them to execute legal contracts.[5] Thus the majority of marriages were more cultural rituals than legal commitments. The success of slavery as a business institution was in direct opposition to the formation of healthy family units among the enslaved. Often, husbands, wives, and children were separated through the trade or sometimes forced to remarry and break marriage bonds for the purpose of breeding. Booker T. Washington argued that the lack of strong ancestral influence and knowledge among African Americans further deprived the black child of a strong sense of self-efficacy:

> The influence of ancestry, however, is important in helping forward any individual or race. . . . Those who constantly direct attention to the Negro youth's moral weaknesses, and compare his advancement with that of white youths, do not consider the influence of the memories which cling about the old family homesteads. . . . The very fact that the white boy is conscious that, if he fails in life, he will disgrace the whole family record, extending back through many generations, is of tremendous value in helping him to resist temptations. The fact that the individual has behind and surrounding him proud family history and connection serves as a stimulus to help him to overcome obstacles when striving for success.[6]

Though black families throughout history have established strong family units and created their own ritualistic marriage bonds, despite the laws of the day, the direct, intentional, and continual role of society in stunting the growth of a family ethic within the African American community is important to note. After decades of constant oppressive politics in America (the Black Codes of the 1800s, Jim Crow of the 1900s, Reaganomics of the 1980s), what has been the result? It is almost difficult to escape the pathology report. The American power structure has in fact caused a life of dis-ease for some. Marian Wright Edelman provided the devastating detail in her text *Families in Peril*. Edelman offered the following statistics on the black family in the decade of the 1980s:

> Black children are twice as likely to die in the first year of life, be born prematurely, live in substandard housing, have no parent employed, and live in institutions; three times as likely to be poor, live in a female headed household, be in foster care, and die of known child abuse; four times as likely to live with neither parent, be incarcerated between fifteen and nineteen years of age; five times as likely to live with a parent who never married. Only four out of every ten black children, compared to eight out of every ten white children live in two parent families.[7]

Edelman went on to refer to William Wilson's belief that the delay in marriage and lower rate of remarriage, which contributed to the number of single-parent households in the 1980s, were most closely aligned with the lack of access provided to black males within the labor market. According to both Edelman and Wilson, black women are facing an increasingly small marriage pool of black men.[8] They define "marriageable" as employed and economically stable. The mix of inferior education, persisting discriminatory practices, and an internalized sense of defeat has proved lethal to the young black male and thus to the black family. Edelman also asserted that an unwillingness to accept jobs perceived as low-end and dead-end and increased urbanization, desegregation, and the black middle-class flight to the suburbs "made a sense of hope more remote for the poor blacks left behind."[9] Written in the mid-1980s, Edelman's extensive critique of the black family was too early to include another factor that has since had a devastating impact on the black community: illegal drug use.

The introduction of drugs into the African American community in the late 1970s served to tranquilize an already socially numb community. The drug-trafficking trade offered alternatives for two very desperate populations: those seeking to nullify the pain of social struggle and those for whom the door of opportunity seemed permanently closed. The effect of participation in the drug scene thus created a subclass of drug-addicted or drug-selling parents. The ill effect of drugs is then added to the long list of social crises befalling impoverished black people: the deterioration of skilled and higher paying jobs in urban communities; less public support for public housing, health care, and education; the breakdown of the economic infrastructure of the ghetto; and newly adopted means of coercion by the corporate and private sector as a means of regulation.[10] So even those families that did not succumb to the nullification of drugs still suffered in some ways from the social suffocation of oppression. And even in families that remained intact, there could have still existed a strong level of dysfunction. As Nathan McCall[11] notes, the presence of a frustrated and oppressed parent can be a dangerous and destructive element in the household. Every member of the family is then affected by these issues as they prevent the parent from fully developing and actualizing the role of nurturer, as did slavery in years past. In the more than twenty years since Edelman's book was published, the statistics for the black family have not seen much improvement. According to the 2007 U.S. Census Bureau report on community in America:

> The average African-American family median income was $33,916 in comparison to $54,920 for non-Hispanic White families. In 2007, the U.S. Census bureau reported that 24.5 percent of African-Americans in comparison to 8.2 percent of non-Hispanic Whites were living at the poverty level. In 2007, the unemployment rate for Blacks was twice that for non-Hispanic Whites (8 percent and 4 percent, respectively). . . . In 2005, the death rate for African-Americans was higher than Whites for heart diseases, stroke, cancer, asthma, influenza and pneumonia, diabetes, HIV/AIDS, and homicide. . . . African-American infants were almost four times as likely to die from causes related

to low birth weight, compared to non-Hispanic white infants. . . . African-American females had more than 22 times the AIDS rate of non-Hispanic white females.[12]

This is a lot to stomach. And it is not every African American's life experience. But we are all affected by the social factors that influence these statistics. The ideas and concepts that surround "wealth" whether as a real statistic or a media-driven cultural myth can often impact the way that young people make sense of and evaluate their families. Images of "wealth" have most often been offered through television. In the 1950s and 1960s concepts of wealth were shaped through shows like *Father Knows Best* and *Leave It to Beaver*; in the 1980s through shows like *Lifestyles of the Rich and Famous* and *Dynasty*; and in the twenty-first century through reality shows like *The Real Housewives*, *Keeping Up with the Kardashians*, and *Jersey Shore*. The incredible access that everyday people have to glimpse the so-called fabulous and overly indulgent lifestyles of the rich is now almost excessive. These images of the "good life" have the potential of influencing how young people measure the realities of their own life—even when that life might be modest but culturally rich and strong. In the book *Rereading America: Cultural Contexts for Critical Thinking and Writing*, Gary Soto tells a story about his childhood and his attempts to get his family to imitate "perfect" families:

> One July while killing ants on the kitchen sink with a rolled newspaper, I had a nine-year-old's vision of wealth that would save us from ourselves. For weeks I had drunk Kool-Aid and watched morning reruns of *Father Knows Best*, whose family was so uncomplicated in its routine that I very much wanted to imitate it. The first step was to get my brother and sister to wear shoes to dinner. "Come on Rick—come on Deb," I whined. But Rick mimicked me and the same day that I asked him to wear shoes he came to the dinner table in only his swim trunks. My mother didn't notice, nor did my sister, as we sat to eat our beans and tortillas in the stifling heat of our kitchen. We all gleamed like cellophane, wiping the sweat from our brows with the backs of our hands as we talked about the day. Frankie our neighbor was beat up by Faustino; the swimming pool at the playground would be closed for a day because the pump was broken. Such was our life.[13]

Young minds are indeed impressionable. As an adult, Gary Soto can look back at his life with great pride and appreciation for the overwhelming love that was present in his home. His story reveals the glimpses of economic disparity that is real for so many families of color: living without the convenience of an air conditioner, living with pests because extermination is a luxury, and living in a neighborhood where the local community center also struggled to keep programs running and to stay afloat. But these experiences gave meaning and shape to his life and his cultural outlook. While reading his story, I thought of a student who came into my office in the University Cultural Center a few years ago. He was a first-year student and clearly at the stage of enjoying college but beginning to miss home a bit. He asked me if I would go home that night, make him an egg salad sandwich, and bring it to campus for him the next day. Students had asked me for a lot of things—never an egg salad sandwich. But he said that egg salad sandwiches reminded him of home. A modest meal of egg salad was his fond memory—not steak or seafood, not lasagna or even spaghetti, which often requires sauce, meat, and pasta. Quite honestly, you can buy a loaf of bread, a dozen eggs, and a jar of mayo for less than five dollars and you can feed a whole family. Time and again, families remind us that money isn't everything.

But even still, money is most definitely an important factor of survival in America. Economics impacts the type of education we will receive, the state of our health (disease, diet, and stress), where we will reside, how we will get to work, and how many hours we will spend there. Wealth continues to be a serious issue in the health and lives of all people, and we can't simply dismiss it by saying, "Money doesn't matter." In 2011, the Pew Research Center[14] reported the largest economic gap in household wealth in twenty-five years. According to the report, which measured social and demographic trends from 2004 to 2009, the median net worth (all assets minus all liabilities) of white households was twenty times that of African Americans and eighteen times that of Hispanics. The net worth of Hispanic households decreased from $18,359 in 2005 to $6,325 in 2009—a decrease of 66 percent. The net worth of black households fell from $12,124 in 2005 to $5,677 in 2009, a drop of about 53 percent. These major drops in wealth have been attributed to the recent housing crisis. But white and Asian populations, though affected by the crisis, still maintain a much larger share of wealth in the United States.

> The drop in the wealth of white households was modest in comparison, falling 16% from $134,992 in 2005 to $113,149 in 2009. Though white households were also affected by the housing crisis, home equity accounts for relatively less of their total net worth (44% in 2005), and that served to lessen the impact of the housing bust. In 2005, the median Asian household wealth had been greater than the median for white households, but by 2009 Asians lost their place at the top of the wealth hierarchy. Their net worth fell from $168,103 in 2005 to $78,066 in 2009, a drop of 54%. . . . About a quarter of all Hispanic (24%) and black (24%) households in 2009 had no assets other than a vehicle.[15]

It is important to note that because the wealthiest in our country belong to the Asian and white communities, their overwhelming amount of wealth influences these numbers. There are many white and Asian Americans who do not have a significant amount of wealth and who also struggle in the face of poverty or suffer because of the disappearance of a true middle class in America.

But overwhelmingly, Latinos and African Americans have been the hardest hit. Homeownership continues to be the major source of wealth creation for African American and Latino communities. The major disparities in business ownership and investments contribute to the lingering economic gap across racial communities. And economic struggle most definitely puts a heavy strain on the family.

Beyond African Americans, subpopulations among many underrepresented ethnic groups also have long histories of struggle to sustain healthy and strong families in the face of economic and social oppression. One group that has faced similar challenge and social struggle has been Puerto Ricans. Also, coming from a history of European servitude on agricultural farms located on the island, Puerto Ricans living in Puerto Rico had very little political agency until 1949 when they democratically elected their first governor.[16] Though they live on U.S. territory and have been U.S. citizens since 1917, they cannot vote for president and have limited representation within U.S. politics. Whether on the island or on the mainland, Puerto Ricans find themselves on the margins of U.S. society. A large wave of Puerto Ricans began to leave the island in the 1950s and relocated to New York—a city with easy and cheap travel and many job opportunities.[17] But as the jobs began to dry up in the 1970s, many Puerto Rican families remained in New York and struggled to survive in an overcrowded, highly competitive, and extremely expensive city. Chavez and Guido-Dibrito explain:

> In 1961, in their influential book *Beyond the Melting Pot*, Nathan Glazer and Daniel P. Moynihan described Puerto Ricans "adapting to a city [New York] very different from the one to which earlier immigrant groups adapted, and . . . being modified by the new process of adaptation in new and hardly predictable ways." Thirty years later the results of that adaptation are apparent. Puerto Ricans are not simply the poorest of all Hispanic groups; they experience the highest degree of social dysfunction of any Hispanic group and exceed that of blacks on some indicators. Thirty nine percent of all Puerto Rican families are headed by single women; 53 percent of all Puerto Rican children are born out of wedlock; the proportion of men in the labor force is lower among Puerto Ricans than any other group, including blacks; Puerto Ricans have the highest welfare participation rate of any group in New York, where nearly half of all Puerto Ricans in the United States live.[18]

Much of what influences these dire statistics has to do with two factors: inadequate education and economics. Inadequate education refers to not only noncompetitive K–12 education but also a lack of lifelong education about core social issues such as health (including nutrition, medical conditions, mental, and sexual health). Unfortunately, health education is often tied to issues of economics.[19] The poorest in the United States (across all races) are the ones with a lack of access to proper health care, health insurance, healthy food, mechanisms for stress relief, and the education to teach them what they should be doing to take care of themselves (although they might not be able to afford to implement these strategies even if they were educated on the issue). In his chapter in the book *The Covenant with Black America*, David Satcher suggests that it will take a broad network of social strategies to address the crack that life in America has put in the foundation of some families. Though not impossible (many oppressed families prove this statement every day), it is difficult for families to concentrate simply on loving and raising children when many are constantly battling poverty, poor health, and an inadequate knowledge base. Satcher writes: "Many things must change to secure the right health care, healthy living, and well-being in America. The solution to this pervasive problem of health disparities is that we must advocate for system changes that include universal health insurance, guaranteed primary medical homes, proportionate representation in health professions, bias-free interventions, nonviolent and exercise-friendly neighborhoods, nutritious food outlets, educational equality, career opportunities, parity in income and wealth, homeownership, and hope. There are individual, community, and governmental responsibilities for achieving these goals."[20]

For some families in today's society, the glass of family bonds is not overflowing, it is not even full. And some families have always been thirsty, always struggling from generation to generation. To paint a picture of family as perfect and always positive would be to offer forth a distorted image. And so I first acknowledge the challenges, shortcomings, and obstacles that some families face. But what this group of young people shared with me is that the glass of family bonds is not empty either. When young people thirst for love and support, their family provides that nourishment regardless of how empty the well might be. And though no family is perfect, there are many healthy black, Latino, indigenous, and Asian family units out there with a strong foundation, active parents, and the sense of family history that Booker T. Washington discussed. So it does make sense that when I asked, "What is culture to you?" the young people replied, "Family."

A Family Treasure Chest

Family, above all else, was the most significant component of anything cultural. The personal relationships that young adults form among family and community friends established the foundation for their basic understanding of culture. Their family structure was more like a community that included many people beyond their immediate parents and siblings. Across all ethnic groups, family was a treasure chest of grandparents, other extended family members, neighbors, and unrelated friends of the family whom they still referred to as "aunt" or "uncle." These extended family networks were actively involved in helping to raise and care for them as children. The members of this community family helped to shape their values and ethics by sharing with these young people important wisdom from their life experiences. But most importantly, these extended family members seemed to model an ethic of stepping in to help out a struggling friend or family member. Typically, single mothers relied heavily on family and friends to help. Therefore, children were never really raised by one, single person but instead surrounded by a community of loved ones. In this cultural world, a mother's best friend became "Aunt" and a grandmother became "Mama." Among African Americans in particular, the concept of extended family networks is not new. In her book *Black Picket Fences: Privilege and Peril among the Black Middle Class*, Mary Patillo-McCoy engages an in-depth case study of the Groveland community in Chicago's South Side. Groveland, a middle-class neighborhood in Chicago, has its share of elder grandparents that are now taking care of their children and their children's children—all of whom had a more difficult time carving out opportunity in America. Patillo-McCoy blames the changing culture in America toward antiaffirmative action, weakened antidiscrimination efforts, and consistently decreasing employment opportunities for the struggle that many children of Baby Boomers have faced trying to "make it" or at the least make it better than their parents.[21] The reality is that in some ways our parents and grandparents had the advantage of feeling the initial breeze as the door of equal opportunity programs opened. This helped initially to establish a middle class of color . . . factory jobs, administrative jobs, and government jobs. But as many of their children attempted to walk through this same door, they first encountered a push back, and eventually realized that the door had been effectively closed and locked. Some of the now adult children of that generation have found themselves and their own children living at home with their parents as a form of life support. The numbers are not large for this scenario, but their story and experience are still important. From the grandparents' perspective, it is simply an example of a parent's love— it never ends. The Groveland parents are good examples:

> Both Mrs. Arthur and Mrs. Waters fear what could happen to their children and grandchildren. They could easily draw on numerous examples of neighboring families who have suffered through drug addiction, unemployment, or plain irresponsibility. When these are the things that parents fear, one way to protect the children is to keep them under one's roof. When adult children continue to live with their parents, the parents get the peace of mind of being able to monitor their children's activities. They do not have to worry as much about drugs, or jail, or homelessness, as they would if they insisted that their children get out. For the second generation, their parents' support allows them to use their money to save for a car or a house, to get back on their feet after a divorce or job set back, or sometimes simply for their own leisure activities.[22]

Beyond Groveland, and within the group I studied, this community and extended family involvement personified a cultural ethic of selflessness and generosity that was deeply appreciated as these young adults reflected on their lives. Bre, a biracial college senior, wrote about the role family played in shaping culture broadly and building her sense of self in particular: "Family is a monumental symbol in black culture. Family played an extensive role in helping me cope with my insecurities. My grandfather, whom I lovingly call 'Pop-Pop,' serves as one of my greatest inspirations. Moreover, he is one of the reasons that I am where I am today. My great-grandmother, my grandmother (Mom-Mom), my mother, and myself are all one."

Bre's comment posits family not only as a major influence on who she has become but also as a *part* of who she is—her family lives *with* her physically and *inside* of her spiritually. Like Bre, many students commented on grandparents playing an active role in their lives. Almost half the students interviewed for this project spent portions of their childhood residing with grandparents or extended family members. Mark, a Filipino American sophomore, related his family experience:

> My parents were both born in the Philippines and moved to the U.S. when they were really young. So while I am technically second generation, I consider myself more of a second-and-a-half-generation Filipino American. It was pretty crazy living with my grandparents, parents, three brothers, and one little sister. My grandparents were semitraditional in that we would always have a dish with rice and that their side of the house was full of clutter. They both loved to garden, so the backyard was split: half grass and playground, half garden with fruits and vegetables. They would invite "aunts" and "uncles" over for dinner that weren't actually related. They had a "barcada," or clique, in Tagalog.

Mark's multigenerational family and community experience immersed him in his native language (Tagalog) and established a special community (which he refers to as a clique) that bound by culture. In many ways, the prevalence of young adults having spent most of their childhood living with extended family seems to challenge the idea that the "It takes a village" ethic no longer exists in contemporary cultural communities. Both cultural heritage and economic realities have made this ethic a contemporary reality. Norris, a young biracial man, says, "It has helped me realize that family is not just people that share the same last name or live in the same house or even people that have the same bloodline as you. Culture is sharing different experiences with one another . . . helping each other."

Many others also called their grandparents by titles that seem to indicate a closeness that may have been motivated by their living situation. "Pop-Pop," "Mom-Mom," and "G-mom," are just some of the titles given to these extended family members, which seem to serve more as terms of endearment than explanations of family position. The opportunity for multigenerational connection is a critical insight as even those who did not physically live with their grandparents or extended family members still referenced the influence of family on their cultural development. For example, Francheska, a Puerto Rican American student, gave this account:

> As soon as June hit and the school year was over, we were on a plane headed to Puerto Rico. My sister, brother, and I spent three months out of every year in Puerto Rico at my grandmother's house. My grandmother passed down to me the values that make me who I am. My grandmother taught me how to pray and how to find strength in God. Every single night, right before bed, my grandmother would pray the rosary on the porch in her rocking chair. With the serenity of the night, with the chimes of the coquís, and with the slight illumination of the stars and moon, she and I could feel God as we prayed. She began teaching me the Our Fathers and Hail Marys and eventually gave me my first blue and white rosary. My grandmother believed, loved, and cared for all of God's creations, which is the reason I have a big heart. I care and love all things because my grandmother taught me that in God's eyes we are all equal and that we should care for all things on this earth. . . . My grandmother taught me that the way to demonstrate God's love was to care about my community. Everyone in Dorado (el barrio where she lived) respected and loved my grandmother because she always gave to others. I would accompany her as she walked el barrio paying visits to the sick and giving away clothes to those in need. Having this as an example of how to care about others at a young age taught me to close my eyes to the individualistic society I had to return to in August.

Several communicated a value for having a large support network through their family—numerous people from whom they could learn or with whom they could socialize. Keith proudly spoke of the size and importance of his family: "My mother's side of the family is extremely large. I have numerous uncles, aunts, and cousins. . . . It's around forty people that I really have a good relationship with. . . . My culture is really around family and family values. I've been raised to respect and believe in your family because they are the only people that really care about you. This culture that I have grown up in has shaped my personality a great deal."

Courtney, an African American student from Philadelphia, told a story about meeting her father's family for the first time. For her, discovering a large family network was similar to uncovering a treasure: "One day while my mom and I were at the mall, she said that my father's mother didn't live far. So I suggested we stop by. That day I went to my grandmother's house for the first time and met a whole host of family members I never knew about. I loved it. Considering that my mom's side of the family is fairly small, I was excited to see that I had so many aunts and cousins."

During our conversations, students gleamed as they talked about their families—the closeness, the size, and the ways in which their families engage one another. For Larren, an African American student also from Philly, the fact that her family is large and that she is provided opportunities to engage with different family members is important. "Each Thanksgiving at least thirty-two family members and friends pile into cousin Debbie's home. Everyone contributes to the dinner. As long as it takes for us to get together is as long as it takes for us to depart one another. But my family is big on holidays, and everyone contributes. Christmas dinner is at Aunt Edna's house; Fourth of July cookout is at Cousin Tanya's; Easter dinner is at Grandmom's; Thanksgiving dinner is at Cousin Debbie and Aaron's home every year.

The idea of having a large community of support (forty people, thirty-two family members) was a source of pride for many. A sense of togetherness is an important part of culture. The bond among family seemed to be very important. In many ways, their family created the initial example and birthed the value for community loyalty and closeness. Thanh, a Vietnamese American student, shared her story:

> I discovered the untold origins of my family. For the first time, I talked to my forty-two-year-old aunt and my fifty-five-year-old father about their refugee experiences. Both the emotional and political aspects of their stories shocked me. "I read about that!" was what I kept repeating in my head as I listened to them. I learned that my family intentionally kept these stories to themselves. My dad did not want to burden us with his pains and hardships. I understand now that my dad was engaging in an act of love. He was embracing my happiness at the cost of his own. My family is my unconditional love. My family is everything to me, and I would not have them any other way. As I took a deep look into my cultural mirror, I see that I was the one who did not know *them*. . . . The American culture allows me to express myself. But the Vietnamese culture allows me to love, know, and celebrate my father, mother, uncles, and aunts as individuals. The appreciation of my family's Vietnamese roots makes me a humble American. I am an American Vietnamese.

It took time and growth for Thanh to come to appreciate the value of being close to her family and appreciating the wisdom that they had to offer. She was like many teenagers, feeling as if her parents did not understand her or could not relate to her struggles. It was when she finally sat down with her family during high school and listened to their stories that she realized that she did not really know struggle. Her family is like many families that come out of very hard life circumstances: the elders sometimes believe that forgetting and moving beyond those experiences is the way to give the next generation a better life. But as evidenced here, taking time to share and center young people in their past gives meaning to their present.

Keith's family is a perfect example of the importance of togetherness and closeness. Keith's last name is Baker. His grandfather was an African American man raised in Opelika, Alabama, who lived on a road called Baker Village, whose residents were mostly members of his family. When Keith shared this information, it resonated with me because this community structure is very similar to my own. My family owned one side of my grandmother's street in South Carolina. It housed aunts and uncles, sisters and brothers who all lived next door to one another. Though Keith's family and my own family no longer live on those old family dirt roads in the South, that heritage has clearly not been forgotten. Larren recalled that last Thanksgiving her grandmother had just spoken about the importance of family remaining close and holding on to family heritage:

> This Thanksgiving dinner, my great-grandmother (Ginny) made everyone realize what our culture stood for. She took us back in time and gave us some history about herself and her siblings. Ginny said, "Everyone walking around here so happy to see one another, but if it weren't for this holiday, you all would not have even thought to visit one another." Ginny never talks, so everyone is looking at her like "Huh?" She said, "Yeah, I said it" and went on to preach about how it takes for us to have a dinner or a funeral for us to get together and act as a family. She went on to say, "I am eighty-eight years old and can count on both my hands how many times my own granddaughter came to my home to visit me. Not saying we don't see each other, but it's not you coming over to say, 'Hey, Grandmom, you need anything?' or 'I just was in the area' or even 'I just want to spend the day with you.' I can count how many times Larren, Sierra, Harry, Jason, been there, and they are my great-grands. You know, I don't blame you grandkids. I blame your mother, my own daughter, because that is the way she raised ya. We've got to keep family close."

Many others began to chime in about the problems with family members moving away and the potential of the family becoming disconnected. With voices of alarm, they discussed how strong family ties are essential to sustaining culture. Without family culture cannot live. For their generation, the ability to seek out opportunity and have new experiences is important. But they all agree that opportunity cannot come at the price of the family unit falling apart and community ties being broken. Shaun, a young African American man who has been listening intensely, nodding and shaking his head throughout the conversation, speaks up for the first time: "Shit . . . we all we got. Excuse my language." I tell him it's okay—I understand. And I do.

Missing Treasures

It was when families were not able to remain intact or when they failed to demonstrate values of love, support, and loyalty that students began to discuss how family could negatively contribute to culture or fall short as a cultural structure.

Many of the students came from homes that were populated by many family members except fathers. The absence of fathers then made the extended family even more important. Norris reflects: "Although I did not have a father, I had other male role models within my community pushing me to do the right thing. My mother backed by my grandma and an array of hood uncles and aunts have helped mold me into who I am today." The importance of these extended networks went beyond providing security or support—they also provided balance to a parental scale that had been shifted completely in the mother's direction. Many saw clearly how meaningful this support was both to their development and to relieving their mother's level of responsibility. Family and friends helped to raise them, cared for them while their mother was at work, and even provided financial assistance. For Terry, an African American male student, it was a community grandfather who bought his mother a home in which to raise her family and who served as an adopted father to him: "At the age of five we moved out of an apartment into a house that my grandfather Carl had bought for us. He was not my biological grandfather, but he was the most positive black male in my life; he was like my father. My sister and I had the same mother, but we were born to different dads; but my whole life my sister never seemed like a half-sister to me because both of our fathers were not in our life, so it seemed as if we shared the same dad—nobody."

Several students spent a significant amount of space reflecting on the absence of their fathers in their lives. Though many of them commented that they "survived" the pain of parental abandonment, that the situation was "just life," or that they had many other family members helping them in place of a father, the fact that when broadly asked to discuss the topic of culture, almost half of the group at least mentioned the absence of fathers indicates that both parents are seen as important cultural tools. One of Courtney's statements illustrates this point:

> I grew up in a single-parent home. Although my grandmother and uncle lived with us, I was still deprived of a father. My mother is a very strong woman, and she made sure I had everything any child could want and need. My uncle was my best friend, the one I looked up to and admired, the one who read me stories before I went to sleep. When he moved, I was left without a father figure. I met my father once before when I was nine, but he disappeared again as usual. My father eventually went back to his ways of not coming around or calling.

Young people clearly communicate a deep love for their mothers and a sincere appreciation for extended family members. However, the missing relationship with the father still leaves a sense that there is more growth to be gained from a father's side of the family. Norris explained how knowing his father and his father's family has always been a desire. He remembered the exact date of the one meeting he had with his father.

I have always wondered what the other side was like—the other side being my father's side of his family; my dad was never present in my life. For all I know, I could be sitting in class next to my half-brother or sister and not even know it. The only time I really remember interacting and meeting him for the first time was on April 5, 1990. . . . All I remember is that he had a darker complexion than I had with a bushy mustache and a Latino accent—he was an immigrant from Panama. He asked me if I knew who he was, and I replied "no," followed by him introducing himself to me. I kind of regret not taking the opportunity to take more time to talk to him then because just as he came, he left, walking down the street waving and walking away. That was the last time I saw my father.

Though many discussed the absence of their father, Stan and Terry are the only two who discuss negative social influences like addiction and the criminal justice system that contribute to parental absence. The pain of abandonment is strong. However, the spaces to reflect on and wrestle with these feelings seems to be rare and few. Terry's portrait reveals where he turned for positive male imaging: "Most of the males in my family were in jail, on drugs, alcoholics, womanizers, or all of the above. I always wanted to be like the men from my favorite television shows such as Heathcliff Huxtable from *The Cosby Show*, a doctor; Uncle Phil from *The Fresh Prince of Bel-Air*, a lawyer; or even Carl Winslow from *Family Matters*, an officer of the law fighting crime."

In Terry's case, television provided access to professional black men. His comment speaks volumes to the need to provide more real interaction across class levels in communities. Though Terry discussed having other male figures in his life, many of these men were in similar socioeconomic situations and struggling themselves. Do not misunderstand me here, the men who struggled with jail, drugs, and alcohol provided him important love and support while they could or when they were sober. The care provided by the men that are present, regardless of their social standing, should not be diminished. It is essential. These men were not perfect, but they were present and they cared. However, Terry still turned to distant images on television for models of *professional* men. Young people need a taste of different experiences to satisfy their thirst for life. And so we need more men of color from various backgrounds serving as extended family in schools as teachers, on playgrounds as mentors, and on blocks as neighbors.

Not all incidents of paternal absence were due to abandonment, the criminal justice system, or drugs. In Bre's case, it was health. Her father died very early in her life, leaving her without a father but still with a positive image of him as a man: "If you look at my family now, we went from having many males in the family to very few. We didn't run them off. My father developed a rare form of cancer. He always worked even in his illness to make sure his family was clothed, fed, and taken care of."

Our conversations revealed a need for greater interaction with older male role models among both young women and young men of color. Sons and daughters miss their fathers enough to mention them when telling their cultural life stories. But more importantly, they clearly saw both parents as critical cultural foundations upon which their identity is built. Though no one expressed sentiments of cultural deprivation or feeling as if they were culturally half empty, many did want to know the other side of themselves—the other family from which they could learn and the other person from whom they were made.

A Half-Full Glass

Of course this discussion would not be complete without devoting space to the clear appreciation, love, and regard young people have for their mothers as cultural gardeners. The role that these women played in planting cultural seeds and harvesting the fruits of their labor through ongoing support of their children in college is incredible. Throughout this section and the others to follow, mothers, mommas, mommies, and mom-moms are mentioned, applauded, and thanked. The classic Maya Angelou poem "Phenomenal Woman"[23] was included by many as a dedication to their mothers and the role that they played in growing them as cultural beings. Upon rereading, this poem—within the context of all that has been shared by the young people here—does, in fact, capture the strength, sassiness, endurance, perseverance, abundance, loneliness, loveliness, courage, and compassion of these women.

> Now you understand, Just why my head's not bowed, I don't shout or jump about, Or have to talk real loud, When you see me passing, It ought to make you proud. I say It's in the click of my heels, The bend of my hair, The palm of my hand, The need for my care."[24]

Whether it was the cultural nurturing that family provided or the cultural void that absent family members created, family greatly influenced the cultural experience.

Despite the struggles and problems, this group spoke affectionately and optimistically about their families. In this sense, culture was a half-full rather than half-empty glass of family bonds. These young women and men were aware that there were missing pieces in their familial structure. But they still appreciated the nourishment that was present, and they were optimistic about future opportunities to continue to grow their cultural heritage. If the image of culture can be metaphorically compared to a home, then family is undoubtedly the foundation—the cement that holds it together. One young woman opened her cultural self-portrait with the following quote from Lee Iacocca, which probably best sums up the importance of family to culture: "The only rock that stays steady, the only institution that works is the family."

Ride or Die:
A Dedication to Those That Believe in the Possibility
of Love, Family, and Marriage
Toby Jenkins

I am ready to fall . . . to leap
To cry . . . to lose sleep . . . to go deep into an emotional journey
Yo, I'm ready to ride
Shotgun . . . without a seatbelt
No doubt about trusting my life in his hands
I'm ready to speed down a soulful highway where his heart and my spirit
are crossroads to our destiny
I'm even ready to break down . . . smoke, fumes, flats . . . all that
Because love is all of that
Only true joy can lead to pain . . . only hard laughs can lead to weeps . . .
And only deep passion can lead to heat and hate . . . but I'm ready to take
    the risk
I don't want to wait, negotiate, or make him do me right
I just want to let him do me right . . . I just want to forget the ones that didn't
    do me right . . .
I just want to fall . . . I just want him to call
me his friend . . . not hang out, small talk, or walk holding hands kind
    of friends . . .
I want to be a friend to his mind . . . a nurturer of his ideas that helps to align
his ability with his ambition
I want to be a friend to his heart . . . human nutrition for his soul . . .
I want to grow old being a friend to his spirit . . . I want to be so spiritually
    connected that when he speaks my soul hears it . . . I want him to make
    my stomach turn . . .
To be so moved by who he is that I yearn for him . . . and I'm not just talking
    physically . . .
I want to know if our synergy can make the world a better place . . . if
    everyone around us can be touched by our soul space . . .
I want to work the job of being his mate . . . I mean I want to love him so well,
    that he'll
Even he has to scream . . . work it!!!
Because that job is fulfilling and his love—it's my healing
Without it I am a motionless verb, a song without words
A beat so weak that you can't hear it . . .
And I'm ready to be consumed by a love so in tuned . . . it finishes my lyrics
I want to bring the humility back to love where it's no longer about him or me
But what we can be . . . together
Reciprocal and humble giving

It may sound like an age-old stereotype but my mother—she ran a bath every
    night for her love because that was love to him
And my grandmother—she cooked breakfast, lunch, dinner, and heated up
    supper
every night for her lover
And he built their house with his bare hands because that's what his love
    expected from her man
Forget—the—world
I'm willing to give *whatever* it takes for us to live . . . in love
And I expect . . . him to make real my ideal definition of love as a verb
    and action
That requires hard work not just physical satisfaction
Forget cards and flowers . . . I want him to spend hours thinking of ways to
    love me
I want him on the daily grind to come up with new ways to blow my mind
    loving me
I want him to invest it all . . . stumble, trip, and fall in love with me
I want him to give me new ways to see partnership and individuality
New perspectives on religion and spirituality
Because I know that he can . . . me and my mothers have a history of loving a
    good black man
You see, my black brother, he's been knowing me . . . been loving me . . .
Been giving me that spiritual medicine for my racial pain
That loving acceptance to counter the social disdain
That empathetic knowledge of my struggle and stress
That inherited history that he won't let me forget
Our love . . . our bond . . . it's indescribable . . . it's unimaginable
Unspoken understanding, solidarity, oneness . . .
A reason to believe in the ability to conceive black love . . . that's what I'm
    looking for in a man
Ride or die
I don't care if we drive or fly
I'm ready to ride with you
I'm ready to ride for you
I'm ready to ride because of you . . . I'm ready to give, do, and be love

3

A Politic of Survival

A Cultural Self-Portrait: Mike
(in His Own Words)

As a young man growing up in Danville, Virginia, I found myself trying to fig-
ure out why having a family was so important. My mother, Newman Maurice
"Nance" Nunnally, was born in Jersey City and was the youngest sibling of three.
My mother was named after one of her uncles. But it was hard being a little girl
with a man's name, so the family began to call her "Penny." The reason they called
her "Penny" is that my mother always had a kind heart and they always told her
that as long as you have a penny you will never go broke. My mother never got a
chance to know her own mother. Her mom was killed by her husband (my mom's
father). He was not found guilty. The family has always felt that in the late fifties
there was no justice—another murdered black woman meant that there was one
less Negro on the streets in the eyes of the law. Her mother was killed before she
[my mom] was even one year old. So my mom was raised by her grandmother. My
mom eventually moved to Danville, Virginia, with her grandmother. For years
she would travel back and forth between Jersey and Danville in order to keep the
relationship she had with her siblings and her father alive. But her father was
later killed by a drive-by shooting while he was standing in the front door of his
home. My mom was sixteen. She never knew her mom, and now her dad was
also dead. She was really between a rock and a hard place, and she was looking
to start her own functional family. My mother got kicked out of school when she
was in the eleventh grade for protecting one of her cousins during a fight. So my
mom went to work. Back in the 1970s you could get a decent job where you could
provide for yourself but not a family. My mother's life growing up was rough, and
she did not want her children to witness what she had throughout her childhood.

In 1977, my mother met my father, Solomon Tyrone Nunnally Jr., who was born and raised in Pelham, North Carolina. My father is the oldest sibling out of eleven children—six boys and seven girls. My father, just like my mother, never finished high school, but he never let his lack of education get in the way of him living life. My father grew up a little different than my mother because he was raised by both of his parents and his grandmother was a preacher. Since my father was the oldest, my grandparents expected a lot from him when it came to helping out with the family. My father was well known in his hometown as "Good Time" because they all knew that when it was time to party, somebody better call Tyrone. My father loved his family, but he was more concerned with making money so he could go out and have a good time. My father was a country boy who didn't mind getting his hands dirty to make a quick buck. He started off working on cars with his brothers in his dad's front yard. But then he realized that he wanted to see and travel the world—to see what was out there. At the age of eighteen he started working for this trucking company so he could live out his dream of being the first in his family to see all fifty states. He did see the states. But during his journey he forgot what was important in life—his family. It was during this time that he also became abusive toward my mother. As a child, I had to face being a part of a family dealing with domestic violence. I am a middle child of four siblings with an older brother named Tyrone, younger brother named Torrance, and a baby sister named Sherita. The first time I saw my father put his hands on my mother, I was ten years old, and I did not know what to do. My older brother, Tyrone, came into the living room and pulled my dad off of her and yelled at me, "I bet' not ever see you sit here and watch him put his hands on Mom." From that day on I never let my dad put his hands on my mother again.

What I mean by my father forgetting about his immediate family is that the lifestyle he began to live involved drugs and women. This has shaped my identity. My father was more concerned with doing drugs than taking care of his responsibilities. When my father was doing drugs, he felt like everybody was against him, so he began to take his frustrations out on my mother. He had it in his mind that my mother was out in the street cheating on him. So he began to cheat on her. This made no sense to me—my mother loved him more than she loved herself. Because of my father's addiction to drugs and women, we were not able to stay in a stable home for more than a year. So we began living with family members. My mother hated when we had to live with family members, so she took matters into her own hands and started working more hours in order to make sure we had our own place to live. With the things that I had to witness as a child growing up in a dysfunctional home, I was able to see the things that I did not want to do as a man. When you see a man who tries to put his hands on a woman, in my eyes it makes that person less of a man. I told myself that I was happy that I witnessed the wrong things that my father did because it helped shape me into the man that I am today. I understand how to treat a woman like a woman at all times.

As I got older, my outlet was music. I started off with poems about the struggles that I had to face as a child growing up, and gradually my poems turned *into songs. My music allows me to open up emotionally. As a child growing up, I turned to sports and music as a way for me to escape from my past. When I was either on the field or in my room writing, I was able to feel free from all my pain. Here are a couple of songs that I would like to share about my struggles and life. The names of the two songs that I am sharing are "No More Struggles" and "Nunn's Life."*

No More Struggles

No More Struggles, No More Struggles, No More Pain
I'm tired of living life and doesn't a damn thing change
I been hurt for too many years
Up in my room full of pain and a whole lot of tears
Hoping that I don't fail that's my biggest fear
Wishing one day that my brother and them meet their career
My momma raised four of us she done her best
Three boys a baby girl she wouldn't settle for less
Keep thinking how we gon' survive off one check
Tryna help moms out take stress off her chest
Picture this sitting home with nothing to eat
Best thing to do man was fall asleep
Waking up same feeling on your mind
I got tired of momma saying everything will be fine
My pops he wasn't always there
But when he was you know that dude showed that he cared
One day the dude just up and left
I can't respect him moms he don't respect himself
Grandmamma said son you just like your father
So every other day I live my life a little smarter
Out in the streets I banged a little harder
I'm nothing like this guy so why even bother
I'm on a different track I'm not going that route
I'ma be a pops one day ain't no bailing out
My brother one luv he was my pops
Taught me how to be a man and how to stay on top
Taught me how to do things I thought I'd never do
He said step number one be the leader of your crew
I put two and two together life is a game
I'm tired of all these struggles and doesn't a damn thing change
the only man that can help me is the man above
but I got to help myself by showing myself love
if you been through what I been through then you know how I'm feeling
I just need the man above to send me a blessing
It feel like I been hurting every since I could talk
Places I had to go . . . I still had to walk

Thinking about the pain every time I'm taking a step
I was crying inside and couldn't scream out for help
Living life as one of those kids who just didn't care
When other kids were happy I thought life was unfair
What I'ma be in life I never knew what to say
Looking up to the sky asking the Lord to pray
for me I made my life straight by the sports that I played
Even though we struggled people thought that we had it made
When times get hard we got down and prayed
Closed our eyes and God already knew what I was going say
"Now I lay us down to sleep, I pray the Lord our soul to keep, and if I die
*   before I wake, I pray the Lord my soul to take"*

I wrote this song when I was eighteen years old. The next song that I wrote is based on my life as a Nunnboy.

Nunn's Life

What you know about Nunn's life . . . dreams of playing ball chick and nice car
Let me tell you about Nunn's life hustling every day trying to get paid
So what you know about a Nunn's life struggling all the time living that fast life
So let me tell you about a Nunn's life living every day like it's their last day
So what you know about this Nunn's life TDott, Slim and Tone's Life
I guess it's up to me to speak our life's right
Now buckle up tight Tone about to take flight
Born in the middle so I was trained to be the toughest
Lil' bruh was the roughest
big bruh he is the compass
Natural born leaders but direction I follow
I'm not worried about today I just live for tomorrow
And tomorrow I did with my sorrows
Never drink my pain away like my uncle's dreams of making it big was on
*   my mind*
You couldn't knock my shine
so I increased my grind
It was all in my mind
on how to make it to that next level
mind got to stay level
All I ever heard is
you Nunnboy's gifted the hard way was the only way we did it
OK welcome to this life that I live in
Grandmother always said that I was different
It must be because I was raised by my mother
Looked up to brothers
but I hustled like my father

Damn right I learned how to hustle from my father
He showed me how to get out of certain problems
See he taught me not to make the same mistakes that he made
Don't let money change you
don't spend it like I do
Don't get sidetracked by laying back in a nice whip
Cuz that lifestyle can get you trapped with the wrong chicks
I was on that same road but changed up
I got it pops thanks for the heads-up
Everything that I did, I did it on my own
And I did what I had to do to take care of home
Don't get this confused this not the life of a thug
This is just how it is by living the life as a Nunn

As you can see I use music as a release in order to express my emotion without breaking down in front of people. I feel that doing music has helped me to grow and develop into the person that I am today. Most of the time people are afraid to express how they feel when they are around people. We have found a way to get our message across so we can begin to relate to and understand our own lives. Culture is an important part of who I am today. If you do not understand your culture, then how are you going to explain to people the life that your family once lived? What I know about my family culture is that family is all you've got and without it you feel lost. And we all know that emptiness is something that no one likes to experience. My culture, my family, and everything that I have experienced in life has taught me that in order to get where you want to go in life, you have to take chances, and as long as you never give up, then you will never fail. As long as you have a penny, you will never go broke.

A Cultural Snapshot of Daniel

D aniel's cultural story was difficult to get through. He is a young man with whom I was able to spend much more time than the others. I worked on his college campus and interacted with him in various capacities—both inside and outside the classroom. Dan had previously taken a few of my classes, and he was also actively involved with the university cultural center that I directed. Dan took advantage of everything on campus. He was involved everywhere—student organizations like the NAACP and Black Caucus, fraternity life, cultural center programs, mentoring programs, leadership programs, and political organizations, and he was an Inroads Intern completing corporate internships every summer. Though he was very popular and very involved on campus, Dan came off as a quiet young man. It was not the kind of quiet that conjures visions of a shy and awkward kid. Dan's quiet demeanor was serious, mature, and reserved. When he did choose to speak, it was often with passion, assertiveness, and critical thought. He was not afraid to disagree, to lead the crowd, or to tell his peers to "be quiet and shut up" if an administrator that he respected was trying to get their attention. Dan was also one of my biggest professional supporters. If I needed anything—a chair moved, a room set up, a volunteer for a program or this study—he was the first to sign up. There was respect present deep in his eyes whenever I spoke to him. I knew that he valued and appreciated my work at the university. I also generally knew that he was from Philadelphia and that he was at the university on full scholarship. He was a true scholarship student, with real financial challenges. If he did not maintain his grades and keep his scholarship, he would not be in school. But after reading his portrait, I saw him in a new light, through a very intimate cultural angle. His story personifies culture as a politic of survival.

"You can grow up looking up to them, like every child is supposed to: his success, her struggle, his manly physique, her motherly beauty, his word, her trust, some things that would stand out to children as they are brought up in this world that would make their mother or father seem like the best in the world." So begins Dan's story. Dan's parents were divorced when he was six years old. Their divorce marks the beginning of a lifetime of struggle. After the divorce, Dan could recall only his parents' hate for each other increasing each year and his sense of disappointment in them following suit. Unlike many of his peers raised by single mothers, he and his brother spent the first six years after the divorce in the custody of his father in Baltimore. As a little boy he wanted to be just like his father. His initial memory of his father was that he had a "good job" at a wire company. When his father was working, taking them to company picnics, and displaying acts of responsible love, Dan had a heart full of love for his father. Each day, Dan's father would pack up the boys' shoes in his work-bag as he prepared to go to work. He did this so that his sons could not go outside and get into trouble while he was away. Dan used to think, "Damn he really cares about us, that's a father right there. I mean he's taking our shoes so we don't get into the streets. That's a father."

But his father was "let go" at his job, and as Dan puts it, "After that, life was like constantly driving up and down the same hill." For several years, his father constantly moved him and his brothers around. They lived with family members, with friends, and at times of severe destitution, in shelters. They would go from periods of constant moving to short stints of having a stable life with another "good job" and a "nice home." But the financial stability never lasted, and so Dan's father would pack up the boys and move again. He recalls that these jobs were the only good memory or sense of respect that he has left for his father. "The good thing was that I remember my father having a job for long periods of time. I guess that's why I looked up to him. Honestly, I don't even know what he did sometimes; the wire job was the only job I can recall . . . but he always kept trying to work." The problem was that the jobs were never steady, and his father often found himself unemployed. Their living situation reached a point where he and his brothers could not take it anymore. He called his mother, who was then living in Philadelphia, and she came to get him in a matter of hours. From that point, around age twelve, he lived with his mother in Philadelphia, which he now calls home.

Dan's mother worked long hours, and he had much more freedom in her house. He went from never being allowed to go outside in Baltimore to proclaiming, "I pretty much raised myself out in the streets of Philadelphia." At fifteen, he started selling drugs. He explains that his "environment and living situation gave him no choice." His mother was struggling but still managing to keep a roof over their heads and food on the table. When Dan first came to live with his mother, he loved her dearly, simply because she was his mother. But he really did not know her. He started to develop respect for her when she began to go to school, but both her pursuits and his pride were short-lived. When she dropped out, so did his faith in her. "During that time and afterward she would consistently lose the few jobs she had. Since I been living with her, she never worked since her last job, which was like three or four years ago," he explains.

As a son, Dan seemed to want to see his parents stay afloat—even if they were treading shallow waters in a low-paying job. "They just need to find any job or do *something* with their lives," he says. Their inability to press through their economic struggles affected his sense of respect for them. This respect was lost for good when his parents both became drug addicts.

> Being as though I was raised in the streets, I know all the signs, behaviors, and flaws of someone being on drugs. Shit, I been knew my father was back in Baltimore hitting that glass dick. What made it official with my moms was that one night I went to the bathroom and on the floor I found a 1212 bag, which was a bag that one would package coke or crack in. I mean, I should know; I was selling it. So I asked her whose it was, and she said, "It's mine. . . ." I started to see my mom turn into something, someone that I could never love nor have respect toward: a crackhead. She would promise things and not follow through with them, go through my stuff in search of money, and when she found it, she would say, "Oh I was just borrowing it; I was going to pay you back; it shouldn't matter; I do this; I do that; blah, blah, blah." Yeah she became a disappointment.

He did not comment at all on the potential hypocrisy of judging his parents so harshly for falling victim to the very drugs he was helping to sell to someone else's parents. But perhaps that is because they were *all* victims to the seduction of drugs. His parents' financial struggles and drug addictions have been a major part of his life. Through all this, Dan has managed to do well in school. He is not an A student, but he persists through school despite his home life and in spite of the fact that he recently became a father himself. He is now getting a college degree to create a different legacy for his new son. Everything that he has experienced has made it almost urgent for him to be both hopeful and hardworking in creating a healthy and strong relationship with his own son. In order to focus on a new future, he understands that he must accept the realities of the past. They cannot be undone. So he has accepted his family's flaws. "That's life," he says.

And his life has taught him how to survive in the face of real turmoil. Through his life struggles he has learned self-determination, perseverance, resilience, and most importantly forgiveness. He even goes so far as to say that he is sure there are others who have had it much worse than him. Despite the financial struggle, the drug addiction, and the instability, Dan still expresses deep love for his mother and father. He describes his father as the "worst factor" in his life but yet proclaims, "I still love him! I mean he *is* my father." He says that he is learning to love and respect his mother. Despite her flaws, she is the only mother he has. Dan ends his portrait in the same way that it begins, but with new insight:

> I started this semi–life story: You can grow up looking up to them, like every child is supposed to: his success, her struggle, his manly physique, her motherly beauty, his word, her trust, some things that would stand out to children as they are brought up in this world that would make their mother or father seem like the best in the world. My life's disappointments have only made me want to be a better person. My culture is my knowledge and experiences that I have had that have made me a more conscious person—more conscious of superficial BS that my generation holds as values, more conscious of others' intentions and morals, and more conscious of social and community needs. In the end, I just hold my faith as a priority and live life as righteously as possible.

Dan is a young man who developed a sense of culture despite there being no steady figure to teach it to him. It seems almost as if the negativity in his life caused him to cling to culture as a symbol of anything positive, anything opposite of what he saw growing up on the streets of Philly. Even tough experiences can help us to better understand and know love when we see it. For Dan, culture is all the life experiences that he wished for his family—responsibility, hard work, strong values, faith, and righteousness. He saw them in glimpses—bits and pieces of a steady life. But he remembers them and holds on to them. Dan's life story is a testament to the strength that culture has to pull us up when our world falls down around us.

Culture as a Politic of Survival Critical Essay

Like a home, culture seemed to be built with an exterior to shield and protect from harm. The exterior was molded with what I call a politic of survival. A politic can mean many things. But in this case, I refer to it as a collection of cultural tactics that are used to survive and to overcome oppression. After having survived the personal storms of racism and poverty in America, these "tools" are often passed on by parents and grandparents. Just as a home shelters its residents from inclement weather, culture provides shelter from the storms of life. While I expected to hear things like "culture is abundance," "my culture is about enjoyment," and "culture is about good times," I was instead told that culture is "hard work," "determination," "resourcefulness," and "respect." The ability to work through struggle was a major cultural skill and value to the young adults with whom I spoke. Many of them were raised by single mothers. Therefore, much of the praise regarding social survival was directed toward mothers. Mothers teach the valuable lesson that success in life requires hard work. Mothers also model the way as family leaders, demonstrating a willingness to work long hours, do hard jobs, or start from the bottom in order to provide for the family. But one of the most crucial lessons learned from our time wrestling with the idea of culture is that these histories of struggle were sources of both pride and pain. Though many saw their family's ability to "overcome" poverty as a source of pride, others viewed their persisting economic struggles as sources of frustration and shame. And all were working as adults to reconcile these feelings and to come to terms with the good and bad experiences in their lives.

Ain't Nothing Going On but the Rent

Money and respect were the two most important players on the everyday field of American life. Almost everyone in the group shared a childhood filled with some form of financial strain. What I found through our conversations was that experiencing social struggle and developing a strategy to tackle that struggle was overwhelmingly valuable to them. Similar to previous generations, these struggles, strategies, and lessons are important forms of cultural heritage—of passing down cultural wisdom. But the differences between generations lie in the social struggles faced in today's society. Economic struggle continues to be the primary social challenge across communities of color. However, the effects of drug addiction, community violence associated with poverty, and the empathy that children develop (most often for their mothers) after observing the stress and pain of single parenthood are equally important in contemporary society.

Shernā wrote about the critical lessons that were gained from her family's struggles:

> Another aspect of African American culture involves understanding that the things we want the most in life are not always granted to us. Rather, we are expected to struggle—to put up a fight for what we want. My mother was forced to cook and clean, doing dishes day after day in order to pay her way through college. Her profound understanding of her culture has shaped her into the type of parent she is today, teaching my siblings and me that if you really want something in life, you are

going to have to work your butt off in order to get it. I asked Mommy how she did it, and she said, "It was hell. . . . Well it wasn't really as hard to raise you two as it was a struggle. Basically, what you had to do was get yourself on a budget. You know how much money you have; don't go over that amount. What I did was budget."

Shernā, like many of her peers, grew up watching her mother work both hard and intentionally to make ends meet.

Like Shernā, many others commented on their family's economic struggles as culturally defining moments—experiences often intertwined with feelings of both pride and shame. Terry saw his mother's economic struggles as a source of pride. The fact that she was able to develop strategies to survive and to communicate an expectation of success to her children influenced his cultural identity: "My mom had to raise me and my sister by herself off of a salary that would seem to most as poverty. She envisioned a future for her kids that would be different from hers. She wanted both of us to graduate, attend college, and have a good job. She did everything in her power to make this happen." Michael talked about the exhaustion his mother faced from day to day. "Although I could tell inside that Momma was unhappy, I knew to stay in a child's place. She would come home after work and start crying at the kitchen table, ordering my sister Erma and me to massage her feet. She developed really coarse feet as a result of wearing the same tired worn-out shoes to work every day to make sure we at least had food and a roof over our heads." Person after person related how hard their mothers worked. They told story after story of how their mothers were "taught very early on about the rewards that are gained through hard work and perseverance."

Money, Power, Respect

For a few in the group, money and success went hand in hand. Their family's economic struggles often led to two life lessons: (1) Success can be gained from hard work. (2) Success is most often determined by your financial situation. Jennifer, a Latina student, began her journal with the following sentence: "In truth, my family is composed of some of the poorest people I know." She went on to relate that her family often sees this as a point of shame and will deny their true financial situation to hold on to "the smallest thread of dignity just so we can proclaim to the rest of the world that we are people too." In a society where dignity and dollars are inextricably bound, an underprivileged family may feel more compelled to deny their oppression than to name it, claim it, and fight against it. In this way, the psychological damage of linking socioeconomic status with social respect continues to be a powerful tactic to sustain social systems of economic oppression. In the same ways that poor white Americans were historically encouraged to be blind to their own poverty and to be satiated by so-called racial difference, so too are communities of color in a contemporary America often blind to their true financial realities and satiated by materialism and consumerism. Whether middle or lower income, families are often in denial about how truly badly they have it. Our families are often victims of the social pressure to paint a picture of a life that will provide them a sense of dignity.

But what sons and daughters are sharing is that it is actually the social struggles and lessons that they value the most. Their overwhelming respect for the power and endurance of their parents and grandparents illustrates that the greatest inheritance is the internal and cultural wealth built inside the self and inside the family. These lessons will continue to accrue value after the last dollar in the bank is spent. But philosophical arguments like this mean very little when the rent is due. And no one who has truly known poverty wants to continue to live in it. Derrick, an athlete, explained his parents' beliefs: "They were better off with an education, which meant more money. Having more money made it easier for the family to live. My parents stress going to college in our household because they believe that graduating makes you more successful, and the more successful you are the more money you make."

But some young people today clearly distinguish between having money and being successful. Courtney's mom had a lot of money and bought a lot of things but still was not stable. "Being as though we lived with my grandma, my mom had a lot of extra money at times. My mom worked at Macy's for most of my childhood. She would come home with a new shirt or a pair of jeans for me every Friday." However, this ability to buy material things did not make Courtney describe her family as successful. Economic stability was about more than brief periods of access to money. Though some parents had fleeing moments of "good jobs," their lifestyles were still symbolic of oppression and struggle. From working several jobs, to still living with their parents, to having their money all disappear because of a lack of financial and legal knowledge, many families never had enough social capital to sustain a true climb out of poverty. As a result, many students saw money and material things as superficial distractions from true culture. Jennifer, whom I mentioned earlier discussing her family's tendency to deny the truth of their poverty, also reflected on herself critically, recognizing how she had also adopted the desire to hide her financial situation: "I even try to surround myself with an abundance of material goods so that I can psychologically envision that I'm just as financially stable as the next person. But is this indeed truly who I am? . . . There is an ever-growing pressure that is bestowed upon me to succeed in a society that has made success an obstacle for anyone who shares my identities."

Lloyd, a twenty-year-old man from the Bronx, New York, feels that the masses are "merely existing (not living, but existing) as products of economic, social, behavioral, and psychological enslavement." He sees many of the extreme struggles that his ancestors endured to create new roads of opportunity as a dream deferred. He wonders how many current dreams are being crushed by the dynamics of the streets—how many talented people are wasting their lives and not living up to their full potential. For him deferred dreams are the product of social failure. Money is needed to escape poverty. But materialism, a value that is persistent in America, often serves as the social chain that keeps people forever bound to their current class position.

Tara, a young woman from Prince George's County, Maryland, tells a family story similar to her peers with a history of economic struggle. But her story changes and has a different ending. Tara talks very candidly about the realities of PG County. It is a suburb of Washington, DC. The wealthiest majority-black county in the United States, PG is plagued by economic extremes. The sections outside the beltway (the major highway connecting Maryland, the District of Columbia, and Virginia) display great affluence, with $700,000 homes in gated African American communities. The area inside the beltway is populated by another set of black and Latino communities that are living in sheer poverty. But PG is a place where even those who live in large homes with Range Rovers parked in the driveway have to face a racist society where business developers refuse to build high-end stores in the area. Tara says that even outside the beltway, the best black people can get are discount stores and maybe Old Navy or Macy's. This situation is a source of anger for many who can afford to shop at Saks or Nordstrom, BCBG or Armani Exchange, which are more high-end stores. So, for her, money does not necessarily guarantee social respect. For Tara, respect is most closely aligned with self-achievement. As she explains this viewpoint, it resonates with me—I've lived in PG County for ten years. I find myself extremely interested in learning more about Tara's story of economic struggle. Would she situate it inside or outside the beltway? Her answer was both. Her family story is a story of determination to cross over to the other side:

> At first my family was not financially stable, and they did not make ends meet all the time. Although it was a struggle to live in this harsh life, they found other measures to achieve their goals. My mother's side of the family opened up a barbershop and hair salon, and it is currently in existence today. There were not many job opportunities available, so this was a great option for them. My father's side of the family began to enroll in school. His two brothers and their wives are now doctors, and all of them have their own medical practices in Maryland. The success on both sides of the family shapes my identity. Business ownership and education changed my family's situation. We were able to move. It was like a pursuit to a higher road. My life revolves around my family—how they have developed and learned and changed our situation and moved to a better area. The more they do, the more I am culturally shaped.

As I read this, I still could not help seeing the obvious tie between economic elevation and elevated self-respect. Moving out of their poor neighborhood was the major marker of success. Business ownership, college degrees, and elite careers allowed this family to gain a sense of social agency. But what about those families that either cannot or choose not to "make it out"? Why do we place so much emphasis on leaving instead of investing in the communities from which we come? Many of these questions continue to be unanswered, and those answers did not seem to be what was truly important here. The bottom line was that when we live lives that are drowned in economic struggle, of course we seek out dry land. Of course we don't want to sustain struggle but instead rise above it. Whether we swim in a direction that is "inside or outside the beltway" is another discussion. What matters in this initial conversation is that the ability to swim out of social oppression is often a skill formed by and taught through culture. Just as the assailant that victimizes you will not be the one that teaches you personal recovery, the society that oppresses you will not teach you how to rise above its own oppressive systems. But family and community members who have made even small gains will save you from drowning. In this case, cultural pride is the bravery that is needed to take the first stroke and to believe that you just might make it. And cultural heritage comprises the lessons that taught you to swim in the first place. Bre, another young woman, illustrates culture's role in helping her to reach what seemed like an extremely distant goal of social mobility:

> "I wish" was a saying I often repeated over and over again to myself. . . . I was never satisfied with my life. Till this day, I admit I tend to let those words break away from my lips every once in a while. I used to think I lived a hard, unfair life, but began to realize how fortunate I actually was. My grandparents and even my mother at certain points have led by example and have worked extremely hard to give me the [opportunities] that I am [experiencing] now. My grandparents have paved the way to progress. They led by example [and showed us how] to set higher standards and that with hard work you can do anything.

Family struggles of the past became life lessons of the present. They inspire and motivate young people to work hard, to do better, and to achieve more. Perseverance was a major cultural value—not only feeling as though you can keep trying but also having people believe in you, encourage you, or pray for you. Perseverance was about believing that, regardless of the situation, it can turn itself around. Looking back in history, at the heritage of many enslaved, oppressed, or colonized communities, the value of having unshakeable faith in life makes sense—if an enslaved person could persist in life, believing with no real indications that things would turn around one day, why would their children not inherit this spirit? When you think about the life of an enslaved person—how horrible it must have been to wake up every day into the same miserable situation and to know that there is no end in sight—you can begin to understand just how amazing it was for them to do something as simple as just live. Just being alive was being a person of greatness. Leading rebellions and orchestrating escapes were incredible shows of bravery—but so was simply waking up each morning. At that time, life was so miserable that thoughts of suicide came often, and mental struggles with whether or not to give birth or abort babies to save them from slavery were a constant. Who would want to go on living knowing that tomorrow you will face the same oppression and it will continue to happen for the rest of your natural life? And so it was an incredible act to do something as simple as wake up each day, persist through, and maintain the hope that if you stay alive, your children or children's children will be free one day. They lived. And because they had the stamina to live through that time, we are able to enjoy living more freely today. We are here because they endured. Resilience through struggle is one of the most important life-sustaining skills that one can inherit. And poor people, oppressed people, marginalized people teach these politics of survival to their children every day. They wake up each morning and live. And their children learn how to persevere in the process. So, of course, young people of color would view culture as a strong belief in their ability to triumph.

Through their everyday lives our families create a culture of resistance. What I mean is that through our cultures we are often given the skills and mindset to press forward even when society is pressing back. When I think of my own parents, who by no means made a lot of money but who provided us a rich life, I see this culture of resistance more clearly. Our families learn how to make it, how to survive through life experience. My parents were masters at living far below their means. They never indulged themselves. But they did give us everything that matters. I never remember feeling deprived of anything as a child. When I needed an instrument, new clothes, or school money for a trip, those things were always provided easily and without strain. I now know that was all possible because my parents always had their eyes on their main life priority—their children. They said no to new cars and clothes, name-brand foods and extravagant gifts for others, so that they could pay for their children to go to college, adequately provide for them until they got there, and as retirees live a debt-free life where social security is actually enough. Sacrifice. This is what my family and all the families in this study have taught—the incredible outcomes of sacrifice.

We Fall Down: Drugs and the Streets

Unfortunately, sometimes dreams do more than fall down—they fall apart as they did for Dan's family. For many, the effects of drug addiction and community crime ripped apart cultural values, bonds, and expectations. Because of drugs, dreams died, families fell apart, and parents were transformed into strangers. Neighborhoods sometimes became war zones, all as a result of the severe pressures of economic oppression and the bleak coping options presented—a life of crime in order to make money or drug addiction to mentally escape the depression of poverty. Keith, a twenty-year-old college athlete from Philadelphia, told a different story of personally falling victim to the lure of selling drugs. His curiosity was motivated by the appeal of the "fast life" and materialism mentioned earlier.

> I fell through the cracks and started to experiment with drugs. I never did drugs, but I did sell drugs for a while. On my mother's side of the family there are nothing but drug dealers, and they all had money, girls, and a nice car. At first, when I started selling drugs, I had all the new Jordans, nice jewelry, and a pocket full of money. But one day, I was chilling on the corner, and these dudes ran up on me and my cousin with guns and tried to rob us. My cousin was much older, and he tried to fight them, but he got shot five times in the chest and died. When I started selling drugs, school started to become less and less important. When I was doing bad, my parents' relationship also started doing bad. They were always arguing. But when I listened and stopped with the drugs, my parents started doing better, and I started doing better in school.

Keith's story illustrates how when materialistic social pressures are combined with poverty the result is a cultural death warrant. Cultural structures and cultural bonds cannot survive in negative environments. In Keith's case not only he fell down in life as a result of drug involvement, but his parents' relationship was also destroyed. God was his bridge over troubled waters. For others, it was school. Terry, another young man from Philly, explains his experience with the challenges of his "block": "On this block were nothing but kids, drug dealers, and little old ladies. School was my key that separated me from everything negative in my life. As I went on to high school, most of my friends were either in jail or dropped out of school doing nothing. Countless [numbers] of my childhood [friends] have lost their lives in the pursuit of the fast life. Gang violence, family casualties, drug addiction, prison sentences, STDs, and the most contagious of all bleak hopes for a better tomorrow [have taken over their lives]."

To Terry, the alternatives to school were bleak—go to school or stand on the corner. Most of his friends who dropped out or did not go to college fell hard in life. Their plight went beyond deferred dreams. Their lives had either exploded and were lost to prison or gang violence or were ticking bombs awaiting the bleak reality of HIV and drug addiction. For Terry, school did not just change his life—it saved it. For Lloyd, his parents (mother and father) rescued him. Lloyd is young, black, and male, and he has had a life filled with most of the experiences associated with the intersection of these identities.

> Some of the largest influences that have shaped my cultural identity have been my childhood experiences. Growing up in a predominantly African American neighborhood filled with gang violence, shootouts, drug busts, and a community whose very lives were filled with deferred dreams, the probability that I would be able to rise above the influence

of my environment was not high. The majority of my childhood friends who sat in class with me are incarcerated, dead, or involved in criminal activities. The only difference between me and my friends (who didn't make it out) was the influence of my parents (mainly my father). He made the difference between me being in college rather than the state penitentiary or a mortuary.

His choice of alternatives is again compelling. The alternative to college is either prison or death. But overwhelmingly, the young black men in this project affirmed that they do not seek out trouble or crime. If anything, they are trying desperately to get away from it. The late rapper Tupac Shakur discusses this reality in the documentary *Tupac Resurrection*:[1]

> The main thing for us to remember is that the same crime element that white people are scared of, black people are scared of. The same crime element that white people fear, black people fear. So we defend ourself from the same crime element that they are scared of, you know what I'm saying, while they are waiting for legislations to pass and everything, we're *next door* to the killer, we're *next door* to him, you know. All them killers that they letting out, they're right there in that building with us. Just because we're black what we get along with the killers or something? We get along with rapists because we're black and from the same hood? What is that? We need protection too.

Lloyd is one of a few young people who came from a two-parent household and who discusses his father as being instrumental in his "making it out" and feeling this sense of protection. During the group interview, he was one of the disagreeing voices in the discussion on "haters" at home. Many people in the group shared mutual frustrations with how the larger neighborhood often responded to their pursuit of education and jobs. They talked about feeling isolated on their block and not being supported. But Lloyd interpreted these reactions differently. When his neighborhood friends responded negatively, it made him want to help them to expand their goals—to see not only his potential but also their own. He mentions that most of the guys in the neighborhood know his father, so they do not approach him with the same negative comments that other students receive. They respect his father and thus respect him. Having a firm and respected family support is his safety net in his neighborhood. But many people do not have this stable foundation to lean on. Donald is a good example. He begins his journal in the voice of his mother and father at the time he was born:

> My name is K.C. and I'm a thirty-year-old crack addict from Philadelphia. I have a one-hundred-dollar-a-day crack habit, no job, and a five-year-old daughter, and my girlfriend is pregnant with my first son. I

currently live in a men's shelter in West Philadelphia. I rarely see my daughter and have no means to support my pregnant girlfriend. For the past couple of months, I have been contemplating suicide, but I know that I must live for my children, so I have decided to continue my worthless life. . . . Hello, my name is Elaine Mae Shirlington, and I'm a twenty-four-year-old pregnant woman from Philadelphia. My life is okay at the moment, but it could be much better. I currently live with my parents, and I'm a food service worker. I'm happy that I'm pregnant with my first son, but in the beginning I contemplated an abortion. After talking about the issue with my mother, we decided it would be best to give the child a chance to live. I'm in love with a pretty worthless man at the moment. But love is hard. . . . What's up y'all, my name is Donald and I'm a twenty-year-old college student from Philadelphia. Before I explain my life and culture to you, I wanted to introduce you to my parents and explain their mind frame around the time I was born.

Donald did not meet his father until he was fourteen years old. Sharing the psychological issues plaguing his parents when he was conceived provided a very intimate understanding of this young man's life. The comment that "love is hard" says it all. It must be hard as a child to know your father wanted to kill himself, to be aware that your mother considered abortion, and to live a life of constant economic struggle. However, what is most important is the idea that all this was experienced because of the dedication that his family had to loving him—regardless of the struggle, despite the circumstances, they simply held on, they simply survived. That says something about culture—it is about determined and persistent love—a love that even society cannot break. This was the case for all of these young people, especially Dan, Mike, and Donald. Donald included a picture collage in his portrait—pictures of him with his mother, grandmother, and sister as well as a picture of a fireplace mantel filled with family photos. In his life story, he says that he has had a good life and that his culture has shaped him into a good person. Because of all his family has been through, he is not willing to compromise his morals and values. If a sense of culture can do that for a person—can help them come out of such a painful start in life with a bright outlook on the future and an uncompromising sense of self—then culture is in fact an incredible life tool. It is probably one of the most important and underappreciated politics in our society.

In her book *The Measure of Our Success*, Marian Wright Edelman[2] offers twenty-five critical life lessons to her sons that might help them to live a more full and meaningful life. The very idea that true "success" is measured not by the size of your bank account or the cost of your car, but by the imprint that you leave on this world, underscores the meaning of living a culturally driven life. Culture does not teach us how to run a meeting, sell a product, or operate on a body, but it does teach us how to do those things with purpose and character, tenacity and zeal. Culture does help us to get to these careers—to make it through any obstacles that may have come our way. Your school may have taught you how to be a lawyer, but your culture has taught you how to be a person. Edelman is an example of yet another mother who has taken the time to share the politics of survival that she has learned. I close this chapter with her twenty-five beautiful insights on life:[3]

1. There is no free lunch. Don't feel entitled to anything you don't sweat and struggle for.
2. Set goals and work quietly and systematically toward them.
3. Assign yourself (don't wait for others to give you work or purpose).
4. Never work for just money or for power. They won't save your soul or build a decent family or help you sleep at night.
5. Don't be afraid of taking risks or of being criticized.
6. Take parenting and family life seriously and insist that those you work for and who represent you do.
7. Remember that your wife/husband is not your mother/father or servant, but your partner and friend.
8. Forming families is serious business.
9. Be honest.
10. Remember and help America remember that the fellowship of human beings is more important than the fellowship of race and class and gender in a democratic society.
11. Sell the shadow for the substance.
12. Never give up!
13. Be confident that you can make a difference.
14. Don't ever stop learning and improving your mind.
15. Don't be afraid of hard work or teaching your children to work.
16. Slow down and live.
17. Choose your friends carefully.
18. Be a can-do, will-try person.
19. Try to live in the present.
20. Use your political and economic power for the community.
21. Listen for "the sound of the genuine" within yourself and others.
22. You are in charge of your own attitude.
23. Remember your roots, your history, and the forebears' shoulders on which you stand.
24. Be reliable. Be faithful. Finish what you start.
25. Always remember that you are never alone.

4

Education, Culture, and Freedom

A Cultural Self-Portrait: Christine
(in Her Own Words)

I begin my story with the first man in my life—the man who would come to my tea parties, play Princess Jasmine and Aladdin, and toss around a football: my daddy. Others may know him as the chief of police of National City, Dr. Adolfo Gonzales. To me, he is my daddy, or Pop, or Dad, or DaaaaaaAaaaadd!!

His story began with his first memory living in Mexico as a three-year-old little boy whose father was hit and killed by a drunk driver. He was the middle child born to Juan Gonzales and Elvira Gonzales de Estrada. After the accident, my daddy's remaining family moved to the United States. His mother's greatest desire was for her children to finish high school, a goal that was seemingly impossible at that time. For the most part, my pop would stay out of trouble, aside from miscellaneous mischief kids get into, like throwing shortening on the ceiling so it would look like snow. Eventually his mother developed epilepsy and had violent seizures. My dad was just too little to help. But he would run across his backyard, to his neighbor's house and knock on the door to ask them to come and save his mom. The neighbor was the only doctor they knew. This was one of my dad's first acts of saving lives. As time went on, my grandmother remarried and had four more children. This marriage also impacted my daddy because he would watch the abuse that my grandma endured. As a result, my daddy swore he would never hit a woman.

My dad remembers going into his kindergarten class and not understanding anything his teacher was saying. He said he would ask his friends next to him for help and he got paddled, not for talking in class, but for speaking Spanish. That was the only language he knew. He tried learning English as quickly as he could so he would stop being sent to the principal's office. Miraculously, he made it to high school, where the counselors decided that auto mechanics was the way for him to go. They did not offer my dad any opportunities for honors classes or any means of putting him on a path to higher education. My dad was told to be a mechanic. So he became one, and he won an award as the best mechanic in all of San Diego County his senior year. With the knowledge he gained my dad was able to "pimp out" his own car. It was the age of hydraulics. I can only assume my dad's car was the best. However, the cops didn't agree and would constantly pull him over. So my pops decided to move to Los Angeles. He packed up and hit the "10"—that's the name of the highway. On his way to a new life and new freedom, he got pulled over again. With less excitement, he turned around and went back to San Diego, where at least he knew the cops. This was just one of many experiences of discrimination that he would face in his life.

My mom's story is a little different. She was born in Chula Vista, California, in a little hospital, which ironically is now an insane asylum. She is the eldest of five children. My mom is a highly complex person, whom I love but don't quite understand. Her story began with a strict household. Her mom stayed at home while her father worked as a taxi driver. My mom always viewed her mother as the fun-sucker in her life, so she would go visit my great-grandmother, "my aby," as much as possible. I understand why my mom loved being around her as a child. I remember my aby being very sweet and kind. In school, my mom was a bright student and wanted to continue her education, but her counselor told her that she "was pretty, and would have no trouble finding a husband," and college was "not for her."

My dad returned from his voyage to Los Angeles during my mom's senior year of high school. This is when history was made. My mom says she saw my dad standing outside, with his unmistakable, healthy, shiny, long, straight hair. My dad says he met my mom when he nearly hit her while she was riding her bicycle in the middle of the street. Whichever story is accurate is beyond me. All I'm sure of is that they met and fell in love—I am proof. My mom graduated from high school June 16th and the next day, June 17th, she got married. My dad cut his straight, belt-length hair to his shoulders in order to look more presentable for my mom's family. I've only heard stories of my dad's hair, because the only picture I've seen of them together is their wedding picture at my aby's house.

My dad applied to the Los Angeles and San Diego police departments, but neither of them hired him. So he went through the cadet academy for San Diego as a volunteer. During that time he also worked construction for the city. My dad has always been a hard worker. He applied again to the San Diego Police Department (SDPD), and they finally hired him. Throughout this time my mom went to the nearby community college and rented a small apartment. My dad worked diligently and thoroughly, so that when a promotion would come up, he would be qualified to apply. As one of the very few bilingual officers, my dad was stationed in San Ysidro, where his friends lived. He asked to be transferred to another area but was told that he was needed in San Ysidro. My dad followed orders and worked according to the police oath: "I do solemnly swear that I will support and defend the Constitution of the United States and the Constitution of the State of California against all enemies, foreign and domestic; that I will bear true faith and allegiance to the Constitution of the State of California; that I take this obligation freely, without any mental reservations or purpose of evasion; and that I will well and faithfully discharge the duties of the office of Police Officer of the City of San Diego, acting to the best of my ability."

A few years later, my dad applied for the promotion available to him and was denied. He went back to his supervisor and asked for feedback. To my father's surprise, he was told it was because he had an accent. In private, my dad took pebbles, put them in his mouth, and practiced speaking and enunciating each word to try to get rid of his Spanish accent. The next time the promotion came around, he was finally promoted, but he still had to work in the same area. My dad was working full-time and struggling with having to arrest people he knew. He decided to work more with the community and gain their respect as an officer.

Once again, another promotion came up, and my dad applied. He didn't get it. This time when my dad went back for feedback, he was told it was because the other person had a degree, so my dad decided to go back to school. He went to Southwestern Community College and earned his associate's degree. The next time, he was promoted. My mom stood by him throughout all of the acts of discrimination and the professional obstacles. He overcame them with her support. My mom slowed down her classes and kept trying to decide what to major in. With no guidance, she decided to "simply" help my dad and take whatever classes she could, while working full-time and raising a daughter. By that time, they had given birth to my sister, Melody Star Gonzales. As the only child for eleven years, my sister had to endure the trials my parents faced raising their first child and working hard to achieve. My dad eventually earned his bachelor's degree from Chapman University and his master's degree from San Diego State University. The motivation? His supervisor told him he couldn't get another promotion because his eyes were brown—the other two Latino assistant chiefs had either green or hazel eyes. My dad risked so much for this job and still had to face so much racism.

One night, when my mom was four months pregnant with me, she and my dad went out for dinner. My dad received an emergency page and parked the car a block away from the incident, then walked to the scene. He left my mom in the car. As he returned to my mom, a white pickup truck loaded with six men drove by. The men in the truck shot fourteen rounds from two different guns at my dad's car, where my mom was sitting. My dad shot back at the assailants, hitting one in the thigh. The truck sped away. Sadly, in the panic of the situation, neither my dad nor mom was able to get a good visual of the shooters or the license plate. The perpetrators were not captured for a long time. It took hundreds of man-hours and a huge investigation to solve the crime. This incident made it real—how dangerous my dad's job was and what he risked every day to take care of his family.

When I was born, my parents were beginning to stabilize their living situation; they had bought their first house, which is still my only home. My dad continued to see discrepancies in the police force that he wanted to correct, so he went back to school and earned his doctorate in leadership from the University of San Diego. My dad was up for promotion to assistant chief of SDPD as my brother, Marc Alexander Gonzales, was born. After about five years there, my dad applied to be the chief of police of National City, where this June will mark the fifth year he has been there. With his degree and his background, my dad is the only chief of police with a doctorate and one of the few that is full Latino.

Throughout my dad's struggles and disappointments, my mom has been there to keep him strong and driven. My dad accomplished all he has because of my mom. But I think my mom was tired by the time I was a teenager. After going through all my dad's struggles, my mom had already put up with a lot. As a teenager, I didn't really know. I didn't see all the struggles from before. I know that seeing me not understand or even care must have been very frustrating for my parents. I can't believe it has taken until now for me to fully grasp that concept. My sister saw more of his struggle, so she pushed herself more. She understood the responsibility she had to make our parents' struggles worth it.

Throughout my father's police work, my mom spent the majority of her time taking care of us—taking us to school, to the theater, to music lessons, to dance lessons, to summer camps, to tennis lessons—with little to no time for herself. I have always appreciated what she was doing for me, but I masked it by keeping quiet. But my family is really the root of my love of the arts. My aby was a great singer, and I miss her dearly, for she never knew how much she inspired me. I still feel her presence during all my performances and also in times of great despair. I started acting at age three because I followed my sister into an audition for a community theater musical melodrama. By age six, I was taking classes in a professional dance company with my sister. In the fourth grade, I was the youngest member of the San Diego Youth Symphony. I was one of the original members of a nonprofit mariachi band. In performing, I feel that I am keeping my aby's legacy going. I always knew that my mom did a lot to support our talent and education. But that didn't help our relationship—we didn't have the typical mother/daughter closeness. But now, as I sit here writing this essay, there is much I want to thank her for, something a simple hug could say . . . but she's thousands of miles away, back home, where I left her. I used college as an escape route to get away from her, but it has actually led me back to her, made me appreciate her even more. She has always been very proud of me; my mother is why I am who I am.

Because of my father, I help everyone I can with whatever I have, even if doing so means putting myself second. I do these things with the slight hope that I might inspire that person to help someone else. Because of my sister, I have learned to be patient. As the eldest, she was the first to have to wait to hear back from colleges; she had to wait in line for her diploma—she knows how long it takes to accomplish *tasks and reminds me that time and dedication are my friends. Because of my brother, I wake up every morning with a smile on my face. He is my unconditional love, who never fails to surprise me.*

My parents' lives shaped the life I lead and the legacy that will follow. I know I can achieve because my dad did. My culture is how I relate to my family, my individual identity, my background and ancestors, the Spanglish I speak, the way we are passionate and love fully, the way we yell, and the way we greet one another with a kiss on the cheek. My culture is seen through the arts and the joys it brings people. I've always wondered which direction to go or which avenue I love best. I have no answers. But I have opportunity because my family worked hard to pave the way. I love making friends, and I love making a difference, so I figure I should do that through every means available to me. I need to put more value into my work, my education, and my family. I want to leave a powerful legacy for my children, even if it takes them, like me, twenty-plus years to even begin to understand the value of family and culture.

A Cultural Snapshot of Fernando

"Who am I really? Looking through the mirror of my past, present, and future." This is the title Fernando gives his life story. I find this interesting. The question seems to imply that exploring culture might provide him insight into a deeper part of himself—a greater understanding of the core of his being. The metaphor of the mirror is equally compelling—that perhaps by looking at his past, present, and future he will see a reflection—a mirror image of himself as a total man. Fernando is a Dominican American student. He radiates a welcoming and almost loving demeanor. When I look at him, after years of working closely with college students, I size him up to be the kind of student who likes to be hugged, who needs caring interaction, and who wants to know that he is important to you. It feels both easy and good to love students like Fernando. Fernando begins his story by telling me about his father leaving the family. His father originally left them in Santo Domingo with the hope of securing work opportunities in the United States in order to help them. But his father eventually disappeared, and even after immigrating to the United States himself, Fernando has not been able to reconnect with his father. "My father moved to the United States to make something of himself and to send money back to the family. As the years progressed, my father was out of the picture. When he moved to the U.S., it was the last time I saw him."

Fernando's parents eventually divorced, and his connection with his father permanently ended. So he shares many of the same life experiences as his peers—being raised in a single-parent household, struggling economically, spending significant time with his grandparents because his mother was constantly working, and valuing the lessons of hard work and perseverance taught to him many years ago on the family farm in Santo Domingo.

My grandfather became a very big influence on me. . . . He was always there for me through so much that I now have a bigger appreciation for how he has impacted my life. As a child, he would take me to the family farm, which was where he made his fortune, and provided me examples about life. I honestly did not know what he was talking about half the time. But looking back at all the things he would speak to me about makes me feel warm inside. All the things he said to me became a lesson I could use through life.

His sense of personal development (or what I deem cultural efficacy) revolves around understanding himself, valuing himself, and possessing a clear understanding of and appreciation for the cultural values taught by his family.

My ethics revolve around my emotions. Whether I like to admit it or not, I am a loving person. If it comes to making a hard decision, I reach down to my emotions and figure out if I could honestly make a mature judgment. But when I get a feeling that something is not right, I know I need to think about it and contemplate what it means for me and how it will affect others. That I got from my grandfather. My mother made me into the person that I am, and I thank her for that. I learned this when I came out to my mother and she apologized to me. . . . I will always remember my mother telling me she was sorry for not accepting me and for hurting me. To me it was profound to hear my family say, "All we hope for our children is for you to become a good person and to not make the mistakes we have made in our lifetime."

His family wanted him to have a better life, to not have to experience the struggles that they had known, and to know for sure that when challenges did come his way he could face them with honor and resilience. This is how his family faced losing their savings. His grandfather made a small fortune on their family farm in the Dominican Republic. However, all the money was eventually lost. But Fernando expresses an appreciation for this loss because he feels that his character has been built as a result of economic struggle:

My grandfather was a very hardworking man. He would make a penny turn into a dollar as if it was magic. He became such a hardworking person that my family became wealthy. This was inspiring—a man who had nothing did so much for his family. Eventually my family lost a big portion of this money. Our government was very corrupt. Those workers would steal the money that the community would make. Fortunately, we lost a big portion of the money. I say fortunately because I probably would not [otherwise] have the same values I have today. Because I had to struggle hard in my life, I look back and think if I had all that money, I probably would have become a different person.

His family, particularly his mother, has worked hard for him to go to college. Fernando is creating a new legacy in his family. He is traveling down new paths with education as his vehicle. His mother and grandparents were farmers and domestic workers, and so he is the first in his family to attend college. College has opened and will probably continue to open many doors of intellectual, professional, and cultural opportunity for his family in the years to come. This is what many students meant when they talked about culture being a value for education. Families have cleaned, farmed, and labored for their children's education. Education has always been a cultural goal. And students like Fernando often dive right into college and try hard not to disappoint. The sacrifices that his family made to get him to the United States and eventually to college changed more than just his opportunities; they changed his life. Attending college was a critical experience for Fernando. When he talks about his college campus he states, "This was my first home." This is an important statement because he often talks about having lived in many different environments—there is a sense that he really does not call any one place "home."

> My sister and I moved to the United States with my mother in 1996. We came here to start a new life and begin a new chapter in our family. My sister and I lived with our grandparents for three years [previously]. My mother was traveling around Venezuela, Puerto Rico, and the U.S. to give my sister and me better opportunities. Eventually she resigned, and we migrated to the U.S. Living in New York City was very influential to me. It was a change of environment, coming from a farm to a big city where the electricity would run and never leave. It was great.

But for Fernando the most cherished environment thus far has been in college. He talks about how he loves his country, but it is very conservative. Education was a different kind of freedom for him. In college, Fernando found the support and freedom to come out as a gay man and as a strong and outgoing leader. He talked often about appreciating the opportunity that college provided him to value all parts of himself and be true to his identity. His experiences in college also pushed him to be more outgoing and outspoken. He found himself having a voice and using it within student organizations and through his involvements with the LGBTQA Student Center, the Cultural Center, and the campus program board. College was a multidimensional and multicultural coming-out process for him. "In my life, I have been through different environments. I think that my most influential years have been college. During the last couple of years, I have come out, matured, and actually represented myself for who I really am. These are things I would never have seen actually happening if I had stayed in the Dominican Republic. College has been my favorite [place] because I am on my own. I get to challenge myself and I get to decide what qualities to accept as the real me."

For Fernando, college as an educational space offered a place where he could put his cultural values in practice. It was not an either/or choice for him—either college or family/culture. Instead, college offered him a both/and opportunity—to both discover new experiences and value his cultural heritage more deeply. He started college at age seventeen and says that at that time he did not know much about himself. He did not even have a strong sense of culture.

> I didn't know what culture was. . . . It took me a while to come to this conclusion. This is why culture is important to me—it is part of every aspect of my life. My ethics and integrity were really "hardened" here [in college]. I think, as time progressed in college, I began to understand what my ethics were and how I derived them culturally. In a way, I was only exposed to the Latino world with a small influence from the American culture. Living at college by myself and experiencing many different things on my own was very powerful because I was able to shape who I am and the ethics that I was originally taught by my family.

Culture then represented a marriage of contemporary experiences, cultural education, and classical wisdom. Both his individual experiences in college and the familial lessons and experiences of the past helped to mold and shape him as a cultural being. As Fernando states, "These experiences have made me who I am, and I feel that they played a role in my personal development." While in college, he has challenged his family to show unconditional love in new ways through being true to his sexual identity. The independence experienced through education has helped him to step back and appreciate the image of his full self—to feel confident in living openly as a gay man. He is the first to do many things in his family thanks to school. The idea that college or education in general changes students in some ways is true. Education changes their minds, their views of the world, their images of themselves, and often their opinions of their communities. In Fernando's case, education brought about a welcome change in his life and made concrete (or "hardened" as he put it) his cultural definition of himself. "Growing up, I was taught to always look at the past because there is a lesson there. But all [aspects] of my life—my culture *and* my college experiences—are incorporated in the definition of *this* me . . . really."

Fernando's story posits college as one of the most important experiences of his life—one that his family worked hard for him to have and one that helped him to appreciate his family and culture more deeply. College helped him to appreciate the cultural lessons learned from his family, and it helped him reach a better understanding of his cultural history. But most importantly, college also provided Fernando the freedom to explore his whole self in a way that being immersed in his cultural environment had not previously allowed. His educational experiences provided him with the personal freedom to pick and choose past values and lessons and merge them with new ideas and experiences to create his own life. For this reason, Fernando's life is a wonderful snapshot of the ways that pursuing an education is an important part of the cultural experience.

Culture as a Value for Education Critical Essay

The Possibility of an Education

The idea that education is inextricably tied to culture was a bit surprising for me. I expected students to view education and schools as institutions external to their culture. After reviewing so much literature that discussed culture shock and cultural isolation in schools and on campuses, I expected education to be a negative "environment" for students. However, what I found was that the *educational environment* and the *ethic of education* were something different for them. Campuses, schools, buildings, classrooms, curricula, programs, and even teachers were in fact viewed as external institutional forces. But nearly all students spoke about education, learning, college, and academic opportunity as being an important value in their culture. Whether the ideal of education was valued because of the past lack of access to education by parents and grandparents or whether it was appreciated because pursuing an education was an act of continuing an important family legacy of achievement, education and culture were bound to each other. Kara, an African American female student, best sums it up in the first line of her self-portrait: "Education alone is an unparalleled symbol of my culture." Several echoed a value for educational opportunity. Lloyd revealed that he could not recall a time when his parents were not working hard to teach him the importance of education. To him, their energy and effort toward making education a life priority shaped his cultural identity and rooted education firmly in the foundation of his culture. In his cultural self-portrait he wrote, "Aside from knowing that education and knowledge would be a large determinant of how far I would go in life, my parents' focus on the importance of education was primarily driven by their [being] African Americans. I would attribute this to my parents growing up in times when schools were segregated and academic resources were scarce. To add fuel to the fire, all four of my grandparents were illiterate."

Lack of historical access to education was most often named as the motivating force for the family's value for education. Many had parents or grandparents who were denied access to quality education or any education, and so these ancestors worked to ensure that their children were provided the opportunities that they had been denied. Many parents saw education as the key to successfully navigating the social struggles of life. Dearra chose to interview her mother as she explored her history and culture. Her mother made a comment during Dearra's conversation with her that is telling: "'If you don't have no skills, you'll be living from hand to mouth,' Mommy said. 'Education is important so you won't have to depend on nobody—no one but yourself. You know what you can do.'"

The focus on and dedication to education that parents have influences the value their children place on it. Young adults see culture as important to get ahead in life, and so this includes education. Education is a means through which deferred dreams move to the front of the line. Education allows for family legacies of deprivation and oppression to be transformed. The achievement of these young people getting to and through college is a source of pride and wonder to family members who had not had that chance. Looking back on Christine's story, we can see that her grandmother always had the education of her son (Christine's father) as her life goal. She only dreamed that he would finish high school, which would have been a major family achievement. Could she have ever imagined that her son would go on to earn a PhD and that the next generation of her family would all be college educated? Shernā, the young woman from Baltimore, tells how her grandmother often checks up on her academic progress on the weekends:

> Momma [Grandmom] is always enthused when school is a topic. Her exhilaration makes me realize how much my education truly means to her. During my freshman year of college, she would often call bright and early on a Saturday morning (fully aware of the fact that I was still sleeping) to discuss my exam grades, which she southerly refers to as "marks."
>
> "Shernā Ann," with emphasis on the Ann because I am named after her, "what kind of marks are you getting?"
>
> "I'm getting A's and B's, Momma."
>
> "B's? Well that's good too," she'd say (not completely satisfied, yet content).
>
> Though discussing my marks on an early Saturday morning was quite annoying, I knew she did it because she cared. She cares enough that I am taking advantage of the many opportunities that she was never given. Going to college was merely a dream for Momma, and in her eyes I am fulfilling a fantasy.

Continuing the Legacy

For other students, this dream began many decades ago. There were several for whom pursuing an education was about continuing a family legacy that other trailblazers in the family had begun. Like Christine, a few had parents who were college educated, and one had grandparents that attended college. For these families, the older family members had worked hard to get earlier generations into college, and so education was an expectation for younger generations—to continue the educational legacy that was started years ago. Derrick says that everything he is today can be attributed to his family's background and his parents' achievements. He explains it this way: "My parents were both the first in their family to attend and earn a college degree. This major accomplishment set the foundation for the future. From then on, we were all better off." Kirin, a tiny and enthusiastic African American young woman from Philadelphia, is the one student who lays claim to grandparents receiving a college education. For her, this is a strong source of pride. She talks about several family members who attended college, illustrating how widely spread the value for education is throughout her family.

> My family is one of the few families that can trace back to their great-grandparents holding college degrees. And because of that, I see the success that my family has had. It was my great-grandfather's vision that all his children would receive an education. My great-aunt Jean went to community college and became a certified public accountant, and my grandmother received a bachelor's degree from Temple University about twenty years after high school graduation. But again the seed was planted—the will to know the importance of education. I am blessed with two parents who went to school. My mother attended George Washington University and my father the University of Maryland. I can remember my parents starting their own private school. . . . It was set at an affordable price so that many of those who normally would not have access to a private education could attend. The most important lesson about that school was they instilled a work ethic within the pupils. It was known throughout the campus that all work was to be completed with NCA standards, which stood for "Neat, Complete, and Accurate." This notion was instilled in me from a young age.

Kirin's story illustrates that education as a cultural value mostly concerns legacy creation. "Willing," as she puts it, the appreciation for education to future generations and continuing the proud academic achievements of past generations. This is true for any of the families explored in this study—those that had been historically denied an education or those that had long histories of educational involvement—all sought to create a long-lasting legacy of educational participation in their families. Contrary to the popularly held belief that a commitment to education is nonexistent among impoverished and oppressed communities, these students affirm that if life can be considered to be a buffet of opportunities, then education was the main course—the main objective in life. People do not seek starvation—it happens to them as a circumstance of oppression. The poor want to be educated. They need to be educated. They often see it as a life support—a chance.

One of the key themes that emerged in this study was the idea that a familial and communal value for education was a critical component of culture. Across racial, ethnic, and economic class, all the participants voiced a strong commitment by their family to education and an expectation for them to attend college. Many of these young people were the first in their families to attend college, and they told stories of mothers and grandparents working extremely hard to get them to and through school. "By hell or high water," they were going to college.[1] This sense of educational expectation and urgency within the family makes college a coveted prize in the familial experience. Rashne Jehangir[2] explains that particularly for students coming from immigrant families, the first marker of success in America is often measured by the educational experiences of their children. Having a child successfully navigate through the school system and eventually attend college makes the hard sacrifices that come with leaving one's homeland worth it. And when examining the ways in which college participation in one generation of any oppressed group can completely change the outlook for subsequent generations, these families are indeed correct in their hope that education will be the answer. Sandria Rodriguez calls this "switching the tracks." In her book *Giants among Us: First Generation College Graduates Who Live Activist Lives*, she shares her own family experience:

> My sisters, my brother, and I are college-educated members of the middle class basically due to my parents' great desire that we make a better living for ourselves than they had been able to. They made tremendous personal sacrifices to ensure our future. I remember that my mother wore the same coat for ten winters when I was growing up. She would go north to the city during the four months after Christmas to work as a live-in maid for rich white people in order to help my father pay college tuition. . . . My parents were giants upon whose shoulders my siblings and I stand. Our children stand there too as will their children. My mother was an agent of total change in her ancestral line. She left the long-worn rails of recent generations and imagined a new way over unfamiliar land. She "switched the track," and her children took off in a different direction.[3]

A college degree changes the possibility of what a future can be for the whole family. Research confirms that many families of first-generation students possess a firm belief that they want their child to experience college, though they may not possess a firm understanding of the college experience.[4] Jehangir states, "Because first generation students often become representatives and models for their communities, failure in school is not just their own to bear, but also a reflection of their families as well."[5] And so it is clear that from an early age, the seeds of "college" are initially planted with the intent of growing a family garden because education nourishes and sustains generations of a family.

Culturally Centered Education

As benefactors of the value for education, many reflected on their particular experiences in college. As Zora Neale Hurston revealed in her work *Dust Tracks on a Road*, college was a space in which students could step back and fully view and appreciate their culture—admire it, miss it, understand it, and fully see it.

College helped to bring the architecture of their culture into plain view. Teddy, a second-generation African student (his parents are Nigerian) explained it this way:

> It was in college where I was finally immersed in the learning of African as well as African American history. When I went to college, I was forced to go outside the classroom to gain more knowledge about my history/culture, whereas in K–12 all my learning was restricted to the classroom. I decided to become a history and education major to hunt for a history and a culture that were all my own. The National Council for the Social Studies made this statement about the field of social studies: "The social studies curriculum is designed to acquaint children with their world, to help them make sense of it, and to give them a sense that they might make it better than they found it." This should be the purpose of all education.

For Teddy, the entire campus was full of cultural knowledge and education to be explored. In the group interview, he talked excitedly about the importance of cultural education opportunities:

> I think cultural education is the most important, critical thing in your four years of college because it gets you questioning your values and your beliefs and why you think this way. It helps you to be reflective. I took a lot of African American studies classes. I would go home, and I would see guys on the street corner, and I'd start talking to them—I would take this approach like, "I know that I don't even know you, but I feel that I do know who you are now." I'm serious. I would come home and all of my family was like, "Okay what did you learn now about black people?" But I feel like if you educate yourself about situations, you have more of a sense of pride in who you are and where you come from. For my parents it's easy, but not me. I went back to my old high school, and I was like, "You guys lied to us"—I actually said it to my history teacher. . . . [I]t hit me more personal. They cheated me of my sense of self.

Erika, a Latina junior, chimed in:

> Yeah, I would agree in a sense 'cause I'm taking a Spanish class. And it's like higher-end Spanish. And we read stories and poems from back in the day. And it's just interesting because growing up, I only learned about the history of America. I didn't learn my own history. It teaches me, you know, José de San Martín, and just different people who have changed Latin America and have influenced it tremendously. And because of them I'm able to be in the United States. It helps me to know what they've done to benefit my culture. And I guess it's kind of like

they're my Martin Luther King or George Washington. So for me
it's important.

For Teddy and Erika, college education is about much more than advancement and transforming family status; it is about gaining a better understanding of themselves—knowing themselves more intimately. Throughout many of
the group interviews, students also mentioned how college was helping them to
learn and appreciate the "fundamentals" of their culture or how cultural programs on campus made them feel "comfortable" and "more at home." Tara felt
that being away from home at a college in a rural community helped her to better appreciate her culture:

> A contributing factor to developing knowledge of my culture is my col-
> lege experience. I was raised in a predominantly black neighborhood,
> but I was not too familiar with my culture until I came to college. I took
> my community for granted. Being in college made me come to under-
> stand what my "culture" was. Before, I was conscious of it, but I was not
> aware of the significance. My surroundings [in college] have allowed me
> to open my eyes and sufficiently value my life. In college, classrooms are
> filled with majority white people. I am lucky to be a part of a class that
> might have two or three African Americans. Experiencing the feeling
> of being alone and being a part of "their" world just leaves you empty
> inside. College has not shaped my personality but more so it gave me a
> better understanding of my personality. My experiences at home have
> shaped my personality.

Tony also spoke about his new appreciation for his culture: "Before I came to
college, I really didn't think about my culture too much, because that's all I
kind of knew. But coming here has taught me to appreciate where I'm from a lot
more. Like before, I never really got to miss family or miss my community or
miss my corner store or whatever. . . . I got to appreciate the small things or the
really big things after coming here."

Many expressed an expectation for opportunities to learn about their cultures and themselves, to gain greater education on social issues, and to have
opportunities for fellowship among peers through cultural programs. Additionally, some expected college to provide them with opportunities to interact with other ethnicities, to connect with students who share their culture,
and to be social [cultural engagement]. Kara commented that she expected that
the campus "would provide some type of cultural programming and opportunities to be around people and various ethnicities." In the group interview,
she explained: "I was thinking that cultural education is important because
of personal development. That is something that should be experienced as far
as culture in college because . . . we think that we know who we are—but we
really don't."

The role that education can play in helping young adults to come to know, appreciate, and understand their culture is significant. As these young people have shared, this learning can take place inside and outside the classroom. It can involve academic curricula, campus programs, community-based experiences, workshops, retreats, and interactive learning exercises. Any educational institution should commit to creating a culturally rich environment—not in isolated spaces of the school or campus—but in the totality of the campus environment. Students thought that their colleges should intentionally create cultural programs and not just "expect for it to happen." In other words, we must work with focused intent and purpose to construct a cultural community in educational institutions. Almost all the students in this study stressed the importance of community. They felt that culture in college was about "creating a collaborative community" among students, ensuring that all students feel "a part of campus," and providing "opportunities to go deep" into learning about their own culture.

This proposed objective of the college experience once again raises the issue of social and cultural capital that can be quite important for students as they navigate their way through college. For first-generation, low-income (FG/LI) students of color in particular, social capital is a critical issue. By social capital, I am referring to the social forms of equity that are possessed by members of society in the form of experience and knowledge. Because the culture of the college campus is not often shaped around the cultures, values, or ways of being and knowing of traditionally oppressed and underrepresented people, students coming from these communities cannot see themselves reflected in the college experience. It can be similar to visiting a foreign country, where priorities, speech patterns, behavior norms, role expectations, and even food choices are different. Though all students are expected to develop and change during their time in college, FG/LI students often find themselves having to change the core of who they are in order to adjust successfully. This pressure to shave off the old culture in order to adopt new forms of social and cultural capital has an immediately negative effect on the student (through feelings of isolation, marginalization, and resentment) and a more long-term effect on the family and community.[6]

Problems with attrition and dissatisfaction among students of color have long plagued the higher education community, particularly at predominantly white institutions. Much of the problem with access, satisfaction, and retention has little to do with individual student efforts or commitments to succeed in higher education. Ultimately it is about oppression. Previous research has indeed shed light on the various forms of social oppression that impact educational environments at all levels. To understand the socially oppressive context from which a student enters the college experience provides important insight on why differences continue to persist in educational participation, preparation, and success. In the past, scholars who have sought to understand the reasons for student departure have often associated college success with the ability to acculturate into the college environment (the ways in which the student must change rather than how the university must change). L. Rendon, A. Nora, and R. Jalomo[7] provided a very important critique of previous theories of college student departure. They suggest that these theories were similar to research ideologies of the 1960s, which often dissected the behavior of the individual without taking into consideration the broader context of the institutional and social forces that impede success. They also assert that this approach failed to privilege the oppositional cultures and forms of community capital that prove to be valuable in the success of students of color:

> It was believed that minority individuals were engaged in a self-perpet- uating cycle of poverty and deprivation and that they could avoid social alienation by becoming fully absorbed (assimilated) or adapted (accul- turated) into the dominant culture.[8] Assimilation required a process of separation, a cultural adaptation that required minority individu- als to break away from their traditions, customs, values, language, etc. in order to find full membership in the predominantly white American society. However, during the 1970s and 1980s critics contested this per- spective, citing problems such as the use of mainstream cultural norms as evaluative criteria, as well as the problematic assumption that minor- ity group norms and cultural patterns were inferior, deviant, and self- destructive when compared to those of the majority culture.[9]

Understanding the significant impact of acculturation on the educational experience is an important first step in understanding the importance of cul- turally centered educational practice. Padilla and Perez[10] describe acculturation as changes in one's material traits, behavior patterns, norms, values, cultural awareness, and ethnic loyalty. Immigrants, both voluntary and involuntary, have often been forced or pressured to acculturate in different ways. Accultura- tion is about feeling compelled to adopt characteristics of the dominant culture in order to successfully navigate American society. So then those whose cul- tural groups are underrepresented in society must yield to the dominant cul- ture and adopt the dominant culture's language, values, and behavioral codes in order to "make it" in America. Padilla and Perez explain:

> There are a variety of factors that influence the different ways in which people acculturate. . . . Moreover, some immigrants experience more social discrimination because of their minority status. Ethnicity, race, religion, language, and/or dress often distinguish many immigrants from the host country's culture. Immigrants from various groups differ on these characteristics. Thus, members of some newcomer groups are likely to be targeted for greater discrimination than others. Some new- comers may be more inclined to undergo cultural changes not because of personal interest or inclination but due to political, social, and/or

economic circumstances that may make certain types of cultural adaptation preferable or beneficial or even to a condition of survival.[11]

Too often educational institutions have been at the center of teaching acculturation. Beginning with the Freedman Schools for African Americans and the Non-reservation Boarding Schools for Native Americans, one of the central roles of education has been to influence the assimilation and indoctrination of the American "other." William Henry Pratt's founding of the Carlisle Industrial School marked the beginning of a long practice of taking Native American youth from reservations and boarding them in schools that engrained American values and ideologies through coercion and often force.

By 1902 there were twenty-five federally funded non-reservation schools across fifteen states and territories with a total enrollment of over 6,000. Although federal legislation made education compulsory for Native Americans, removing students from reservations required parent authorization. Officials coerced parents into releasing a quota of students from any given reservation. Once the new students arrived at the boarding schools, their lives altered drastically. They were usually given new haircuts, uniforms of European-American style clothes, and even new English names, sometimes based on their own, other times assigned at random. They could no longer speak their own languages, even with each other. They were expected to attend Christian churches. Their lives were run by the strict orders of their teachers, and [the system] often included grueling chores and stiff punishments.[12]

American colleges and universities played a significant part in the initial efforts to "educate" and "civilize" Native Americans. Schools like Harvard College, the College of William and Mary, Dartmouth College, and Hampton Institute all established some form of Indian education program whose goal was to successfully acculturate and assimilate Native Americans. Native American parents were convinced to send their youth away for long periods in order to gain access to educational opportunity. Bobby Wright explains that these parents had no idea what an "education" would actually look like for their children:

Those native parents who perhaps sought a better life for their children or who were coerced to surrender their young for education probably could not fathom the hardships and tragedy to which they submitted their offspring. They had no way of understanding the cultural shock, which their children must endure. The Indian children's customs—indeed their entire way of life—were different from those they found in the towns of Virginia and New England. When they traveled the hundreds of miles from their home communities, they were ill prepared for the physical and psychological assaults they encountered upon their arrival. The schools certainly did not prepare the children for the dramatic environmental change. If anything, they compounded the stress by enforcing a sudden and direct change in lifestyle—in their dress, language, behaviors, values, and diet.[13]

Similarly, the early freedman schools constructed throughout the South originally sought to acculturate African Americans to European cultural norms and like Native Americans relinquish the "savage" spirit that many white Americans at that time associated with the African American community. These were schools created by white northern missionaries who supposedly sacrificed the comfort of their northern lives to travel south and construct schools in a foreign territory—one largely populated by African Americans. But Marvin Lynn offers a critical perspective of these early missionary efforts:

> When white missionaries and politicians from the North set out to build dozens of "Black schools" in the South during the Reconstruction period, they were not simply concerned about the welfare of ex-slaves with no skills and no means to support themselves. . . . [T]he missionaries were not benevolent do-gooders who sought to lift the African out of poverty and ignorance. Rather, they were concerned about the impact that a population of physically and mentally free Negroes could have in a white supremacist patriarchy. Eurocentric and patriarchal schools could ensure the continuation of white male domination, even if the Negroes were free. Carter G. Woodson's often quoted statement sums it up well: "Taught the same economics, history, philosophy, literature, and religions which have established the present code of morals (oppression), the Negro's mind has been brought under the control of his oppressor. The problem of holding the Negro down therefore is easily solved. When you control a man's thinking you do not have to worry about his actions. . . . [H]e will find his 'proper place' and stay in it." . . . As history shows, this system of education has not served African Americans well. While ex-slaves and their children were taught to read the word within a European culture that denigrated other forms of communication and learning, they were not taught to "read the world."[14]

One such perpetrator of acculturation and cultural oppression was the Penn School situated on St. Helena Island, South Carolina. Originally founded by white northern missionary Laura Townes of Pennsylvania, the Penn School brought "mainland" culture to the Gullah community in South Carolina. The Gullah had a history of strong cultural roots primarily because of their physical isolation on the islands of South Carolina. The water offered a shield that protected language, customs, folk life, and traditions. The Gullah spoke a language similar to the Caribbean patois or the southern creole that was a mix of African and American speech patterns. The Gullah weaved sweet grass baskets, made bateau boats to travel across the river,; fished to make a living, practiced their own unique forms of spirituality, told folktales, and let loose at juke joints.[15] A personal reflection from Emory Campbell (2008) explains:

> The foods we ate, the songs we sang, the spirits we embraced, the no-ble families in which we were loved, and the language we spoke, I had taken all for granted. Through the years each of us had thought that our lifestyle was as American as lifestyles elsewhere. But as peo-ple from elsewhere came to the islands we got inklings that something about "we islanders" was different. Sensing that being different cul-turally presented difficulty in assimilating with mainlanders many of us would take advantage of every chance to learn new folkways and abandon our own. . . . [Many] made concerted efforts to become im-itations of mainland Americans and the Penn School was where we learned how to do this. . . . When my older siblings and other relatives would return after a full year at the Penn School there was no trace of their Gullah speech. . . . The school was teaching them to look and act like European-Americans so that they would be accepted as main-stream Americans.[16]

Though at the most basic level, the intent of the missionaries was a wor-thy one, the school curriculum was most often Eurocentric and forced a sup-pression of existing language and culture. This educational approach seemed to be driven by an ethic that placed very little value on African American cul-ture. Students had to be "taught" culture because it was assumed that they did not have any. The history of the Gullah community in the South is a complex history of how culture is sustained by local communities while being unappre-ciated by larger society. More than any other regional population of African Americans in the United States, the Gullah people are known for preserving African language and cultural patterns both during and after slavery. Due to the isolation and socialization patterns in the low country of South Carolina, the Gullah community has been able to retain strong cultural legacies born in their native Africa.[17] Campbell explains:

> In a brief word, Gullah is a culture comprising a system of beliefs, cus-toms, art forms, food ways, and language practiced among descen-dants of West Africans who settled along the coasts of North Carolina, South Carolina, Georgia and Florida from slavery to the present. . . . It is widely believed that the regularity of enslaved Angolians arriving at various coastal ports gave rise to the term "Gola Negroes" which later became Gullah. Until the last half of the 20th Century the coastal com-munities of South Carolina and Georgia were populated almost entirely by African Americans. The harsh, humid climate and accompanying malaria disease deterred white occupancy during slavery, thus allowing

for ethnic purity and development of a hybrid West African culture that would become known as Gullah.[18]

The physical isolation of African Americans in the coastal regions of the South during and immediately after American slavery allowed for the community to sustain key components of their culture and to resist the slow death that many cultures experience when assimilating into a new society. Gullah is a unique subculture of the African American experience because of its history of having held on tightly to West African cultural folkways. Broadly, the history of the Gullah community is relevant to second- and third-generation immigrants of any origin. But the Gullah history and experience are particularly salient for underrepresented immigrant groups such as West Indian, Latino, Middle Eastern, and Asian immigrants that are facing the challenge of maintaining strong cultural ties in a contemporary America. Today, we see Latino populations faced with a negative backlash against their language and the full inclusion of their culture in U.S. schools. Time and again history repeats itself. The cultural story of the Gullah community sheds light on what culture means to a community—why it is important to sustain your language, rituals, and religion while all around you society pressures you to change them.

Despite the many pressures to denounce their culture, the community held on. They fought to sustain their culture. The language was sustained. The folkways persisted. And the residents participated in cooperative land buying, knowing that land was the key to sustaining culture. The history that is present in soil is critical to the growth of culture. Much has changed since those days. Today, the Gullah community's special contribution to American life is being recognized both within and beyond the low country of South Carolina. The Penn School (now the Penn Center) is one of only a few fully functioning freedman schools still operating in the United States. The leadership has changed several times over, with Emory Campbell having at one point served as executive director of the very school that once sought to suppress his love of his culture. With Campbell's leadership, the school was transformed into a cultural education center. The center has become the major preserver of Gullah heritage and culture. It is a strong example of how educational and community institutions can be transformed and work to benefit and support local culture. The Gullah story is a story of culture on life support—attacked by society, resuscitated by the local community. Today, the battle over land and cultural sustainability continues in the low country of South Carolina with the development of new, gated resorts on many of the islands. And so once again the community is organizing itself. For the Gullah their culture is everything—culture is community and culture is education—and so they continue to fight for culture's right to live.

The way in which the Penn Center was reappropriated by the local community and transformed in to a culturally centered institution is reminiscent of the critical work that many colored schools managed to do. As Lynn states,

"Of course Black independent schools and churches have historically played a significant role in providing Blacks with emancipatory forms of education."[19] Not all colored schools have been bad. In fact, many have been exemplary. One of the major contributions of colored schools to the understanding of critical and engaged pedagogy was the way in which these schools unapologetically tied education to the lived experiences of African American students. I can remember my mother sharing stories of her experiences as a student in colored schools: the ways in which they were taught spirituals, how the home economic students were taught to cook the soul food lunches that were served to the entire school, the ways in which teachers were more than teachers (they were neighbors and friends of parents), the ways in which occupations like agriculture were included in order to ensure that families continued to survive across generations, and the ways in which blackness was never villainized, demeaned, or unappreciated—it was central to everyone's world, students, teachers, and the institution itself. Kmt Shockley, a professor at Morgan State University, has done significant research on culturally centered education. Though his work focuses specifically on African-centered education, the broader cultural implications are relevant for all groups. At the center of the issue is the failure of educational institutions to simply educate.

> The inability of the American educational system to properly address the cultural and educational needs of blacks is one of the most perplexing problems in U.S. Society today. Even as the population of blacks and other groups has continued to increase, many scholars have reported that the culture of schools has remained ethnocentrically white.[20] For example, according to the National Center for Education Statistics,[21] from 1986 to 2001 the population of blacks, first-language Spanish speakers, and Asians enrolled in U.S. public schools grew from 29.7 percent to 39.5 percent. However, the teaching force remained overwhelmingly white and female, and the academic achievement gap between whites and other groups (such as blacks and Latinos) persisted. . . . African-centered education involves the act of making the education that black children receive relevant and meaningful to the black community. In order to do so, it is necessary for those who teach black children to assume the task of conducting careful historical and cultural studies of Africans.[22] . . . [B]lacks need an education that places them at the core of their own learning.[23]

In the book *Integration Matters*, C. P. Gause[24] stresses the importance of the role that educators play. Gause conducted a study that explored the voices of educators, examining the ways in which educators successfully include culture in the educational experience. At the core of the best practices that came out of this study were the spirit, respect, and cultural efficacy that educators bring into their work. As Gause states, "These educators understood the plight of the [student] and were committed to making a difference in their lives by assist-ing many of their students with navigating the multiple identities they were asked to construct particularly while attending public schools." The teachers at the school in Gause's study saw the purpose of both education at large and their careers in particular as more than simply "depositing" knowledge in the empty minds of students. In his critical work *Pedagogy of the Oppressed*, Paulo Freire explains the deposit or banking theory of education: "In the banking concept of education, knowledge is a gift bestowed by those who consider them-selves knowledgeable upon those whom they consider to know nothing. . . . The oppressed then internalize the image of the oppressor and adopt his guide-lines. . . . But, freedom is acquired by conquest, not by gift. It must be pursued constantly and responsibly."[25]

Education is a dynamic process. But most importantly it is a respectful and responsible one. Educators must first bring to their career a respect for the stu-dent, her community, and her culture. And they must, in turn, possess a strong sense of responsibility to truly affect the lives of students. A part of this pro-cess requires the educator to affirm the knowledge and life experience that the student brings into the classroom, the campus program, and the workshop or retreat. To experience racism and oppression is one thing; to be provided opportunities to understand it, study it, and dissect it is one of the first steps in the process of liberation. The educators of color in Gause's study affirm that education is about more than "receiving" a gift or "opportunity" from the priv-ileged, it is a birthright for both the student and educator: "It is our moral duty to transform the lives of students . . . because of what our forefathers and fore-mothers endured."[26] To help students come to know themselves more deeply, perhaps educators must first experience the reward of coming to acknowledge and value their own experiences with oppression, interactions with racism, and histories within their cultures.

Education Policy and Purpose

Of course, teachers are not the sole players in the transformation of educational institutions. And they often are not the most powerful. The term "educator" includes all those engaged in an academic, student-development, or adminis-trative role in a school. Faculty on college campuses, practitioners in student affairs, K–12 teachers, and school administrative leaders have the responsibil-ity to provide significant cultural learning experiences for students—dynamic experiences that cause even the facilitator to grow as a result of being a part of the educational community. But beyond creating significant cultural learning experiences, educational administrators must be challenged and questioned on the cultural norms and values that are associated with institutional policies. So-called high academic standards and policies at all levels of education have often retarded the development of the whole, intelligent, and productive citizen that Du Bois imagined in his classic essay mentioned earlier. Those deep within the educational pipeline know this all too well. In a 2011 interview with *Education Week* magazine, Jonathan Kozol offers the following insight:

> In inner-city schools, where principals are working with a sword of threats and punishments above their heads—for fear that they'll be fired if they cannot "pump the scores"—they inevitably strip down the curriculum to those specific items that are going to be tested, often devoting two-thirds of the year to prepping children for exams. There's no time for arts or music or even for authentic children's books like the joyful works that rich kids still enjoy. "What help would lovely books like these be on their standardized exams?" Instead, the kids get pit-pat readers keyed to the next miserable tests that they'll be taking. So culture is starved. Aesthetics are gone. Joy in learning is regarded as a bothersome distraction. "These kids don't have time for joy, or whim, or charm, or inquiry! Leave whim and happiness to the children of the privileged. Poor kids can't afford that luxury." So NCLB, in itself, adds a whole new level of division on the basis of a child's economic class or race. An apartheid of the intellect. One class enjoys the treasures of the earth and also learns to ask demanding and irreverent and insightful questions. The other class is trained to spit up predigested answers.[27]

Beyond primary and secondary schools, colleges and universities are also guilty of devaluing culture, community, and public scholarship through campus policies that reward certain types of research, value particular types of publications, and distribute inequitable budgets and resources across the campus. Often, the ways that budgets are structured on college campuses create a "ghetto" of an experience for some departments while other departments have so many financial and human resources that they end the year with money still in the bank. Ask any multicultural affairs department if they have ever had a budget surplus come May and the answer is likely no. They spend the entire year holding out a departmental "hat" and asking for cosponsorship after cosponsorship just to plan the programs that they were created to provide. We still live separate and unequal today on many of our college campuses. The term "handicap" comes from the practice of having hat in hand and begging for money to be placed in it. That is why this term and image are so offensive to disabled people. But this is in fact the identity of many cultural departments on college campuses and in schools. Our departments are handicapped by the lack of resources and support provided to them by the larger institution. I once heard the media personality Tavis Smiley say that budgets are moral documents. This observation is clearly true. Budgets are moral documents that illustrate the truth about an institution's values and priorities. Public statements and rhetoric espousing a commitment to diversity are merely empty words. Budgets tell the true story. And so if many of the ethics that underscore education are still steeped in oppression, we must extend our memories to those times and places that, in the face of oppression, still managed to get it right. This is about re-membering education from its current unequal, individualistic, and often oppressive state into the ideal that education is supposed to represent for the individual and the community. Many education scholars, such as Ernest L. Boyer, affirm the need for institutions to embrace their responsibility to educate for the public good:

> Higher education leaders are acknowledging that diversity brings with it important new obligations. We have, on campuses today, students of many backgrounds. Colleges and universities are being called upon to respond to a large and increasingly varied group of students, many who have special talents, as well as special needs. . . . Indeed, the real danger is that . . . students will become specialists without perspective, that they will have technical competence but lack larger insights. . . . The aim of education is not only to prepare students for productive careers, but also to enable them to live lives of dignity and purpose; not only to generate new knowledge, but to channel that knowledge to humane ends; not merely to study government, but to help shape a citizenry that can promote the public good. Thus, higher education's vision must be widened if the nation is to be rescued from problems that threaten to diminish the quality of life.[28]

So how do we do this important work? Beyond a complete overhaul of education policies, at the most basic level, how do we begin to understand and approach cultural practice within any type of educational setting? In his book *Scholarship Reconsidered: Priorities of the Professorate*, Boyer again points out the growing need for colleges and universities to connect with communities in more meaningful ways: "The scholarship of engagement means connecting the rich resources of the university to our most pressing social, civic and ethical problems, to our children, to our schools, to our teachers and to our cities. . . . I have this growing conviction that what's also needed is not just more programs, but a larger purpose, a sense of mission, a larger clarity of direction in the nation's life as we move toward century twenty-one."[29]

In essence, Boyer is arguing for a return to the values, commitments, and visions that so many of the good colored schools upheld. The strength of community-centered and culturally relevant educational experiences still holds weight today. Public scholarship initiatives that bring students onto reservations for deep cultural learning or that take students to birth lands in other countries to better understand their cultural histories contribute to this type of learning. Courses that center learning around community experiences, that include world views and opinions from diverse cultures, that involve and privilege local community leaders and even family members as guest teachers also help us to create more significant learning experiences for students of color. Engaged learning, public scholarship, and critical pedagogy are important staples for developing culturally relevant education. Beyond curricular innovations, we must also approach our cocurricular work with more intent and purpose. During my time as a practitioner creating campus-based programs, I identified three primary types of cultural experiences that should be created on a college campus (both inside and outside the classroom). A colleague and I developed this approach into a model that we called the "Tri-sector Cultural Practitioners Model." The model is primarily derived from actual practice but also utilizes national research on diversity in higher education, college student development, and cultural studies to create a practical guide that educators can use to help structure their program offerings.[30]

> The model is a multi-layered approach to creating institutional programming that focuses on challenging students to explore and to develop the multiple facets of their culture and in turn understand how their culture impacts their personal and professional character. The model identifies three sectors that may be critical in the holistic development of the student of color. These sectors include the Cultural Education Sector [focusing on cultural learning and scholarship], the Cultural Student Development Sector [focusing on cultural leadership, civic engagement, and the intersections of gender and ethnicity], and the Cultural Engagement Sector [focusing on the celebration, participation, and artistic expression of culture].[31]

Throughout this study, I have asked students to comment on the particular types of cultural experiences that they seek in school and to specifically evaluate the benefit of cultural education, cultural engagement, and cultural development programs. Again and again, they stressed the synergy that is created when offering a mixture of various types of learning experiences. Cultural experiences should be many and varied, take different formats and approaches to learning, be innovative and creative, and occur often and everywhere on campus. Students found cultural education programs to be particularly beneficial because they offer opportunities for "critical thinking," build a sense of "self-importance," allow students to "better understand the community and family," and fill the cultural knowledge gap created in high school. The benefits of cultural engagement programs included providing students of color with social options ("something to do"), contributing to their level of "comfort" on campus, reminding them of home, providing opportunities to "better understand the meanings of their rituals and traditions," "bringing together all types of people" across cultures to participate in cultural celebrations, and providing opportunities for them to "relate and interact with similar people." And, cultural development programs were seen as beneficial because of their ability to offer opportunities for more reflection, dialogue, and processing rather than "memorization." It also helped to influence how students "see themselves" and "build self-esteem." Finally, the ability to share the cultural knowledge that they acquire in college is important. Students overwhelmingly voiced the need for college to provide them with the knowledge and ability to help others who are still in their home communities so that their neighborhood friends can also better understand themselves and become more culturally aware. This is truly at the core of the idea of education as a practice of freedom and liberation. A college education must build awareness, agency, and cultural and social capital among students and by extension their families and communities whose members worked so hard for them to get there.

5

Art, Land, and Spirit

A Cultural Self-Portrait: Francheska Marie Soto-Gonzalez
(in Her Own Words)

I Am

I am the curly hair that seems out of control
I am the curvy figure that defies some mainstream clothes
I am the dance that is created from drums that beat bomba, plena, and salsa
I am a shade that confuses because I'm neither black nor white
I am tall and even taller with high heels
I am a woman who is confident within her skin
and at the same time self-conscious when it comes to others' perceptions
I am a Catholic who prays the rosary yet feels uncomfortable in a church
*   that judges*
I am an American revolutionist who refuses to see her island pillaged and
*   abused by the U.S.*
I am a compassionate soul who yearns to cease the suffering of others
I am a compassionate soul who can't seem to solve my own suffering
I am an orphan who lost her mother at the age of eleven
I am a loner who lost connection with her family in the island
I am an optimistic lover, who seeks to be loved unconditionally
I am an encourager to all those who believe in me
I am an individual who relates to the rawness of graffiti, hip-hop, and
*   slam poetry*
I am a foreigner who wants to learn about other cultural identities
I am an aimless soul who wants to touch all corners of the world
I am a sister, a daughter, an aunt, a friend,

and eventually a girlfriend to someone who deserves it.
I am a person who could fall into many categories, but to help you define me
I am Puerto Rican
I am Latina
I am bilingual
I am a creation of God who keeps evolving
I am Francheska Marie Soto-Gonzalez.

Everything Boricua

It's not that I don't have a history or a connection with the past. It's that I am in search of my past. When I refer to the past, I mean being completely aware of the history that constructs both you and your cultural identity. I haven't caught amnesia and forgotten the story and history of my family or myself. It's just that my mother passed away [when I was] eleven and I've been putting the pieces of my life together since that shattering event. [When I was] eleven, my sister woke me up in the middle of the night. She told me that my mother, Carmen Teresa Gonzales, had given up the fight against breast cancer after two and a half years. My sister's announcement marked the end of a concrete understanding of who I was. Mothers are irreplaceable. Mothers are the source of our past and cultural identities. They play a huge role in piecing the various parts of their children's lives together so that the children can fully understand themselves. A missing mother leaves a child wandering forever. So I am constantly wandering between my past and my present to learn how to identify myself. So I cling to my memories and seek guidance in the God that my family taught me to love.

My childhood was the best years of my life. I yearn to re-create them now. I wish they could come back—years filled with family unity, summers in Puerto Rico, child play, and carelessness. Family unity was the key factor that made these years utopia. My mother was the glue that kept our immediate family functioning and our extended family close even though they were in Puerto Rico. The connection that my mom maintained between Virginia and Puerto Rico was the lifeline of my evolving cultural identity. I cannot remember a childhood of speaking English or traditional American sleepovers. Any time spent stateside during the school year took place in my Puerto Rican townhouse, where Spanish was the only language permitted and weekends were filled with boleros and salsa.

My mother was the iconic symbol of everything Boricua to me. My mother's spirit of determination and resistance made her a Boricua. My mother went from teaching a classroom full of eager math students in Puerto Rico to managing a Dollar Store and then a Kmart on the mainland. She spent endless hours managing these stores so that she could assist my father in providing a home, transportation, clothing, and food for us. I have one memory in which my mother had to go to work so early that she left clothes out for my siblings and me. My mother's spirit of joy and zest for life made her a Boricua. Unfortunately, my strongest memories of my mother are those that are haunted with tears and silent screams of breast cancer. I hate that my most vivid and everlasting memories of my mother are those of her with breast cancer. My mother suffered, battled, and was defeated by breast cancer, but she wouldn't have told anybody that. In my mother's opinion, she wore scarves because they were pretty, she visited the hospital for routine checkups, she cried and hugged onto me for support in the bathroom because she loved me, not because of radioactive reactions to treatment. My mother fought cancer and sadness the best way she knew how, through laughing, singing, and dancing. My mother never feared cancer because her spirit was bigger than cancer. Breast cancer caused her to deteriorate physically, but it never took her joy or zest for life. My mother's spirit of unconditional love made her Boricua. I continue to feel her presence and love in everything Boricua.

La Isla del Encanto: Puerto Rico

There are two important women who have impacted my life: my mother, whom I've touched on, and the next is my grandmother, Teresa Torres-Gonzalez. As soon as June hit and the school year was over, we were on a plane headed to Puerto Rico. My sister, brother, and I spent three months out of every year in Puerto Rico at my grandmother's house. My grandmother passed down to me the values that make me who I am. My grandmother taught me how to pray and how to find strength in God. Every single night, right before bed, my grandmother would pray the rosary on the porch in her rocking chair. With the serenity of the night, with the chimes of the coquis, and with the slight illumination of the stars and moon, she and I could feel God as we prayed. She began teaching me the Our Fathers and Hail Marys and eventually gave me my first blue and white rosary. My grandmother believed, loved, and cared for all of God's creations, which is the reason I have a big heart. I care for and love all things because my grandmother taught me that in God's eyes we are all equal and that we should care for all things on this earth. My grandmother taught me that God's way is the only way to live fully in this world. Regardless of how people pray or to whom they pray, believing in God is what is important.

My grandmother taught me that the way to demonstrate God's love was to care about my community. Everyone in Dorado (el barrio where she lived) respected and loved my grandmother because she always gave to others. I would accompany her as she walked el barrio paying visits to the sick and giving away clothes to those in need. Having this as an example of how to care about others at a young age taught me to close my eyes to the individualistic society I had to return to in August. I enjoy giving to others and find it unnatural to solely think about myself. I don't live this life for me. I live this life for others, a way of life which in turn fills me and allows me to experience the best this world has to offer. My grandmother passed down the value that giving is getting because you feel as though you put in five cents toward a better world.

Puerto Rico to me is more than just the beaches and perfect weather that create a paradise. Puerto Rico is a living memory of my grandmother and mother.

Puerto Rico encompasses my mother's spirit and my grandmother's values. Puerto Rico is spiritual to me. Puerto Rico is the key to my past and a haven where my wandering soul can find a definite cultural identity. Without a doubt in my mind, when asked where I'm from I say, "Puerto Rico!" Though I was born in Germany and have lived in Virginia for more than 90 percent of my life, I still say, "Puerto Rico!" Saying I'm Puerto Rican is more than just an ethnic category or a racial explanation; it is a title that symbolizes the heritage that my mother and grandmother have left in my heart and one that I must carry on.

Puerto Rico en Mí/Puerto Rico in Me

Aunque no se nota
En la forma que hablo
En mis características físicas
O en la forma que bailo
Te cuento que soy Boricua
Aunque viva en los estados
Puerto Rico vive en mí
Y si te preguntas como
Yo te respondo así
Mi madre me enseñó tener alma Boricua
Querer a mi isla con una pasión
Amar al campo como el mar
Y a jugar dominó con mi papá
A jugar pelota en la esquina
A comprar limbel de la vecina
A escuchar al coquí hasta el atardecer
A agradecer a Dios por mi barrio
Que me da tanto placer
Ser de Dorado
Mi abuela fue otra que me enseñó
Que ser Boricua es lo mejor
A cocinar y querer a Dios
Porque él fue el que creó
La isla del encanto
Dónde soy yo
Aunque viva en los estados.

Even if you can't tell
By the way I talk
By the way I look
Or by the way I dance
Let me inform you, I'm Boricua
Even though I live in the States
Puerto Rico lives in me

And if you ask yourself, "How?"
I'll respond like this
My mother taught me to have a Boricua soul
To love my island with a passion
To love the farms and the beach
And to play dominos with my father
To play baseball on the corner
To buy limbel from the neighbor
To listen to the coquis at sunset
To thank God for my barrio
That gives me such pleasure to say
I'm from Dorado
My grandmother also taught me
That to be Boricua is the best
And to love God
Because he created
The island of enchantment

A Cultural Snapshot of Derrick

Derrick is an incredibly friendly and outgoing young man. During his group interview he very quickly comes out as the "life of the party," joking with almost everyone and generally bringing an overwhelmingly positive attitude into the space. Derrick does in fact have much to be happy about. He is a star athlete at a university where football is a major tradition. His choice to attend Penn State was heavily covered in his hometown. Both of his parents went to college, and his father played in the NFL. He is popular on campus and, it seems, rightfully so. He is not only a well-known athlete but also a very nice person. He smiles warmly each time we interact and is always respectful and courteous. He is the type of student who makes even the researcher feel comfortable enough to relax and let go of any anxiety and anticipation. Derrick helps us all to enjoy the experience.

In hearing his life story, it is very clear that his family has also played a major role in shaping his sense of culture. The first experience that Derrick chooses to share is being taught how to prepare soul food as a child and the Sunday dinners that followed. He confides that Sunday dinner has been passed down from generation to generation, and for his family it is a time of reflection. Over Sunday dinner, his family discusses school, family, and of course sports. During these dinners his father told old sports stories that helped to give shape to his son's future sports dreams. For Derrick, food represents a "sense of togetherness" and is a "gift from the women" in his family.

> Our Sunday dinners come from the women in my family. To make sure
> our family stays connected, my mother, aunts, and my grandmother

before she passed away would prepare dinner together. My family concentrates on soul food such as greens, black-eyed peas, yams, and cornbread. Some of the best food I have ever tasted came right from the table on Sunday. Maybe the men in our family should start a tradition and cook for the women. It's really about all of us coming together. We talk about sports, jobs, relationships and future goals. I find it helpful to talk to my family because they give me advice so I will not make bad decisions.

Derrick clearly reveals the broader importance of cultural dinners as an experience to connect family and a space in which issues can be reflected on and talked about. It even seems that he recognizes the importance of balance and reciprocity in maintaining tradition—perhaps everyone in the family needs to get involved and play a part in creating tradition, not just the women. Religion was also a very important aspect of Derrick's life. His grandfather was a preacher, and his family was heavily involved in the church—as choir members, ushers, and participants in daily worship. He recalls that his family would "pray every morning and night." The ethical model that his family provided has impacted him deeply and made him into a more thoughtful person. For him, prayer is not a ritual; it is a purposeful and useful daily activity. Prayer allows the mind to get clear and priorities to come into focus: "When I pray, I thank God for allowing me to see another day. I am thankful for the ability to get through the struggles of the day, and I think about how I need to handle everything that I am facing. I am fortunate to still be able to breathe and have mobility, and so I give thanks for that [good fortune]."

Religion as a functional tool reminds a student athlete that the gift of mobility is a privilege. Derrick uses his religion to make sense of the world—to quiet himself and reflect on his life struggles and to sift through those struggles to identify his privileges. He also discusses how gospel music serves as a stress reliever. He talks about how hearing Kirk Franklin's voice automatically makes him feel "relieved from stress, happy, and expressive." And so music is yet another tool used to get through the day. Derrick also tells about another important musical legacy that for him is a symbol of his regional culture:

In the DC area, culturally we developed a different type of expression of music called "go-go." It is a continuous and complex heavy rhythm arrangement focused through cong[a]s, cowbells, and drums. Modern-day bands use keyboards, horns, and snare drums to give it a different sound. We attend a lot of go-go concerts—it's an expression of love. One common form of go-go dancing is called "beating your feet." Another type is called "battling." Teenagers and young adults usually battle each other through dance instead of fighting each other. It doesn't stop crime, but it is a step toward positive energy.

There is a sense of pride in his roots in the Washington, DC, area. This pride seems to be tied to his interpretation of the usefulness and positivity of popular forms of local culture. Though he recognizes that not all forms of pop culture are positive, he speaks of the good in go-go music—the benefits that the community can reap from pouring their energy into artistic expression rather than violence. Even clothing (as an extension of urban popular culture) was mentioned. In local clothing stores where hip-hop music often blasted, regional clothing lines with a meaning and a message are sold in DC. "My culture also supports local clothing lines in the metro area. The clothing lines were invented to show positive work. The clothes that we wear all have positive meaning for our community—for example, a clothing line that I personally wear called 'HOBO,' which means helping our brother out. When I wear HOBO, I feel like I am contributing to a constructive environment."

For Derrick, both family culture and popular culture play important roles in positively impacting the community. Derrick is one of the few students raised by both parents in one household. And he points directly to his father as a major influence in his life. The most salient aspect of his father's presence in his life is the intentionality in his father's approach to parenting. For his sports-minded father, parenting was a well-thought-out field play of exposure, experience, and advice. Whether through the wisdom shared during family dinners, the exposure to and support of positive local businesses, or consistent involvement in religious activities, Derrick's family approached culture as a functional tool to build a better future.

To help me better understand his cultural experience, Derrick shares with me a copy of a card that his father gave to him. As he hands me the small laminated card, he says, "I wanted to include this but I can't give it to you. I keep it in my wallet at all times. My father gave it to me when he dropped me off at college. So I can't risk losing it. But I read it every morning and it really says everything about my culture." He and I walk to the copy machine and make a copy for me to keep. As he walks away, placing his card carefully back in his wallet and then patting his back pocket as he secures his wallet there, I begin to read the card:

God, my wife, and my family mean more to me than gold!!!

Williams Family Guidance and Values

Life

1. Trust in and believe that the Lord will make a way through your worship, trust, and obedience.
2. Pray before each event and ask the Lord to be with you before and after.
3. Stay humble and respectful to everyone.
4. Never forget where you came from, and always remember to give back to those who are less fortunate.

5. Be a leader through hard work and dedication.

6. Maintain your family and religious values.

Sports

1. Run, run, run, and when you get tired run some more (stadium steps, track, hallways, etc.).

2. Maintain a weight that you can easily move with.

3. Drink water and make sure you have at least 10–12 cups a day.

4. Stay confident that as long as you have put in the work and have God on your side, you will be successful.

5. Be determined to be the hardest worker with a positive outlook on each event you participate in.

We will always love you!! . . . Mom and Dad

After reading this card, I think about all my observations of Derrick—his respectful manner, his positive attitude, his performance on the football team, and his peers' sincere belief that he will be in the NFL one day (he has since become an NFL player). I am deeply impressed by the type of man his family has raised him to be, and when considering the potential model he could be to younger black male athletes, I cannot help thinking, "Thank God."

Art, Land, and Spirit Critical Essay

When I began this study, I assumed that things like music, dance, folklore, and worship were what most of us automatically think of when we think of "culture." And they indeed greeted me as I journeyed into the cultural lives of these young people. But I found myself staring religion, art, and cuisine in the face and not recognizing them. They were not the overpowering and central figures that I assumed they would be in the students' life stories. Some did not even mention them at all. Instead, they talked about other issues like the pride and pain associated with place—homelands, mainlands, and hoods. This emphasis provided important insight on the utility of culture in the lives of young adults. Typical cultural constructs like religion, music, and food were important, but they were simply a quiet presence in the room, background and supportive figures that allowed other factors like family, place, and education to take the spotlight. These concepts were about much more than organized spirituality, entertainment, or a home-cooked meal—instead they were seen as important only if they were functional, approachable, and real. Though they are different concepts, throughout this chapter I use the terms "religion" and "spirituality" interchangeably to reflect the ways in which the participants went back and forth using these terms. It was clear that young adults understood their past experiences as "religious"—taking place in formal churches or Catholic schools—but the ways in which they described the benefits of "religion" were actually aligned more with the freedom of "spirituality."

Religion: A Community of Spirit

For many, religion was an important part of their cultural experience, particularly their childhood. Several were "raised in the church" and in families that saw the church as an important symbol of tradition, values, and ethics. Religion served for many as an ethical foundation of their culture. For some, like Terry, it was a cornerstone of childhood: "Growing up and being so involved in my religion played a major role in shaping my values." For others, like Dan, religion and spiritual practice came later in life, during college, and helped them to navigate their own struggles as adults. I recall Dan's statement in his self-portrait, "In the end I just hold my faith as a priority and live life as righteously as possible." A functional approach to spirituality situates it as a guiding force that directs how one lives one's life—the ways in which people demonstrate a sense of righteousness and the ways in which they seek to serve and help others. It is a practical, not philosophical, experience. Overwhelmingly, when these young people described the role and importance of religion and church, it took the shape of another tool to help them navigate life. Spirituality less often involved abstract concepts of morality or organized rituals of religion and more often involved concrete venues for community safety and social relief. Kirin explains it through a historical context, "Church was the place to go because it was one of the few places blacks could feel safe." In her self-portrait, Tara describes spirituality as a form of relief and release: "Church was the place to be when all hope was lost, but when you came to church you had faith that God will make a way." Greta, another African American student, also discusses this topic in her self-portrait: "A significant component of my culture is God. In my household, on Sundays we are not allowed as a family to listen to nothing besides gospel. Gospel music is an inspiration. . . . [Y]ou can release all your troubles, worries, happiness, and praises through gospel music." In his self-portrait, Keith tells how his family would regularly attend church meetings in their community and why these meetings were important as a community vehicle for change: "Prayer meetings were a time when anybody from the community could come and pray about anything that was on their mind, and then they would discuss things they wanted to change in the community."

As I read these portraits, I was reminded of the student town hall meetings that regularly occur during turbulent times on my own campus and the weekly "Sankofa" community discussions held by our black caucus. No longer attached specifically to prayer or religious ideologies, these gatherings still seem to be connected to the spirit of prayer meetings from long ago—an attempt to continue the tradition of bringing the cultural community together to talk to one another about relevant community issues. The church and other spaces of spiritual worship have long been the primary gathering place for the oppressed to network, organize, and help the community. There are not many institutions that manage to regularly bring people together across multiple generations and in such large numbers. In church spaces distant neighbors become a "church family." At their best, churches and other houses of worship are organizational and community spaces that welcome those who might miss the political association meetings because of long hours and late shifts, those who are not invited to "after-work socials" or "networking receptions, and those who may not have the funds to invest in a fraternity or sorority. But they can join the church. Historically, African Americans formed churches in this manner—to establish a space of inclusion, to generate hope and courage, and to organize and keep in touch with the community. Undoubtedly, God was adored, loved, studied, and praised, but a deep examination of spirituality in the lives of most historically oppressed communities reveals the church to have served both the soul and the social condition.

When I think of church as a community safe haven, I am reminded of a famous moment in a local church in Alabama when Martin Luther King Jr. and several hundred black community members were trapped in the sanctuary of the church, unable to leave because an angry mob surrounded the building. Of course, it was active leadership that secured the necessary protection for the people. But we cannot discount the role of place—the ways in which the church was a space that initially allowed the members to convene and then eventually offered walls of protection against a real and serious physical threat. It was a long night as they waited for help to arrive, but the video shows people settled in—comfortable in their church and comfortable with their people. During the civil rights movement many meetings and public speeches took place in the church—the community safe haven where even the ostracized could organize.

This dual purpose of spirit and community has also been the case across other cultural communities in America. Sweat lodges within Native American communities have served similar purposes. The Ontario Associates of Religious Tolerance describe a sweat lodge as "a structure which generates hot moist air, similar to a Finnish sauna. It is used for rituals of purification, for spiritual renewal and of healing, for education of the youth, etc."[1] This has also been the case with mosques. In a 2010 *Washington Post* article, Edward Curtis addresses five contemporary myths that persist about mosques in America. One of the major myths is the idea that mosques are venues through which anti-Americanism and terrorism are taught. He stresses the historical legacy and contemporary practice of mosques to serve as spaces for community engagement.[2] "To the contrary, mosques have become typical American religious institutions. In addition to worship services, most U.S. mosques hold weekend classes for children, offer charity to the poor, provide counseling services and conduct interfaith programs. Through their mosques, U.S. Muslims are embracing the community involvement that is a hallmark of the American experience."

From their start in the very early 1900s, mosques have been community spaces constructed by a religious family that included global immigrants and

Americans. Across racial lines and joined by faith, more than two thousand mosques have been constructed in the United States. These spiritual spaces not only have been *for* the community but also have blended *into* the community—visually reflecting the community in which they are housed. Curtis continues: "Most Midwestern mosques blended into their surroundings. The temples or mosques of the Nation of Islam—an indigenous form of Islam led by Elijah Muhammad from 1934 to 1975—were often converted storefronts and churches."[3]

Above all else, our first spiritual spaces were modest dwellings that made the community feel at home, reflected, and included. Today, particularly within Christianity, there are a significant number of "megachurches" with congregations into the thousands. As I see it, there are both positives and negatives that come with the contemporary transformation of the church experience. One of the most important positive contributions that these churches make to society is that they continue to gather significantly large masses of people of color each week. Not many contemporary political, social, or community agencies are doing the same. The church is one of the last enduring community town-hall spaces that exist for those who are underrepresented in the United States. At the least, these churches convene and gather people on a weekly basis in a way that nonprofits and even national associations have not been able to duplicate. But this discussion of popular success brings us to one of the major failures of the church. Though the people are present, the legacy of civic involvement, activism, social awareness, and mobilization is generally weak. The church, like many other American institutions, is no longer a space where revolutionary ideas, relevant community education, and critiques of the social experience can take place. I often find it interesting that many people are shocked at the thought of revolution and religion occupying the same space. The very idea that religion and revolution do not mix is contrary to the history of most religions. Many of the great religious prophets have been activists—revolutionaries. In his book *Son of Man: The Mythical Path to Christ*, Andrew Harvey[4] declares, "The Jesus movement, as we have seen, embraced outcasts, celebrated the religious truth of women, praised, even venerated the poor, and implicitly and explicitly critiqued all the ways in which religious power was mediated."[5] In the *Bhagavad Gita*, an epic poem of Hindu tradition, the spiritual figure Krishna states:

Know what your duty is
And do it without hesitation.
For a warrior, there is nothing better
Than a battle that duty enjoins
Blessed are warriors who are given
The chance of a battle like this,
Which calls them to do what is right
And opens the gates of heaven
But if you refuse the call
To a righteous war, and shrink from

What duty and honor dictate
You will bring down ruin on your head[6]

In an artistic piece like a poem, a "battle" can metaphorically mean many things. We immediately think of countries at war. But poetry compels us to think philosophically and metaphorically rather than literally. True citizens "battle" and "go to war" with many evils in life, not just other countries. This battle can be something as approachable as taking an active role in fighting oppression, organizing politically, or helping communities in need. And so the *Bhagavad Gita* stresses that refusing to answer the social call is to refuse your call to righteousness. In his book *Strength to Love*, Martin Luther King Jr.[7] critiques the lack of social action by many religious institutions and religious leaders. The fact that these critiques come from a deeply religious man and a devout Christian make them all the more powerful. His words still ring true today.

> Even the Christian church has often been afraid to stand up for what is right because the majority didn't sanction it. The church has too often been an institution serving to crystalize and conserve the patterns of the crowd. The mere fact that slavery, segregation, war, and economic exploitation have been sanctioned by the church is a fit testimony to the fact that the church has too often conformed to the authority of the world rather than conforming to the authority of God. Even we preachers have manifested our fear of being nonconformist. So many of us turn into showman and even clowns, distorting the real meaning of the gospel, in an attempt to conform to the crowd. . . . I'm sure that many of you have had the experience of dealing with thermometers and thermostats. The thermometer merely records the temperature. If it is seventy or eighty degrees it registers that and that is all. On the other hand the thermostat changes the temperature. If it is too cool in the house you simply push the thermostat up a little and it makes it warmer. And so the Christian is called upon not to be like a thermometer conforming to the temperature of his society, but he must be like a thermostat seeking to transform the temperature of his society.[8]

Ultimately, this is about purpose. It is about doing more than just guiding people to live righteously, but more importantly energizing them to help co-create a righteous world. We need space to understand and break down politics and policies. We need spaces that commingle our spiritual doctrine with our social history—that give us the type of insight that we might not be able to get from the schools that we attend or the corporations for which we work. We need spiritual spaces that truly are community centered—unintimidating, approachable, welcoming, and at the core just basic. Beyond the grand halls, the million-dollar technologies, and the fancy instruments we need a space that can explain the most basic realities of our current world. We require spaces that will share those facts, ideologies, and insights of which so many people are simply unaware—building consciousness as well as inspiring souls. In her book *All about Love*, bell hooks explains:

> Our national spiritual hunger springs from a keen awareness of the emotional lack in our lives. It is a response to lovelessness. Going to church or temple has not satisfied this hunger, surfacing from deep within our souls. Organized religion has failed to satisfy spiritual hunger because it has accommodated secular demands, interpreting spiritual life in ways that uphold the values of a production-centered commodity culture. This is as true of the traditional Christian church as it is of New Age spirituality. It is no accident that so many famous New Age spiritual teachers link their teachings to a metaphysics of daily life that extol the virtues of wealth, privilege, and power.[9]

That's what these young people stressed—the need for a more of a community role and functional role for religion and spirituality. In his interview, Norris states, "The church was the center of the community. It was the social center, it was the political center." These statements made me wonder how many of them currently seek out church, whether on or off campus. If religion and spirituality are important markers of culture, do they regularly visit a place of worship? When I pose the question, only one student said she regularly attends church. Others answer that church is "another superficial institution." Instead, the "church" that they described as meaningful is more of an ideal than a reality. It is a religious space with a community purpose, the spiritual space that is a place where everyone has a voice, and the educational space where strategies can be developed to address contemporary politics and social struggles. The actual "church" that they saw both on and off campus was steeped in "conservatism" and "superficial rituals." This response has important implications for the ways in which colleges and local communities approach spiritual spaces and initiatives. Embracing the cultural nature of spirituality and offering space where the past, present, and future of our world can be examined through a divine lens is important. Spirituality must be functional, and it must be linked to action. Spirituality should teach us how to live love in action. It should compel us to actively create a love-driven social ethic. In a contemporary world, none have championed the ethic of love as a lived action more than His Holiness the fourteenth Dalai Lama. The poem "The Paradox of Our Age," often attributed to him, intertwines spiritual awakening with social critique and awareness.

We have bigger houses but smaller families;
more conveniences, but less time;
We have more degrees, but less sense;
more knowledge, but less judgment;
more experts, but more problems;

more medicines, but less healthiness;
We've been all the way to the moon and back,
but have trouble crossing the street to meet
the new neighbor.
We've built more computers to hold more
information to produce more copies than ever,
but have less communications;
We have become long on quantity,
but short on quality.
These times are times of fast foods;
but slow digestion;
Tall man but short character;
Steep profits but shallow relationships.
It is a time when there is much in the window,
but nothing in the room.[10]

What is in the rooms of our spiritual centers? Are we creating simple and sentimental spaces, or are we facilitating a divine social intervention to transform our world? In her book *The Soul of Education*, Rachael Kessler[11] discusses the findings of her research study that also collected the stories of college students but through a lens of their spiritual experience. She writes, "Through their stories, students reveal the need for an enduring frame of meaning. Through religious beliefs or connection to lineage or nature; through concepts of social justice, evolution, or progress; or through creative expression, students respond to the 'challenge of finding or composing some kind of order, unity, and coherence in the force fields of their lives.'[12] When we as teachers create opportunities at school for students to articulate these frames of meaning, we can substantially contribute to their spiritual development."[13] In *Sensing/Thinking Pedagogy*, Laura Rendon urges us to reenvision the spiritual nature of education:

> In many ways, we have lost sight of the deeper, relationship-centered essence of education, and we have lost touch with the fine balance between educating for academics and educating for life. It is time to reconnect with the original impulse that guided many of us to education—to bring our passion for teaching and learning and our minds and hearts into a profession that many educators, like me, believe is based on service to others and the well-being of our society.[14]

All these scholars seem to agree on the need for spirituality and religion to be relevant, critical, and enlightening in the lives of community members. And they are calling for it to be thoughtfully integrated into how we educate our young people. The participants in this study affirm these opinions. "Church" was more than anything else a symbol of a community center where the problems of the community could be honestly discussed and the very best of the community could be celebrated.

The Politics of Place

Beyond religious spaces, the broad role that space and place play as important supporters and sustainers of culture is important to discuss. Just before writing this essay, I posted a comment on the writer Kevin Powell's Facebook page about this very topic. He had posted that his family's native South Carolina was calling to him increasingly as he grew older—that the need to have access to the land, the serenity, and the heritage of those southern spaces was becoming ever more important. I shared my own sense of commitment to South Carolina, as it was where I was born, raised, and went to college. South Carolina is deep in my spirit. As an adult living away from my native state, I also sought to intentionally create opportunities in my life that would bind me to South Carolina in a sustainable way. So I bought the house next door to my parents. I did this for several reasons beyond my desire to stake my own claim in South Carolina soil. As I watched my beloved community where I was raised struggle under the weight of joblessness, crime, and drug selling, I felt that those of us that were raised by the community needed to take action to help raise it back up. Oppression is a sneaky and dirty character that invades a community gradually but steadily and destroys any remnants of the culture that was once present. Our neighborhood, our block, our land was critically important to sustaining the culturally rich community that I had known for the first twenty years of my life. Land is so critically important. It is where families are housed, communities are constructed, and institutions are built. It is on the land that we sit and talk, play sports, or dance at a barbecue. Having our feet planted firmly on our cultural ground sustains us through life. Lucilla, a young Argentinean woman, explains this necessity in her cultural self-portrait:

> I grew up with a foot in two hemispheres: southern and northern. To say I am American is a totally true statement for both pillars of my upbringing. My little brother and I are the only two members of my entire family—which to this day I have no idea how large it is—that are true "Yankees," United States citizens. At the same time, we are Argentineans, with a deep history of struggle, love, perseverance, and place running through our veins. Unlike the U.S. students who learn about living off the land through case studies of Native Americans or the Homestead Act in their textbook, my legacy is intertwined with the land in which my family culture and history flourished.

Many students shared stories of spending summers in their native lands, whether it was Argentina, Puerto Rico, Jamaica, or "down south." These stories always included the memories associated with the land—playing outside, help-ing with chores, or just sitting on the porch listening to old people talk. Place making has always been critically important to communities that do not have much. In the book "*We Shall Independent Be*": *African American Place Mak-ing and the Struggle to Claim Space in the United States* edited by Angel David Nieves and Leslie M. Alexander, Mark Santow[15] explains that people do not just experience things like racism, classism, homophobia, or any other sort of social oppression as a general life experience. They often specifically experience dis-crimination in a particular place and at particular time. On the other side of the coin, this can also be said about experiencing the loving nature of culture. The politics of place determines what type of social experience will take root in its soil—good or bad. Santow explains:

> What does it mean to speak of the importance of "place?" Even a brief journey through America's largest cities reveals an unmistakable con-nection between where (and how) people live and who they are. . . . Urban scholars generally refer to this relationship among place, iden-tity, and social structure as "social geography." The conception of space is critically important for understanding urban life in general and race relations in particular.[16]

Understanding social geography is important to understanding culture, particularly in a contemporary world. Space has historically shaped the types of experience any person will have within it. Living on a farm impacts one's daily life priorities, activities, experiences, and values in a different way than living in a suburb or a housing project. Each space has its own character and its own set of codes that are a condition of occupancy. In this regard, some spaces and places have actually been sites of great pain for many communities. In-ternment camps, plantations, fields, forests, jails, and even some schools have all been places decorated by ideals that simply do not match—the premise of beauty and the presence of terror, the premise of opportunity and the presence of oppression, the premise of justice and the presence of racism. Many places in the United States have served as philosophical burial grounds for freedom and cemeteries for culture. But that history has not stopped people from digging up the soil and resurrecting culture or putting feet to pavement to create a place of inclusion and love elsewhere. In my article "The Culture of the Kitchen," I de-scribe the critical interplay of space and place in the lives of African Americans: "African American history has been situated within many types of 'spaces'—farms, fields, churches, classrooms, courtrooms, juke joints, and homes. Both modest and grand, some have been places of pain. But many of these environ-ments have been spaces of love and cultural inclusion. They have often served as the venues through which the African American community has culturally raised its youth. And they have also been the places where cultural education took place when schools were either segregated or noninclusive."[17]

Robin Bachin[18] points out that many community spaces have been places of inclusion where an ethic of pride could be developed among communities that were ostracized from so many other places in society. Both in a historical and contemporary world, many communities have known this experience—Chinatown in New York and Little Havana in Florida. In her essay, Bachin describes Langston Hughes's experiences when he first set foot on the "Stroll," the part of State Street on Chicago's South Side where most black folks lived: "South street was in its glory then . . . a teeming Negro street with crowded theatres, restaurants, and cabarets. And excitement from noon to noon. Midnight was like day. The street was full of workers and gamblers, prostitutes, and pimps, church folks and sinners. It was here on the Stroll that Blacks met friends and relatives, caught up on the days news, and established community ties. This was a site of local knowledge, a gathering place, where community concerns could be discussed."[19]

A place to gather. Whether on a block, a plot of land, or as discussed earlier in a place of worship, a space to gather is extremely important. Places where the culture could be practiced, respected, experienced, and set free have always been seen as valuable to those whose cultures were otherwise ignored. The simple condition of being Asian is not used as a tool of marginalization in Chinatown. Instead, it is celebrated, appreciated, and vested. In these local streets or areas of commerce, folks invest in sustaining their culture. In the Gullah Islands of South Carolina, the residents engaged in a different kind of investment. When local families faced the threat of losing their land because of a lack of money, the community engaged in cooperative land buying—multiple families come together to co-own the property and keep it in the community. People build opportunity and enterprise on land. They also build a sense of self. As Yi-Fu Tuan affirms, "Human groups everywhere tend to regard their own homeland as the center of the world. A people who believe they are at the center claim, implicitly, the ineluctable worth of their location."[20] Home is all some folks have. And even for those that have much, a sense of home is often the most valuable possession. In her book *Belonging: A Culture of Place*, bell hooks describes the ways that her native Kentucky was also calling her home. Despite living in many fabulous places like New York and California, Kentucky turned out to be the place that spoke to her soul and her memory of self.

> Like many of my contemporaries, I have yearned to find my place in this world, to have a sense of homecoming, a sense of being wedded to a place. . . . Kentucky hills were where my life began. They represent the place of promise and possibility and the location of all of my terrors, the monsters that follow me and haunt my dreams. Freely roaming Kentucky hills in childhood, running from snakes and all forbidden outside terrors both real and imaginary, I learned to be safe in the knowledge that facing what I fear and moving beyond it will keep me secure.[21]

As with culture, the home place is a unique mix of good and bad experiences. It is where our joys and fears were first nurtured. And like culture, even those memories of place that bring up moments of fear, hurt, or lack have still taught us some very important life survival lessons. I am always a bit offended when people tell impoverished youth that their community is just where they live, that it is not who they are. It most definitely is who they are. The achievements and failures, positivity and ignorance of our home neighborhoods influence us, inform our view of the world, and help us navigate life in general—as in, if I can make it there, I can make it anywhere. In my 2005 article in *Gloss Magazine Online*, I discuss the problems that I see with the use of terms like the "hood": "It is important that we understand a 'hood' is a place where people do not enact the role of neighbor—where creating a sense of kinship and being a neighbor [are] absent from the experience. So, a hood can be created within an urban ghetto as well as in an affluent suburb where people don't speak to or look out for one another. If you were raised in a government housing project but had neighbors that looked out for you—then you were a part of a neighborhood however poor it might have been."[22]

Perhaps we need to begin to help young people see the value in their communities, even if that value is only one very small nugget. Is it possible to see these places in a new light and acknowledge that all places, both grand and modest, are rich in value? In my past review of literature that focused on the challenges of educating black males in American society, I discuss at length the viability of hip-hop culture as an "intellectual space of inclusion" for young black men. As a culture, it is a space that welcomes the rage, critical voice, and modes of expression of black men.[23] And also, as a culture, it is clear that hip-hop views place as critically important. Whether it is in the "dirty" South, "Bk" (Brooklyn), or the "Boogie Down Bronx," when home is either a ghetto or a trailer park, artists remember it, claim it, and talk about it. This idea conjures up a memory from the film *Notorious*, which focuses on the life of the rapper Christopher Wallace, also known as Biggie Smalls.[24] At the end of the film, there is real footage of his funeral processional as it traveled through the streets of Brooklyn. For the first time in a long time Brooklyn was silent. And then someone turned on their radio and blasted a Biggie song. Everyone began to sing and dance. Everyone remembered their beloved "home" boy. I recall thinking as I watched that for some communities, all they have is where they are from and the artists that represent these places. Biggie was more than a rapper; for young Brooklynites he represented Brooklyn itself—he represented place and home, and that is why they claimed him so constantly.

In urban centers and suburbs young people today still innately value place. I have worked with many college students who yearn for education-abroad experiences—experiences that immediately force them into a slower time, rural lands, and cultural rituals. Many education-abroad programs give students the ability to see the ways in which people around the world value and make meaning of place. The respite from the typical American pace of life is often valued, even described as life changing. When I worked as the director of the cultural center at Penn State, I offered several education-abroad experiences for our student leaders of color—students who would never be able to afford to participate in a traditional study-abroad experience. One student who participated in a trip to Dakar, Senegal, discussed the impact of this experience:

> The pinnacle of the program was our week-long visit to Dakar, Senegal, in West Africa. I would have never had the opportunity to make a purposeful trip like that on my own accord. For one, we were able to engage with different types of leaders on various levels of the political, social, and communal scopes of Dakar. I was able to engage with African and American leaders who worked, lived, and served in Dakar, which gave me perspective on my own ideas of community and leadership at the time. . . . If I had to put into a single word what the entire cultural exchange experience was for me, it would be "perspective." I gained so much understanding of myself and how I relate to a broader community of people who serve and aspire to serve beyond what is expected of them.

Surpassing expectations frames the foundation of the idea of culture as place. Whether in internment camps, concentration camps, plantations, schools, companies, homes, city blocks, porches, or stoops or whether coming from migrant farms or so-called hoods, people of color have indeed created spaces where they could surpass the world's deficient expectations of them. Through place we have often convened both community and memory. As one young person eloquently states:

> Regardless of the symbols I decide represent my cultural identity and social consciousness, they will always express the same values: kinship, discipline, hard work, sharing, honesty, and love. I am driven to succeed as an individual not because I desperately seek economic gain or personal strength, but rather because I am building myself within my community. The idea of community to me is also not static. Because I am used to maintaining relationships from over six thousand miles away, community is an abstract idea, where the memories and values learned from one geographic region and their people are carried with me wherever I go.

Cultural Cuisine: A Place Where Culture Can Be Mixed, Stirred, and Allowed to Rise

In her cultural self-portrait Lucilla writes:

> Uncontrollable laughter erupted from the table. Five women giggling to jokes I could not understand, exchanging stories of my grandfather's

strict rule, of my aunt's trickery, of my mom's naivety, and the pet chickens that planted eggs everywhere. A maté was slowly being passed around the table, as though churning the memories to the surface of the conversation. From afar it was hard to tell my mother apart from her three sisters; they all move in sync, dictated by a deep bond of sisterhood. There is a photograph of my mom and her sisters in the living room. None of them are looking at the camera, but rather at each other, with a twinkle dancing in their eyes. Every time I see this photograph, I remember Pipa and the sisterhood that ties me to my family. "Pipa," as we called her, was the most honest, hardworking, disciplined, and sweet woman I have ever had the privilege of knowing. Hers was a history of living off the land; she was born on a semitropical prairie with nothing more than a precarious tin roof propped over her head. . . .

The Argentinean maté custom is integral to my perspective on community, relationships, and sharing. Maté is often confused with the tea, but it is really the wooden cup in which loose tea, *yerba*, is placed, with the *bombilla*, a suction straw, nudged inside. Hot water is poured to the rim of the maté, either with a thermos or a teapot. The idea of drinking maté is that the drinker serves water for the next person to drink. The tea gets passed around the circle for hours over conversation, games, jokes, stories, etc. . . . When people suggest drinking maté, they are referring to this practice of interaction and relationship building. The idea is to devote a solid amount of time, every day, to slowing down with your loved ones—friends and family—in the spirit of kinship. I cannot remember a moment when my mom had company over, or we were visiting someone, and the maté didn't get whipped out. Maté has had a deep influence on my life. In the United States, people are very used to having acquaintances, people in their lives they casually call their friends but do not share the intimate details of their lives with. This structure seems convenient to the fast-paced lifestyle in the northern Virginia area; you can't have a true network of deep relationships if you can't devote the time to it. Although I have learned to appreciate certain aspects of American culture, this is something that inspires loneliness in my heart when I remember the days in Argentina. In recent years, I learned to combat the looseness of relationship structures in my U.S. environment by taking on the values of maté: sharing of responsibility, devotion of time, and intimacy. Regardless of how busy I am, leading the "American" lifestyle of a million and one tasks a day, I make sure to let my friends and family know I care about them. If I can, I take an hour or two to sit down with a friend and let time pass us by; building of relationships can be more constructive than working an extra hour.

For Lucilla, teatime was an important cultural moment and the venue through which folks gathered, shared, taught, and loved. Her value remains strong not for the tea itself but for the environment that was created around the tea. Many family reunion activities are accompanied by a meal—Sunday dinner, holiday meals, or neighborhood cookouts. These meals offer more than just "food for the soul" as Tara calls it. They also provide important opportunities for fellowship with family and close friends. She explains this idea in her self-portrait: "Cooking became one of the most important traditions in my family because it was a symbol of love and togetherness. Even though the foods we prepare are not that expensive, it's still our tradition. The types of food we eat are fried chicken, yams, collard greens, black-eyed peas, turkey necks, ham hocks, cornbread, and macaroni and cheese. Whether it is after church, holidays, birthdays, births, funerals, there is always a well-prepared meal."

Larren echoes this in her group interview, "Food is a big part. We do almost everything with food. It could be a funeral, and we have food—family dinners. You know, rice and beans and curry and macaroni pie." Others nod their heads, and someone comments, "Sharing food is actually a huge part with mine too."

Teddy says that the central focus of his family's meals is cementing the family bond and understanding one another: "Our dinners make sure our family stays connected. We eat traditional African food. I believe it is a sense of togetherness for my family. Yes we come together to eat, but we also express our feelings and views on different subjects in our daily lives."

For Keith, meals tie together family and religion: "On Thanksgiving, before we eat, we get in a circle and thank God for at least one thing that He has done for us, and then someone will say grace. My grandmother would cook up a big meal, and all of her kids would come with their kids. It was a time of fellowship."

These meals, like the cultural celebrations and rituals that they accompany, serve to bring the family together. The stories shared seem to weave a cross pattern with every thread leading back to family. So again, we see the deeper meaning of a very traditional component of culture. Yes, these young people confirm that whether it is soul food from the South, rice and beans in the Caribbean or South America, or maté in Argentina, communities of color appreciate and find comfort in their indigenous forms of food. The individual body may find sustenance in the plate, but each person, as a cultural being, is fed by the fellowship. Reading about family gatherings and meals again causes me to reflect on my own life. Years ago, when I was in graduate school, I had a good friend who also used to bring friends together around food and fellowship. He used to call our gatherings a meeting of the minds. Indeed, meals are where minds meet and where cultural values are built.

Arts of the Impossible

Finally, of course, art is a critical component culture. But art, in this sense, was not about galleried and formal forms of art. Instead, like religion, land, and food, art was valued for its approachability as well as its relevance in the lives of young people. In a contemporary world, our lives have changed and our daily cultural practices have evolved. And so many forms of art have also developed into creative expressions of today's lived experience. Hip-hop culture, including things like music, graffiti, dance, knowledge production, and fashion is one such example. What makes it an approachable form of art are the ways in which it was born and is still based in the community experience. For years, graffiti art gave young, talented canvas artists a platform to share their art with the world when galleries did not welcome them and when society saw them as criminal. As an art form, graffiti is another example of place making and claiming. Artists paint themselves onto the bricks and mortar of their community. Today, graffiti art has been embraced and included in many community arts programs, providing a structured way for young people to develop themselves as artists. These programs are also examples of how communities have transformed their opinions of graffiti and now see it as a valuable tool to help beautify communities through murals. This provides important social and political agency for young people. It allows them to assist their communities in their own unique way. Hip-hop as a culture has always provided a physical space that brought marginalized communities into the center. This is what makes the visual image of the "cipher" so compelling. A cipher is a circle of energy created by members of the community standing shoulder to shoulder, forming a circle and giving each person in the circle an opportunity to "spit" or rhyme. Hip-hop has always been a space of inclusion. African American, West Indian, and Latino youth in New York City were the creators of hip-hop—they were creative visionaries who sought to develop their own inroads for expression and inclusion.

"Rap music and Hip Hop culture factored heavily in the shaping of the United States. In the late twentieth century this dynamic music and subculture bubbled up in the early 1970's and gave voice to Black [and Latino] Americans who had previously existed on the periphery of the nation's consciousness. . . . The music not only highlighted their struggles, but also shed light on their aspirations."[25] Bynoe goes on to call for a continued political evolution of hip-hop culture, stating, "True revolutionaries will demand a new thing, rap music that not only tells stories, but also speaks truth to power and encourages folks to image new realities."[26] The idea that art created by marginalized communities should have a responsibility to move beyond pure entertainment and include a social and political consciousness has actually been around for some time. Mulana Karenga suggests that art must first and foremost be socially responsible—conscious of the significant role it can play in transforming minds and respectful of the influence and impact that it makes on the communities that consume this art. His work focused primarily on black art, but has implications for all forms of contemporary art that, like hip-hop, is now embraced across various communities.

The best of . . . culture insists that our creative production or art not only be technically sound but also socially purposeful and responsible. It is at its best functional, collective and committing. To be functional is to self-consciously have and urge social purpose, to inform, instruct and inspire the people and be an aesthetic translation of our will and struggle for liberation and ever higher levels of life. It also means searching for and creating new forms and styles to speak our truth and possibilities. To be collective, Black art must be done for all, drawn and synthesized from all, and rooted in a life-based language and imagery rich in everyday relevance. It must be understandable without being vulgarly simplistic, i.e., so pedestrian and impoverished that it damages art as a discipline and the social message it attempts to advance. And it must celebrate not only the transcendent and awesome but also the ordinary, teaching the beauty and sacredness of everyday people and their struggles to live full, decent, and meaningful lives. . . . [I]t must demand and urge willing and conscious involvement in struggle and building of a new world and new men, women and children to inhabit it. And it must move beyond protest and teach possibilities, beyond victimization and teach Blacks to dare victory. The best of the Black aesthetic teaches that art, then, must commit us to what we can become and are becoming and inspire us to dare the positive in a world often defined and deformed by the negative.[27]

Karenga's ideas were echoed by the students in this study. Too often "art" is something so delicate and so privileged that everyday people cannot find themselves in it. Galleries become too formal and performance halls too intimidating. Viewing art as a functional cloak in which all people can wrap themselves for the cultural warmth of inspiration, relation, and inclusion is to understand art as a tool of possibility. The idea that art is for both the poor and the privileged is at the core of Karenga's belief that it must be collective—including all. Like any form of production, some live up to the task and some fall short. But there have been many artists embracing the idea of being both social storytellers and political seers or visionaries. Another contemporary form of art that demonstrates this idea is spoken word. Spoken-word artists creatively mingle the foundation of classical poetry with both hip-hop culture and theatrical performance. Poems can make you laugh about the everyday, shake your head over the challenges of relationships, or stand on your feet motivated to take social action. Open mic nights are yet another nontraditional venue through which the community can gather and speak. Poet Ishle Yi explains: "Performance poetry has made the transition from hip downtown clubs to Broadway show to touring company with its soul mostly intact. The scene began in the late '80s as scores of writers flocked to such venues as the Nuyorican Poets Café, Café 13 and the Bowery Poetry Club to deliver their verse in a style and cadence inspired by another art form: hip-hop. I loved the visceral energy that you see onstage and how the words translate to the stage."[28]

As forms of verbal expression, music and spoken-word poetry offer an opportunity for young people to speak—loudly and unapologetically. In many ways, hip-hop music and spoken-word poetry are a contemporary continuation of the great intellectual tradition that began in the Harlem Renaissance. The strong social, economic, and political critiques of many of today's artists echo the artistic resistance of Langston Hughes's works, such as "Let America Be America."[29] The ethic behind songs like Tupac Shakur's "Changes," Mos Def's "Mr. Nigger," or jessica Care moore's "What Language Does a Black Girl Scream In?" conjure up memories of Claude McKay's "Outcast."[30] Undoubtedly, Harlem Renaissance artists are the reason why hip-hop artists and performance poets have a platform to speak so freely today. The foundation of creative energy, passion, and courage that this group of intellectuals created during the renaissance ushered in a new form of political license for writers, poets, and musicians. Everyone was included in the cause—everyone was considered to be a thinker. Using a new genre of music, contemporary artists are still critiquing, reflecting, and artistically navigating the racial and class-based experience in America. They carry forward the torch. And so new forms of cultural production deserve broad social respect because truth expressed through a politic of imagination and creativity is worthy of praise whenever it is exhibited. In their recent book *Born to Use Mics: Reading Nas's Illmatic*, Michael Eric Dyson and Sohail Daulatzai[31] acknowledge the depth and critical meaning often found in the lyrics written by rappers. Because many underrepresented communities have a history of valuing community-based knowledge and of understanding that knowledge is produced in our homes, on our streets, and through our cultural production, it is important that our communities continue to challenge the notion of who is allowed to be considered knowledge producers and what venues (beyond educational institutions) are allowed to be viewed as points of knowledge production.[32] When they are at its best, the lyrics penned by young hip-hop artists and the poems written by spoken-word artists are a valuable form of nontraditional knowledge and social critique of the American experience. Hip-hop and performance poetry are cultural spaces where individuals who have been kicked out of schools, locked out of opportunity, and imprisoned in oppression have created a space where they can shine, excel, and be great.[33]

And generating a sense of greatness is important when you have lived a life on the margins of society. In their creative work, hip-hop artists have always talked about their greatness, their skill, and their aim to be the best. At its core, hip-hop is about truth, nonconformity, and excellence. The rapper Nas constantly pays homage to Muhammad Ali by proclaiming that he is the "greatest man alive." In the song "Step into a World," KRS-One flippantly jokes, "I'm number one, oh wait sorry I lied. . . . I'm number 1, 2, 3, 4 and 5." Veteran entertainer Doug E. Fresh's signature line is "Give it all you got, give it all you got." The incredibly talented emcee Black Thought speaks to the ethic of diligence, purpose, and commitment in his work: "What I spin put 'em out on a limb . . . got tears, got blood, got sweat leaking out of the pen." And Jay-Z constantly affirms his brilliance and ability, "I do this in my sleep . . . difficult takes a day, impossible takes a week." It is questionable whether this ethic of excellence has been clearly seen through the smog of social stereotypes obstructing our view of hip-hop culture. Too often, the minds and work ethic of these artists are ignored, and they are simply seen as the things that they possess. Even if you do not care for Lil Wayne—he does work hard. That is more important for young black men to hold onto than some of his destructive lyrics. As a form of mass cultural production, hip-hop is definitely not perfect, and in some instances it is actually hurtful to the healthy formation of a politic of love and hope in our communities. Popular culture consumes our society, and the daily realities of our lives often cause us to interact with the media (smartphones, iPads, iPods, and laptops) more often than we interact with one another. According to bell hooks,[34] internalized self-hatred is actually more pronounced now then in the era of segregation. This fact has important implications for the content of the art that is produced in a contemporary world and the people who consume it. Hooks[35] discusses the critical differences between a time period when African Americans were demeaned, stereotyped, and caricatured by a larger society that openly admitted to hate versus the current era where white-supremacist, patriarchal thinking is cleverly hidden behind curtains of verbal democracy and inclusion.

> When we watched shows like *Tarzan* or *Amos 'n' Andy* that we enjoyed, we were ever aware that the images of blackness we saw on these programs were created by folks who, as Mama would say, "did not like us." Consequently, these images had to be viewed with a critical eye. In my own family this critical vigilance began to change as the fruits of the civil rights struggle became more apparent. Mama's last child would watch television alone with no adult voices teaching her a resisting gaze. . . . Once laws desegregated the country, new strategies had to be developed to keep black folks from equality, to keep black folks in their place. While emerging as less racist than it had once been, television became the new vehicle for racist propaganda. Black people could be represented in negative ways, but those who had wanted there to be jobs for Black actors could be appeased. Nothing pushed a white supremacist aesthetic more than television, a medium where even dark-haired white women had to become blondes in order to succeed.[36]

Though written primarily about television, hooks's comments can be broadly applied to all of mass media, as the industry is now more blended and less segmented than in the past. Music is no longer relegated to radio—it is a television-, radio-, and Internet-based form of entertainment. In general, art has become much more accessible and significantly corporate. The stereotypical images of which hooks spoke are now sold to us through songs, music videos, and Web sites. And many people often fail to critically analyze and dissect the art or media that they consume. In America we are taught how to do a lot of things—drive, read, and write—but we are not provided any type of formal education on how to "read" the media and pop culture—how to be a critical consumer. So I was pleasantly surprised to hear young adults say that there is a need for art to be positive and functional. If art is to be reflective of our "real" lived experiences, then the lives of these young people have shown us that hope and love are present even through struggle. Our art must tell the truth about poverty, crime, addiction, love, commitment, and hope—all are present in the lives of those who experience struggle. The young adults in this study saw music in particular as a quintessential tool for communicating who they culturally were. They valued everything from hip-hop to go-go to gospel. According to Breanna, music is important because it is a tool to express struggle and perseverance: "Hard times are often expressed in hip-hop and R&B music. Some songs portray the negative and positives of our culture. These songs are sometimes facts and opinions. We use art to depict moods, struggle, reality, and detail."

This statement illustrates that for Bre, music in particular and art in general are not valuable simply for art's sake. Rather, they are critical communication vehicles. For Erika, music is a source of historical reflection: "Like when I hear some drum beats, it makes me think back to the influence. It kind of puts me in a place where I think of the influence of African music on the youth today and how it transcends from then until now. You can see how we still have some of this stuff. And the influence of that into Latin culture. Even though someone may be dancing to the rhythm differently, I can dance to it with meringue."

To Erika, music in many ways is one of the true and honest reflections of the interconnectedness of our cultural histories. The original rhythms found deep in the music and her organic response through sway, tap, and dance tells the story of her historical and cultural ties to Africans, Europeans, and the Taino of Latin America. The drum calls to attention history, culture, race, and ethnicity. Through art, the best and the worst of the culture can be placed on a public table for discussion. The thread is again working and weaving this pattern connecting music and art back to elements mentioned earlier like struggle, history, and family legacy.

This research has called me to question my approach as an educational practitioner. In our university cultural center, we began to transform the structure, format, and texture of our programs so that art could be more relevant to the students' real experiences, could include the family unit, and could be something so unintimidating that even those who do not view themselves as artists could explore their personal creativity. One such program, Recipes of Resistance, was cocreated by my colleague Crystal Endsley and me. Through the program, we took materials that have been normally associated with sexism and oppression—aprons and tablecloths—and encouraged the students to artistically turn them into materials of resistance. The program began with a weekend arts workshop in which students selected either an apron or tablecloth and painted images, stories, and poems on it that shared the politics of survival, stories of hope and love, or memories of pain that they had experienced in their families. To further underscore the idea of elevating family members as knowledge producers, we had our own mothers, who were artists by hobby, to facilitate the arts workshop. In their spare time, Crystal's mother made quilts, and my mother painted aprons. Neither of our mothers had ever been to college and had never "taught" college students, but we wanted the students to understand that we valued our mothers as brilliant and talented women. The aprons and tablecloths that the students produced were put on display as an exhibit in the cultural center, and within the exhibit space we sponsored various events throughout the week—spoken-word performances, lectures, and group dialogues. We now take this program to other colleges in the United States—schools that are seeking to mix art, family, and social justice. Through this program, we made art into something functional, personal, and interactive for students. But most importantly, through this initiative we lifted up, analyzed, and gave voice to the talents, knowledge, and experiences that are present within family and culture.

It is important to state explicitly that cultural production in communities of color is more than just a cultural convenience—a form of entertainment. There is intellectual and educational merit in culture, art, and community folkways.[37] A community often uses culture (cultural production, engagement, education) as a politic of social survival—as a life raft for those drowning in oppression.[38] In her critical work *Black Feminist Thought*, Patricia Hill Collins[39] suggests that wrestling with the ways in which nontraditional knowledge has been used to educate, create self-awareness, raise self-efficacy, and steward social change among communities of color offers important insight into the complex relationship between culture and education in America. No one illustrates this idea more than Tupac Shakur. Shakur's music was a mix of black power consciousness, contemporary critical critique, and violence, misogyny, and nihilism. He was not perfect. But he was definitely compelling. In *Tupac Resurrection*, Shakur discussed the reasons behind the initial aggressive transformation of rap music. He comments that in the 1950s the black community "asked" for their rights, asked for inclusion. During the Black Power movement, folks became more demanding but were continuously pounded by the fists of the U.S. government and power structure. Now, many of those former young leaders have grown old in jail or have been forced to live as American exiles in other countries. And so Shakur wonders why people would even suggest that today's generation of citizens, students, or artists should continue to simply and respectfully ask for their freedom. His comments are important, as we now live in a society where young people do not just have the general "belief" that other folks have it better—we are actually given an opportunity to see for ourselves their fabulous lives. Wealth, greed, and privilege are tauntingly dangled before our eyes. In his book *Where Do We Go from Here: Chaos or Community?* Martin Luther King Jr.[40] foreshadowed the growing frustrations of young adults: "If they are America's angry children today . . . it is a response to the feeling that a real solution is hopelessly distant because of the inconsistencies, resistance, and

faintheartedness of those in power."[41] Three decades later, Shakur painted the
following picture:

> You have to be logical. You know? If I know that in this hotel room they
> have food every day, and I'm knocking on the door every day to eat,
> and they open the door, let me see the party, let me see them throw-
> ing salami all over, I mean, just throwing food around, but they're tell-
> ing me there's no food. Every day, I'm standing outside trying to *sing*
> my way in: "We are hungry, please let us in, We are hungry, please let
> us in" After about a week that song is gonna change to: "We hungry,
> we need some food" After two, three weeks, it's like: "Give me the food
> or I'm breaking down the door" After a year you're just like: "I'm pick-
> ing the lock coming through the door blasting" It's like, you hungry,
> you reached your level. We asked ten years ago. We was asking with the
> Panthers. We was asking with them, the Civil Rights Movement. We
> was asking. Those people that asked are dead and in jail. So now what
> do you think we're gonna do . . . *Ask*?

Indeed, young artists are no longer asking; they are screaming for their realities to be heard and for the world to change. Through what other venue are
people of color who have nothing but their talent and their name given a mi-
crophone to talk to the entire world? Many companies pay serious money for
commercial media time. Others struggle for PSA and publicity opportunities.
To have a platform, a moment in time, where you are allowed to speak to mil-
lions of people is so incredibly special—why waste it by saying nothing useful?
In many ways, our contemporary art, whether it is edgy street-based painting,
music, or spoken-word poetry, liberates both the young artists and the many
ancestors who struggled so that these young people might live today and have
the freedom to be artists. I am sure that if we were to look deep into the lives
of young artists today, we would find ancestors who willed them their talents.
And so if not for the community, this sense of social responsibility should be
embraced for our great-grandmothers and great-grandfathers who did not have
this chance and opportunity to speak. I close this chapter with the work of An-
thony Keith, an incredible spoken-word artist, educator, and community activist whose work exemplifies the ways in which young adults are using art to
speak truth and bear witness.

Poetry to the Rescue!
Tony Keith

You can save someone from drowning
And my daddy's a preacher and he says that if your sermon is good,
you can save a man's soul
Well, I've never been the type of person to ask for help,

but if I need some saving, trust me, you'll know
But I won't be sending out an S.O.S. message or interrupting
your regularly scheduled program
I won't be sending you an e-mail, a text message,
or sending anything via telegram
But instead you'll find me on a stage
Usually with a piece of paper in my left, and a pen in my right hand
My mouth will be wide open and a vain poking out of my neck
My eyes will be shut tight as I focus on every . . . single . . . breath
Just to make sure my lungs have enough capacity
To create words that defy the laws of gravity
And swirl up into a vortex of knowledge
that causes supernatural catastrophes
And while this poem is not a tragedy
There might be some casualties
If you're not prepared to battle me
But, if you're feeling froggy . . . then jump
And if you can't jump to reach my level
then I suggest you ball up some of that garbage
you've been writing and create yourself a stump
Because I am not interested in entertaining the words
of whack poets and false prophets
That string together any words that rhyme
just to create themselves a profit
Selling ignorance to their audience, spectators, and watchers
Got them digging for some of your common sense inside of their wallets
But they don't realize that their cost of admission
Is really just your cost of admitting to stealing your words
from a powerful poetic 3rd grader you heard spitting
the last time you was babysitting him
And yes below the belt is where I'm hitting
It's because you're hollow at the top
and I'm trying to prevent you from tipping
You see, I don't want you to fall
I'm just trying to prevent you from slipping
into some of these puddles that I'm spitting
So please . . . just listen
I write this for those of you with terminal diseases
I write this for those of you who want to have sex
but your parents are preachers
I write this for those of you who want to learn
but you lack good mentors and teachers
I write this for those of you who love your momma
but all she does is scream at you

I write this for those of you who love your daddy
although his eyes have never seen you
I write this for those of you who miss getting a good night's sleep
after hearing your grandma sing a sweet song to you
I write this for those of you with negative energy
and so like a magnet, bullshit just clings to you
I write this for those of you that work so hard to create change
You get frustrated, but you still maintain
I write this for those of you whose sexuality is unacceptable
until it's received society's stamp of approval
I write this for those of you who don't have an answer,
yet one is always being forced from you
Sometimes saying, "I don't know" is a lie
but sometimes saying, "I don't know" is the truth
I write this for you
I write this for those of you whose egos have been
destroyed by gossip and rumors
Blown up and exploded like cancers and tumors
I write this for those of you who want to earn love,
but don't know it's already given to you
And I write this for those of you who want to claim
your birthright as a daughter of Osun
I write this for you
Been battling poetry until my ink bleeds black and blue
I'm just a superhero with a cape made of metaphors
trying to use my words to simply save you
And yes,
At some point in time, I may need a little bit of saving
But I've been investing and paying in to my Bank of Poetry
account for a little while now, so I can afford a little misbehaving
And yes, some of the words in my poems do rhyme,
but I've been doing this for a while so it just happens sometimes
And yes, the memorization can make my performance good
But I will pick up and read from a book every single time,
just to make sure my messages never get misunderstood
Because I do this for a reason
This gift is not temporary, it does not change with the seasons
That means I can spit fire while the sky is hot
Or cool it down while the water is freezing
And if "words having power" isn't something you believe in
Then I can spit on my fingertips, reach out my palms,
and turn this poem into an altar call
and I'll start saving all of you heathens
Because I care about your futures

I care about your destinies
I care about your legacies
And I want ya'll to remember my name
I want ya'll to look up in the sky and say, "Is that a bird?" . . . "Is that a plane?"
And I'll look down screaming,
"NO! It is poetry and I'm a poet! A social agent of change!"
Piecing letters to words and words to sentences and sentences into sounds
Leaping over metaphors with one single bound
Powerful enough to spark protest for equality in "ghetto" communities
Talk slicker than those politicians
that create policies that grant rich folks immunities
You see, I didn't choose to be saved by poetry
Poetry chose me
Crept up inside my momma's womb and poetry started tickling me
I've been spitting in rhythmic patterns since I was in grade 3
And will continue until I'm through
So who am I?
I'm just a simple, superhero with a cape made of metaphors
trying to use my words to simply save you.

6

Cultural Heritage Still Matters

A Cultural Self-Portrait: Mimi
(in Her Own Words)

I am a Vietnamese American. A naturalized citizen, I was born and spent a short period of my younger years in Vietnam. I left my country at the age of six to move to a place completely new and scary to me. I didn't know the language, the customs, or the lifestyle. I was a scared child uprooted from the place I called home, desperately wanting to belong somewhere. And so I dove right in. I took every chance I got to learn to be an American. I didn't want to be the subject of ridicule by those who thought that because I'm Vietnamese, I must be a Viet Cong (communist party in Vietnam). I worked hard to get rid of my accent and the customs and ways of my people because it represented something alien among my American friends. Most of the people (non-Vietnamese) that I meet are often surprised that even though I wasn't born in the United States, my American accent is flawless. But no matter how much I wanted to be rid of my culture, it never left me. Fortunately, I grew up and realized the beauty of my language, people, and culture. The Vietnamese people that I meet are always flabbergasted by my ability to fluently speak the Vietnamese language and my knowledge of the history, food, and culture of Vietnam. My response to them is always "I was never given a choice." In fact, no one is ever given a choice as to what culture they're born into. It's who we are! It's who we're destined to become.

My parents are true lovers of the Vietnamese culture. They are musicians who specialize in Vietnamese traditional folk music. Their number-one goal is to travel the globe so that they can share the richness of the Vietnamese history and culture. Because of my family, the culture of my people is very much within me. One major component of my culture is family. And by "family" I don't mean just you, your siblings, and your parents; I mean your grandparents, uncles, aunts, cousins, great-uncles, great-aunts, second cousins, and so on. There is never a holiday that goes by when we do not see one another. And growing up, we sought the advice of other members of the family as well as the advice of our parents. Everyone knew each other's stories and life circumstances. And if someone was struggling, everyone pitched in to help in some way. We believe in the idea that it takes a village to raise a child. The close-knit but extended family is a part of who we are. I'm very appreciative of this because I know that I'm never alone. And my family, they also know that I'll always be there for them. This thought is comforting to me given that we live in such a self-centered world. And now that I'm a mother, I'm determined to keep this tradition alive so that my son will grow up to care for those around him and not just for himself. Now that I'm a mother, I can understand the importance of knowing and respecting one's culture and heritage.

The history/story of the Vietnamese people is as long and as ancient as those in China. In fact, Vietnam was once a southern territory of China and has had a long history of fighting to keep the Chinese at bay. However, the recent history of Vietnam is one that has personally affected my family. Two generations of my family are immigrants. My grandparents' generation immigrated from northern Vietnam to south[ern] Vietnam during the Vietnam War. And my parents' generation immigrated from Vietnam to the United States. My grandparents on both my mother's and my father's sides had to escape the threat of communist power in northern Vietnam. My paternal grandfather worked for the Communist Party, but because he came from a wealthy family, they threatened to kill off his family to gain access to their wealth. Afraid for their lives, they fled to the South. My maternal grandparents came from an agricultural background. At the time, they had three young boys, one of whom was still a baby. They knew that if they stayed put, they would either be killed or be forced to join the Viet Cong forces and their sons would be brainwashed by the communists. They had to escape to the South in order to survive. And so one hot summer night in 1954, that's what they did. They set out on foot and left for the South on a boat known as the Open Mouth.

When they finally established themselves in South Vietnam as business owners, they were hopeful that their country would eventually be rid of the communists. To their dismay, the South was taken over by the Viet Cong in 1975. They were forced to sell almost everything that they had in order to avoid harassment from the communist police. My uncles who served in the southern army were forced to go to concentration labor camps and then left Vietnam the first chance they got. By the late seventies and early eighties, everyone in the country was starving from the limited amount of food that was given to them by the Viet Cong government. My mother has told stories of how she had to steal eggs right out of the chicken's bottom just so that I could have something to eat when I was a baby.

My mother was a well-known singer in Vietnam. She traveled in circles of activist performers and artists who witnessed the oppression of the government. There were restrictions on what they could and couldn't perform. And those who created anything that was resistant to the rulers' agendas were immediately dealt with. Tired of dealing with the daily struggles of life in Vietnam, my mother wanted to get out. But because of her musical talent and social visibility, the government would not grant her permission to leave. She had to escape. In 1986, my mother and I left our home. Although I was only six, I still remember it as if it was only yesterday. I remember my mom telling me that we were going to the beach for a vacation and how troubled I was that people were crying as we left. Our first attempt to escape was not successful. We were caught by the border police and imprisoned for a week and then sent back home. I had never been so scared. We were kept inside a dirty, wet room for the entire week. They gave us very little to eat, and the adults were constantly questioned by the guards. I was even questioned. It was a good thing that my mom told me we were going on "vacation," if you know what I mean.

The second time around, we actually joined an underground group that we paid to get us out of the country. We took vans toward the southern border of Vietnam, then went on foot across and into Cambodia. I remember being told to be absolutely quiet while I was running and thinking to myself what an ordeal it was to go on vacation! We stayed in Cambodia for a few days, moving from house to house and hiding in attics, storage spaces, and so on. And then one night, some men rushed into our hiding place and told us we needed to leave immediately because the police were on their way to come get us. We bolted out of there in the middle of the night. The moon was so bright that we could see almost everything as if the sun was out. The only refuge we were able to find was underneath the tall grass fields. We were told, once again, to be extremely quiet. And it was extremely quiet; not one sound was heard except for those that were made by crickets and the wind blowing against the grass. I must have held my breath in for a long time because I can still remember telling myself not to breathe so darn loud. Then, finally, we set out again on foot toward the beach. There were thirteen of us crowded on a small boat that was only meant for a few people. We carried nothing except what was absolutely necessary. We ate dried noodles from instant noodle packages. We were only allowed to bring very little water. Hunger and thirst set in for me after one day on that boat. This was when I finally realized and was told that we were, in fact, not on vacation. I remember how scared I became when someone on the boat mentioned that we were at risk of being robbed, raped, or killed by pirates and how quickly my mom jumped in to change the subject. To everyone's relief, we saw land after two days on the ocean. We ran as soon as the boat hit the sand. But even though we were on land, there was still a chance that we might never make it out of Cambodia, which was heavily patrolled. The men who led the way kept yelling at us to run faster to avoid being shot in case we were still in Cambodian territory. I remember being scooped up immediately by one of the men in the group because I was too small to run fast. The feeling that I felt at that moment, even as a child, was terrifying. I wasn't fully aware of the reality of it all, but the sight of a group of people running for their lives on a dark, empty beach will never escape me. The next thing I remember was hearing people yelling and cheering. One of the men yelled out, "We're in Thailand! We made it!"

Indeed, we had made it into Thailand. The Thai tribal people greeted us with cheers and hugs. They brought us food and water and threw flowers around our necks as if we had arrived at some exotic vacation resort. Relief swept over us as we made our way to the immigration camps just a short distance from the coastal village. We knew from that moment that the hardest part was over and a new life was waiting.

When I finally made it into the United States two years after leaving Vietnam, my world had completely changed, and the anticipation of what was to come played a huge role in shaping me. The hardest part for me, and perhaps for other people like me, was the feeling of not belonging anywhere. I never lived in Vietnam long enough to connect with or understand my culture. And being an alien in the United States, I've had to overcome a lot of discrimination. Imagine being told by your classmates (and a few adults) that you should just go back to where you came from because you're a Viet Cong and you don't belong here. I was being called a Viet Cong, the very thing that I've been taught to hate—the reason for our hardship! My parents never knew any of this because they were too busy working hard just to survive. As mentioned before, I learned to adapt and assimilate as much as I could to prove that I belonged here. I was not going to give them a chance to tell me that I didn't belong or that I didn't deserve what I worked hard for because of my ethnic background. After years of trying to conform, I finally moved to a community where I felt a little more accepted. This move has allowed me to freely rediscover the culture into which I was born.

Now that I'm older, I'm finally able to appreciate and embrace the things that represent my ethnic background. I'm rediscovering my roots through the gathered experiences of those who have come before me. My family's stories and my own story are testaments to the hardship we've faced to guarantee a better life for the future. My roots have nurtured and groomed the person that I am today. No matter how often I've neglected them, they will always be a part of me. This is the cultural education that I will provide for the generations that follow me.

A Cultural Snapshot of Breanna

Breanna, better known as Bre, is a nineteen-year-old biracial young woman from East Orange, New Jersey. In her self-portrait she states, "I am Breanna Miller born July 7th, 1988, in East Orange, New Jersey, to my mother and grandparents of African American descent, with black heritage so powerful and inspiring that it changed the world." This reveals a lot about this young woman. She is another student who belongs to both her mother and grandparents. She is another student whose life story is filled with economic struggle and extended family support. She balances a deep love and appreciation for her family with some sincere regrets and disappointment in that same family. In her mind, culture has been what has kept her going, and it has also been the missing link at times of struggle. And she, like many of her peers, expresses a deep appreciation and desire to take the lead in transforming and growing her family's cultural heritage. But for Bre, this has been a long and difficult road to inheriting her cultural legacy. She describes her history as a "saga" that has molded and shaped her. She views each day as history in the making, and the history that she inherits and creates is shaped by her culture. "I am history," she declares. "It is my responsibility to carry on this history and my beautiful culture." Throughout her narrative, Bre claims culture—she calls it her own. She says, "It is the very essence of our survival." She declares, "I believe each person alone defines and creates her culture according to family, values, traditions, and experiences." To Bre, culture is personal, meaningful, and all her own. She learned this through her own struggles with racial identity.

"Mom, am I really black?" Bre often asked her mother this question as a child, not understanding what "black" meant. Reflecting on her childhood, she describes herself as a "skinny, light-skinned girl" who was surrounded by all shades of color at her black Catholic school. As a child, her entire understanding of black identity revolved around "the shade of your skin and your physical appearance." She tells how everything she learned about African Americans was associated with "blackness": "We learned about the first 'black' everything (scientists, athletes, etc.). But in the way that they appeared they looked very different from me. Brown skin and black hair were just some of the features that seemed to be the typical look for black people, which caused me to feel different. Mom, am I really black?" Throughout her childhood, her peers confirmed Bre's uncertainty. She was called horrible names in school, like "light-bright" and "so-white," which she says made her feel awkward and alone. She came to hate school. And she was on the brink of hating her cultural community. The black kids at school were the ones taunting her. But it was her family and their firm dedication to having her understand her cultural heritage that turned things around for her: "You have to know where you came from to know where you can go."

Indeed, understanding that her place in her culture and race was about where she came from, not what she looked like, was an important lesson. It helped her to understand her cultural legacy.

> I had no idea there was so much more to being black and proud than the cover. The real definition of culture is family. Family is an important symbol. Family played an extensive role in helping me to cope with my insecurities. As I grew older, maturing into an adolescent, they encouraged me to always hold my head up and be proud of who I am. [They] constantly enlightened me [on how] being different made me special. Reminding me to not let anyone tell me I wasn't black or black enough. I thank my pop-pop for this.

Her "pop-pop" shared with her important stories of family history and family survival that taught her critical lessons. One of these lessons was that her black family struggled and shared the same history of oppression as other black families. Their lighter skin color did not shield them from struggle. This history was her admission ticket to confidently enter her cultural community and to truly understand what community looked like (a shared experience and not necessarily a shared physical appearance).

> Pop-Pop serves as one of my greatest inspirations. He was born in the country. And by "country," I mean endless fields, hills on the prairie, silent streams, clear bright skies, and tractor country—Accomack, Virginia. He was born during the start of the civil rights movement and during a time of midwives and gigantic families. He picked vegetables in the field. He always worked hard. He is the epitome of a revolutionary to me. My mom has struggled too. Although I didn't live the [same] extreme hardships and adversities [that] my family did, I still know struggles. . . . Culture has become a crucial sphere of influence in my life; it has taught me to cherish the beliefs, values, and customs that have been bestowed upon me by my grandparents. It has also taught me that there is no reason why I should walk around holding my head down. I have too much pride, dignity, and respect to do anything other [than uphold my culture]. My family history and legacy are things that I hold very dear.

Her family's history and experiences and her own sense of struggle legitimize her as a cultural group member. She may not "look" the part, but she has certainly lived it. If culture is about struggle and perseverance, then Bre feels she has earned her place. She has known struggle both at home and at school. Though she speaks about her past "racial" experiences in school with pain and anger, she offers a much more forgiving tone for the shame of family disappointments and failure. On the same page that she talks about family being a major symbol of her culture and how important family is to her, she also states that her family is dysfunctional: "My family is the epitome of dysfunctional. I don't even know where to begin. Domestic problems became our way of life. Anger and resentment were common. Family gatherings were rare, and the holidays were solemn sometimes. But whether it gives me a sense of pride or shame, my culture is my history and my family, which has shaped my life and me as a person."

Again, one's cultural experience is not always perfect—it sometimes involves both "pride and shame." Bre's life illustrates how you can both hold up your family for the rich cultural lessons they taught and at the same time shake your head at their wrong turns and bad decisions. She says that her mother was the first to gain an opportunity to experience "the good life," but did not take advantage of it. Her mother made bad decisions that led to their economic struggles and dependence on her grandparents. She acknowledges that her father's abandonment of them before she was born also contributed to their struggles. It has been a difficult process, reconciling that all of her family's ac-complishments and failures, strengths and weaknesses have shaped her.

> People often say that every one of your ancestors is a part of you spiritu-ally, mentally, and physically. I didn't believe it. However, as I began to grow, I soon realized the theory to be true. Surprisingly, my mom and I possess some of the same qualities, both virtuous and ghastly. Mak-ing this discovery petrified me to the point where I obsessively tried to change myself in a desperate attempt to be a different person. . . . I am living and learning through these struggles. I believe that until you encounter failure, real success is an absent achievement. "What doesn't kill you makes you stronger."

Once again, it is culture that has the potential to make students whole. Bre's story is a story of coming full circle—settling into her cultural place in society, appreciating her family, and coming to value her culture—the good and the bad. Whether in acknowledging the dysfunction of her family or acknowledg-ing that her cultural experience has not been perfect, Bre still admits and for-gives the shortcomings of culture and family. Family "togetherness" is viewed as a critical marker of a positive and healthy cultural experience. When it is not present, as in Bre's case, life is often judged as dysfunctional. But there is some-thing about culture and family that compels us to be a bit more forgiving than we might be toward race and society. Amazingly, after sharing her disappoint-ment in her mother, she was one of the students who included the Maya Ange-lou poem "Phenomenal Woman" as a tribute to her mother. As an adult, she can now see with more clarity and greater focus her mother's struggles and for-give her shortcomings. She realizes her "mother" was a person not a concept. She failed sometimes, but Bre has learned from her mother's mistakes. And she is ready to take the lead. She expresses her desire to assume the role of doing the difficult but important work of valuing her culture more rightly, loving her community more wholly, and transforming her family's legacy:

> It is my destiny to be a phenomenal woman for my ancestors who have achieved this status and better yet for those who have not. Whether my calling is to be a doctor or a writer, my goal is to make a true differ-ence in this world by making it a better place than I found it. The Miller name will never bear shame despite our past, present, and future fail-ures and misfortunes. It is my legacy, my heritage, and it is who I am. My general black history classifies me as "black"; however, my individ-ual experiences, values, and traditions define me as African American. My black history is extraordinary, but my African American inherited culture is PHENOMENAL!!

Cultural Heritage, Leadership, and Legacy Critical Essay

> Throughout history we've witnessed countless Asian American women who have overcome adversity and celebrated personal triumphs. The best way to recognize our many triumphs as Asian American women is by paying homage to these women . . . filling the empty space in the "American" consciousness with our stories, visions, and dreams.[1]

This passage is taken from Vickie Nam's book *Yell-Oh Girls*, and it expresses the power in sharing the cultural story. All the young adults in this study are benefactors of valuable cultural legacies. Their stories revealed that culture is most definitely a toolbox packed full of experience and skills, disappointments, life lessons, values, and struggles. But this study also reveals strong agency among young people toward changing their future cultural realities—in other words, a commitment to cultural leadership. This represents their desire to will to their children and community an even greater cultural inheritance through the futures and families that they will one day create.

Many saw cultural heritage as an important tool for gaining greater personal understanding. They shared beliefs like "Knowing about your culture helps you know who you are" and "Culture is very important to me because I believe you have to know where you come from to know where you are going in life." For Teddy, cultural knowledge was tied to feelings of self-worth (what I have considered in this study as cultural efficacy): "Knowing where you are in life and more importantly where you come from can assist with gaining great qualities of worthiness. I absolutely love my culture, so there is no doubt in my mind that culture is important."

Because of the emphasis placed on learning family history and values, many talked about their desire to play an active role in carrying on their cultural heritage and telling the family stories. As young adults, they were beginning to transition into becoming more intentional learners within their families. This transition seemed to be motivated by the goal of one day stepping into the role of teacher and leader in their families. Tara recognizes that her cultural development is an ongoing process. But she now listens intently, seeks out information more fervently, and heeds advice more willingly. She understands how inheriting culture is important not only for herself but also for her future children: "On a personal level, I am still growing. I want to develop wisdom and an interest in preserving history. I hope to carry on my traditions, family values, and let my children form their own views on life." For Larren, it is just about continuing what is good in her family and maintaining continuity. She remarks with a "matter-of-fact" tone: "Hey, I may take over Thanksgiving dinner sooner or later, my brother may take Christmas from Aunt E—that's what it's about; it's about to be our turn."

What Culture Means to Me

Whether in a firm or passive voice, through stories or poetry, for the most part these young people were in harmony—they describe culture in much the same way across multiple institutions, races, and ethnicities. Vicki Nam[2] found the same outcome during her project, which analyzed the personal essays and poems of Asian American girls. Across the many cultural and ethnic groups that exist in the Asian American community, the girls' stories still had similar basic threads. "To say that our stories don't reveal threads of shared experiences however would be inaccurate. While each girl's perspective is unique, common themes echo throughout, evoking the group's subtle yet distinctive collective consciousness."[3]

This was the case for the college students in my project. Regardless of ethnicity, socioeconomic status, or geographical location, culture was simply a warm memory, a personal treasure, an important story to tell. Bre offers insight in her self-portrait: "I find it very interesting how some nonblack people define black culture as only religious spirituality or an urban experience. Although these presumptions are undeniably true about black culture, I believe each person defines and creates one's own sense of culture according to one's family values, traditions, and experiences. My family, in addition to my goals, the obstacles I have overcome, and the triumphant achievements I have attained overall, molded me into who I am and what I have become."

Lloyd's beliefs support her statement: "'Culture' is a word that can't really be defined as one thing. For me culture was more about knowing exactly who I am and understanding my beliefs, values, and customs that have shaped the lives of my parents. It [culture] doesn't necessarily reflect the most obvious things like the way you dress or things you eat. Rather, it's a more complex process that deals with understanding and interpreting factors that have forced the generation before you to wise up."

Keith also describes it as a personal process: "Culture is about coming to terms with who you are as an individual and embracing every aspect of it, whether it be through the food you eat, the way you dress, or simply by what you believe. My culture has developed through my experiences."

On the surface, it seems as if Keith and Floyd disagree. One student rejects food and clothes as cultural. The other sees culture as an act of coming to terms with these concepts. But when I examine their comments, I am compelled to think that they actually agree. Both men agree on culture being about insight, understanding, and interpretation. For them it is not simply food, clothes, music, and religion—it is the answer to the questions: Why these clothes? Why this music? What is the purpose of religion? These critical experiences that inform the process by which someone is shaped into a cultural being were most often expressed as life lessons that young adults personally experience or the lessons taught to them by their parents. This sharing of insight and wisdom, advice and information underscores the idea of cultural heritage—passing down legacy. It seems that this is what Lloyd means by culture being a process. It is an act of receiving a lesson, wrestling with its meaning, and then settling down to allow the insight to shape your values and actions.

Laying Down a Legacy

Most values and ethics were learned through a process of lesson sharing and storytelling—this is the essence of building cultural heritage. For cultural heritage to be built, we must talk, listen, learn, teach, and lead. By either demonstrating the lesson through their real life experiences or verbalizing the lesson through reflective conversations, the families in this story laid down legacies of survival and perseverance for their children and grandchildren to pick up and carry forward. Undoubtedly, Mimi, whose story was featured earlier, has learned some incredible lessons about having the tenacity to survive from her mother who fearlessly led her out of Vietnam. Through the cultural self-portraits, student snapshots, and critical essays, I have shared an extensive amount of information on what cultural lessons were actually learned by these young people. Now, I want to spend time with the process of passing on cultural heritage. For many this process or action is as much a marker of their culture as the lesson itself. They placed a lot of weight on the act of creating legacy—remembering, teaching, advising, and sharing.

Larren sees creating legacy as a value inherited from somewhere deep in her cultural past: "From the beginning of time, my ancestors were adapting to the world around them. They did the best they could to survive in the time period in which they lived. Then they took what they learned and handed those teachings on to their children and grandchildren."

Courtney also reflects on history and cultural legacy in her self-portrait: "My family's history has definitely shaped my identity. I am who I am today because of my ancestors and past history. Even though I was not a part of slavery, it has affected certain views and beliefs that my family has. Therefore, my beliefs are similar to theirs."

Families will to their children all of the lessons that they have learned from their past experiences. Through sharing survival tactics like "If you don't have skills, you will be living hand to mouth" or sharing motivational wisdom like "Don't depend on nobody—you know what you can do," these families passed on cultural lessons that shaped the lives of their children.

"My culture has provided me with the essentials of life. Family is there to support you and bestow specific values inside of you. The backbone of our history can influence the knowledge of our mistakes." As I read this statement it sounds familiar—that any loving parent or grandparent is merely a farmer planting seeds of cultural heritage to be harvested later in life as insight and wisdom. Many of the stories that were shared echo this idea. But I distinctly recall Fernando's words whispering again to me: "I honestly did not know what he was talking about half the time. But looking back at all the things he would speak to me about makes me feel warm inside because all the things he said to me became a lesson I could use through my maturity."

Like Fernando, Norris also recognizes his cultural inheritance—a bank of values that have molded his cultural identity: "My family has had a profound effect upon my sense of cultural identity. Values such as determination, work ethic, and persistence inherited by my ancestors and passed on to myself contribute to the very essence of my culture."

Lloyd, in his typical insightful and critical fashion, takes a broader outlook on the importance of cultural heritage. To him, the ills of his generation are tied to their lack of connection to past generations. This disconnection has made them physically unable to fully receive their cultural legacies: "Oftentimes there is a disconnect in the African American community where the current generations don't have an accurate or healthy knowledge about extended family members who came before them. We can only have a sense of why or what we are because of our history."

Lloyd's comment reiterates the earlier discussion on keeping family bonds intact but extends the conversation by his focus on the role of family in teaching history and passing on heritage. Keeping the family together and talking is the most important act of legacy creation and personal understanding. His comment that you gain a sense of who you are because of history demonstrates that he sees how powerful history and heritage are—without it you cannot recognize your own image because you have no point of reference.

The Identity Wars: Race versus Culture

The literature reviewed in preparation for this study warned of the complicated and often contentious relationship between culture, race, and ethnicity. They are distinct yet similar, separate but still broadly tied. Racial identity is an important aspect of the development of a person of color. However, it very rarely escapes the tendency to frame identity based on categorizations of skin color and how individuals experience or interpret life based on these racial experiences.[4] Racial identity has been seen as "a surface level manifestation based on what we look like but that has deep implications in how we are treated."[5] Ethnic identity has also been socially constructed, but it is most often constructed through a community experience. Baghir-Zada definition of an ethnic group is a group defined by shared geographical, racial, and cultural roots, sociohistory, and a sense of group identity. To bring together all these concepts, it is important to distinguish between race, ethnicity, and culture.[6] Culture and ethnicity come from within (derived from the family and community). Race comes from without (derived from society). These terms are sometimes used interchangeably though they hold very different meanings. An extension of the famous quote by Simone de Beauvoir ("One is not born a woman, but becomes one") captures the nature of culture, race, and ethnicity as processes: "One is not born white, but becomes white. One is not born a Latina, one is not born Norwegian,

Arab-American, Afro-Caribbean, but becomes that."[7] In this sense, frequent cultural experiences in college may facilitate the process whereby a student continues to become fully African American, Puerto Rican, Haitian, and so on. Regardless of the various differences, it is almost impossible to explore issues of culture without having discussions about race and ethnicity. And these issues are a critical part of the stories shared in this book. But you will find that these stories affirm that culture and race intersect but are still separate roads along which people of color travel through life. As issues of race and ethnicity surfaced in our group conversations and within cultural self-portraits, I found it interesting how the various stories and beliefs that were shared helped to distinguish between these concepts.

Racial issues were most often presented as very negative and unacceptable. From psychologically damaging racial experiences to family members being in physical danger because of racial prejudice, race was yet another externally imposed struggle to overcome. For some, racial lessons came from their family's past. Keith relates the stories told to him by his grandfather: "My grandfather told me there were times when some white person would try and fight one of his siblings and all of his brothers and sisters would be there for one another. His dad, my great-grandfather, got shot and killed when he was young. He got shot for fighting a white man who hit one of his daughters."

As a young child, Keith learned of the physical danger that race often presents. He tells how he was warned to be careful in the world, particularly when interacting across racial lines—careful negotiation of race was literally a matter of life or death to his family. His story, like those of many of his peers, illustrates how negative issues of race often made culture even more important. In his example, when facing racial threat, the cultural bond of family offered protection by "being there for one another." This was also the case for Greta's mother. "For my mother, growing up in a society that was racially divided between blacks and whites forced her to embrace her African American culture even more." Again, culture seems to appear as a foundation and support to help family members counter negative racial experiences.

But parents and grandparents were not the only ones with racial struggles to share. Many of the young adults themselves had experienced their share of racial encounters within and beyond their families. Norris told how racial issues, specifically colorism, broke into the cultural comforts of his home and family, causing his own grandmother to treat her children and grandchildren differently because of race. Colorism is a form of intraracial prejudice based on skin color. Undoubtedly, the standard of beauty in America has been overwhelmingly white. Historically, the preference for lighter skin, straighter hair, and keen features has plagued many populations of people of color—Latino, African, African American, Asian, West Indian, and indigenous communities have all contended with various forms of internalized racial hatred. Many groups have fought the self-defeating ideals that darker skin is negative and less desirable. Knowing the psychological dangers of colorism makes me cringe when someone uses the term "fair" skin to describe a person with a lighter complexion. We are often unaware of the underlying implications of using the term "fair," as we aren't called to face the corresponding opposite—to be dark is to be "unfair." It is all unconscious, negative socialization. Norris's story is a perfect example:

> We will begin with the interracial discrimination I experienced as a child. I always noticed how my great-grandmother Dorothy, a very dark ebony woman, always put an emphasis on skin tone. To her, I was her "little light-skinned baby," and my cousin Teesh was always referred to as her "little dark chocolate baby." Years after her death, I have become even closer with . . . Grandma Betty, discovering that we have a lot of similar experiences. After talking with Grandma Betty, she revealed to me the dark side of Grandma Dorothy. Grandma Betty was one of two girls born to Grandma Dorothy, who was "jilted" by her boyfriend after she got pregnant. After Grandma Betty was born, Grandma Dorothy finally got married and everything seemed perfect, except the fact that everyone else in the household was darker in complexion and Grandma Betty was a "red bone" with sandy red hair. Grandma Dorothy was always the butt of jokes from her friends, who said that her daughter was the milkman or insurance man's baby. (At that time most of those jobs were held by white men.) Aggravated and annoyed, Grandma Dorothy took her racial issues out on Grandma Betty. "Reds," as Grandma Betty was often called because of her skin color, was abused physically and mentally by Grandma Dorothy. From old-fashioned beatings to washing her hair with coffee grounds to make it more dark, in addition to sitting outside in 90-degrees-plus days to seal in a darker tone— these were just some of the things . . . Grandma Betty had to endure in her youth. As a child, I was also teased because my cousins felt that Grandma Betty showed me favoritism because I was lighter. Before I learned black and white, I learned light skinned and dark skinned.

As Norris points out, through his family he learned that racist beliefs can be internalized and engaged even within the home. As he says, sometimes it's "black on black." His story prompts me to remember a past conversation with another group of students that I had many years ago. I collaborated with the television show *20/20* to do a segment on colorism, and it featured a group interview of African American student leaders with whom I worked at my university. All of these students told similar stories of prejudiced behavior and hurtful comments expressed by friends and family members. Darker students told how they were made to feel ugly and inferior and often prayed to be lighter, and the lighter students told how they experienced either extreme privilege or deep hatred from their own racial communities. These experiences often left all, whether dark or light, feeling shamed. To those students and to Norris it seems clear that race and colorism were also a part of those negative environmental influences that stunt the healthy growth of loving and affirming cultural bonds. Darri directly names race as a persisting and negative social construct. Race is a label imposed on people by a racist society. "Unfortunately race has always carried a negative connotation with it within the context of my American society. And as sure as the wind blows faithfully, it continues to do so today."

For Darri, Norris, Bre, and several others in this study, race is what *other people* feel that they look like. Culture and ethnicity actually identify who they are. Race is seen through a social lens, culture and ethnicity a personal one. Race divides, ethnicity distinguishes, and culture re-members. Students did spend time discussing ethnicity and how it distinguishes them and ties them back to a homestead. Erika related how she began to truly appreciate ethnicity when she started dating her Dominican boyfriend, Aristides. Their broader cultural ties serve as a starting point for them to share their specific ethnic differences: "I'm, you know, Colombian and he's, like, Dominican. There's some things that, like, even just food or how he prepares foods that are different. It makes you really aware of regions in Latin America. We share the same holidays but we may take a different twist to it. So to me, I'm learning and sharing a lot because we can still relate, so it's easy to share."

Tara also provides an example of culture as a unifier and ethnicity as a distinguisher: "When I got here I was like, okay, me and Kat we're a part of a culture. 'Cause, you know, we share similar values and our families—they struggled. So we identified with each other. But Kat's Caribbean, and then I have friends who are African American in the sense that they're from Africa and they immigrated here. And then there's me, who has been here, my family has been here for generations. So I consider myself a part of this culture of people with some of the same experiences, but when you get to the heart of it, we have some practices that are completely different, and it's cool."

Terry thinks that there are a lot more cultural similarities than differences. For him ethnicity is about minor deviations in practices. But he thinks that beliefs that focus on "differences" are really influenced by stereotypes and racism:

> I'm an African American. Growing up, all my mom's friends were West Indian. And it's like all of my friends are West Indian. And my girlfriend is Haitian, and we have conversations all the time about the differences between African American and West Indian. But when you get down to the real nitty-gritty, there really isn't a cultural difference. My family is full of strong hardworking people. When I say if they got to scrub a toilet, they are going to scrub a toilet to provide for their family. And I get really offended when I hear West Indians talk about how they are different from African Americans—that we're lazy. 'Cause it's really them believing racist stereotypes. They believe African Americans are lazy. What makes that different from a white American who stereotypes? It's really race and racism. You know what I mean? Unless you live with me and you completely understand my culture, you can't stereotype us. I'm

not allowed to disrespect my grandmother. I was raised in the church just like them. Everything we learned is the same—culturally.

Courtney chimed in, "Yeah, I mean the real differences are just in like our music, our food, the way it's cooked, the spices, the language—you know, patois as opposed to how African Americans might say "grill," and that means face. It's just little differences that are special." Courtney and Terry's comments about cultural divisiveness are definitely true. And we must discuss these issues, say them out loud, and debate these divisive ideologies if we are to change them. A historical context is needed to understand the root of these divisions in cultural heritage. Students primarily referred to as "black" come from a variety of culturally distinct backgrounds all factoring into some unique cultural issues for young adults. Often reference to the "black community" in the United States has focused primarily on African American issues, broadly using the historical experience of African Americans as a context. It is important to note, however, that within the black population are also first- or second-generation African and West Indian immigrants, who bring with them a stronger connection outside the United States and a strong identification with their ethnicity rather than their racial group.[8] Though many second-generation immigrants become subject to the racial designation of "black American" by white American society and often suffer under the same discriminating educational systems as African Americans, their familial and cultural histories are different from African Americans, a fact which sometimes creates a cultural division.

West Indians share a history of slavery with African Americans. However, after liberation the civil laws and systems in the West Indies were not as repressive as the Jim Crow laws and Black Codes in the United States.[9] In the United States, African Americans enjoyed a very brief period after emancipation when there seemed to be some optimism and hope for true social inclusion. African American men proudly voted and successfully ran for political office. It's not quite clear what tipped the hat—it could have simply been a fear of what might happen if African Americans became too free. But their moment of hope was quickly destroyed by terrorist practices—thousands of African Americans being burned at the stake, lynched, kidnapped, or murdered. This reign of terror on African Americans did its job in spreading fear and preventing them from trying to exercise their freedoms through voting and other basic civil rights. Eventually, Jim Crow laws stripped African Americans in the South of any hope of inclusion by separating them and giving them substandard resources in every public sphere of life.

Meanwhile, in most islands of the West Indies, black people were an overwhelming majority, causing white power brokers to permit them to be educated and to learn skilled trades to become educators, civil servants, shopkeepers, and farmers. These postslavery differences in society had a significant impact on cultural efficacy and ideology as the first major set of West Indians began to immigrate into the United States. From the early nineteenth century to 1924, a large group of Jamaicans and Barbadians began working on the building of the Panama Canal and then continued on into the United States. They began to send "Panama money" to their relatives in the West Indies to pay for their passage to America.

In the 1960s, a second wave of immigrants flooded the United States thanks to this Panama money. This group came primarily from the professional class in their home countries and sought to take advantage of the economic opportunities in America. The difference in education, self-identity, and professional capacity influenced the ways in which West Indian immigrants were initially received by white Americans. Their language accents and professional skills made them distinguishable from African Americans, and therefore designated as the "better blacks" by white America.[10] Therefore, white Americans were more willing to hire immigrant blacks over native-born blacks for domestic and labor-based jobs. The effect of this preferential treatment in America, coupled with a different postslavery experience in the West Indies, sometimes caused an inability for West Indians to understand the oppression of African Americans. They would quickly adopt a belief in the racial stereotypes regarding the culture and the work ethic of African Americans.[11] West Indians were not being hired because African Americans did not want to work. Rather, they were being hired as a by-product of discrimination against African Americans. In *Black Identity*, a documentary film made by Breanna Brown, a college student at Rensselaer Polytechnic Institute, I comment that an additional factor mitigating these divisions was the difference in immigration status. West Indians were voluntary immigrants and thus invested a significant amount of time, money, and personal sacrifice to come to the United States. It would not be of any benefit to move here and associate themselves with the most oppressed of American society. People immigrate for opportunity or to escape poverty, not to simply relocate their oppression to a different land. Therefore, many West Indians embraced the stereotypes and the idea that they were "different" from African Americans simply as a form of social survival. More recent research has shown that second- and third-generation West Indians have now become subject to the same oppressive obstacles as contemporary African Americans. The children of immigrants who were born in America are being educated in the same poor school systems, live in the same crime-infested neighborhoods, have lost their West Indian accents, and are largely identified by society as "African American" and not West Indian.[12] With this history in mind, it is definitely time to put an end to these cultural divisions within the African diaspora. This serves as yet another example of racial discrimination preventing the formation of healthy cultural bonds and alliances.

And what the young adults in this study affirm is that racism is unforgivable. They are insulted by it, oppressed because of it, and psychologically hurt as a result of it. Over the course of this study, there were many more examples of *negative cultural experiences* than *negative racial experiences*—from parental abandonment to economic struggle to general social oppression. Yet the failures and shortcomings of culture were still seen as important and defining moments. Unlike race, culture, even when possessing negative aspects, was still seen as an uplifting, character-building experience. Cultural struggle taught valuable lessons and served almost as a rite of passage, giving students their own cultural stories of struggle and perseverance to tell. Dan stated this lesson in his self-portrait in Chapter 3 as he shared how his life challenges have made him a better person:

> My life's disappointments have only made me want to be a better person. My culture is my knowledge and experiences that I have had that have made me a more conscious person—more conscious of superficial BS that my generation holds as values, more conscious of others' intentions and morals, and more conscious of social and community needs. In the end, I just hold my faith as a priority and live life as righteously as possible.

Kara also supports this sense of reconciliation with the mistakes of the past, "Some [of my family members] are strong and others are weak, but I am reminded to never be ashamed of where I come from no matter what the hardships, failures, and even triumphs that may remain." And Norris considers the idea of a cultural self-portrait to be *rooted* in telling the story of cultural struggle. These stories are a source of pride, "To me a cultural self-portrait is representative of the personal struggles and victories that we go through in life. It represents not only my life but also the life experiences of my ancestors who came before me."

As an important part of their lives, culture was easily forgiven when it fell short. Its imperfections made it easier to love and to appreciate. Culture was how they were raised, it was their family, their values, and their personal priorities. Even when it involved struggle and stress, to disown culture was to disown themselves. So instead, they accepted it, wrestled with it, dreamed of making it better, and committed to using it to fight racism by taking their rightful place as cultural leaders of the next generation.

7

The House That Struggle Built

A Portrait of Culture

T his closing portrait of culture is painted specifically for college educators. It provides a summary image of what all these stories and perspectives come together to tell us as educators. But just as art is not appreciated by only artists, this chapter is open for all to enjoy. Any parent with a student in college, anyone who works in or is studying the field of higher education, anyone who plans to have a child in college one day, or any community member who is simply concerned with the growth and development of our future leaders can find meaning and insight in how we culturally educate young people who are moving into adulthood. We must all work together as a community to push educational institutions to live up to their promise and to serve students more fully.

Painting a portrait of culture is similar to painting a portrait of home. The home that I found myself observing was not a large and flashy suburban home. Rather, it was a small and modest dwelling. It was the type of house that, at first glance, you know has some stories to tell—it has known years of laughter and tears, triumph and tribulation. This simple image brings your imagination to life. In an instant you envision its small rooms overflowing, crowded with family during the holidays. But this house has also known quiet and lonely days. It needs paint. A shingle needs repair. The doorbell does not work. It is not perfect. Yet, despite all its imperfections, the door is always open. The interior is always comforting. The residents are too busy cleaning and cooking, birthing and raising to fix all the external problems. However, the thought is always there—one day I am going to fix this place up. One day I will find the time, energy, and creativity to renovate and design the cultural home of my dreams.

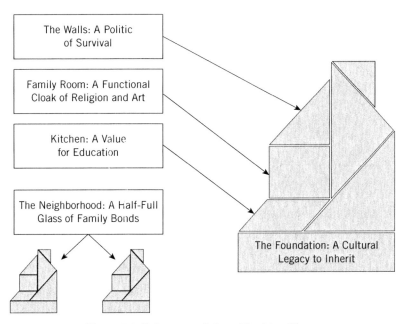

Figure 7.1 Culture as a Safe and Inviting Home

The young adults that welcomed me into their cultural home as a visitor were like any household residents. They walked through the house with comfort and modest pride and gave the tour as if it were second nature—this is my house; this is my culture. Expressed through their attitudes was the thought "Of course this is what it looks like." But for me, I stood examining the picture that they painted of their culture and saw a unique and intriguing structure. I looked at it but I also stood *in* it. And I must admit that while looking at the portrait of their culture I saw my own. I was indeed looking at a picture of home. Whether it is a mansion or a cottage, there is nothing like a warm and clean house . . . or a warm and clean soul. This image of culture as an inviting and safe home appears in Figure 7.1.

The Exterior

Like a home, culture seemed to be built with an exterior to shield and protect from harm, an interior to cultivate life, and a foundation to help it stand for generations. The exterior was molded with what I have called "a politic of survival." These were survival tactics and strategies that were shaped by experiencing years of personal storms. When oppression and racism rained down on the family, the walls of survival and perseverance kept the family going. This ability to withstand the hardships of life was seen as a critical component of culture to the students in the study. Years of struggle chipped the wood, and so culture was not seen as perfect. It included issues of failure, abandonment, and poverty. But the students revealed that a house does not have to be pretty to still feel like home. In fact, many thought that these imperfections gave their culture its character. Each chip or missing piece was linked to a story of survival, triumph, or struggle. Like communities that survive a natural disaster, the students enjoyed the opportunity to come out of the house, observe the damage, and tell their storm stories. Because of the protective walls provided by culture, they survived, they lived, and they appreciated the vitality of the house they call culture.

I interpreted my interactions with these young adults as an important revelation that more opportunities for young adults to tell their own stories of culture in their own words and from their own perspectives should be provided within educational environments. Young adults may become more culturally aware and centered if they are provided opportunities to share the beauty of their culture with their peers. Their portraits of their culture revealed the deep impact of some of the dilapidated areas. From economic struggle, racial challenges, and parental abandonment, students named and pointed out the ugly and rough patches without shame. The willingness among students to share very personal and hard life stories also struck me as salient. Students of color are ready to talk through their own encounters with racism, oppression, and family failure in safe and personally therapeutic spaces. They do not want to be spokespersons of their race, but rather a spokesperson of their own experience, and they want to speak to empathetic, understanding, and knowing ears.

As a practitioner, I do not view providing such student centeredness as simply allowing individual students or student organizations to plan campus programs as a means of empowering student voice. The idea of "student centeredness" has been approached much too literally and without a vivid imagination. Student centeredness is not about allowing students to create, plan, or lead an initiative—that is student governance (giving students agency to lead their college experience). Student centeredness is a philosophy in which we make students central to everything that we do. We allow our deep knowledge of their interests, their experiences, and their generational outlook to mold and shape what our educational programs and services look like. Even if they cannot tell us directly what they want, we should know because we know them— we know their community, we know their generation. In practice, practitioners should develop complex, safe, and creative *institutionally created* programs for personal reflection and story sharing among students. We cannot place the responsibility to create a cultural environment solely on students—the institution has a role to play. During the interviews, many students shared the frustrations of being asked to participate in class discussions on race and culture for the benefit of teaching white students or representing the race. Others spoke of their exhaustion when their organization planned most of the cultural events on campus. Educational institutions must work to commit more resources to cultural education and engagement. Additionally, we must raise professional expectations and challenge campus staff to create deeper, more relevant, and more meaningful cultural learning experiences for students both inside and outside of the classroom.

One of the most important implications from this study is the need to provide critical spaces to sort out issues regarding parental and family experiences. The vast majority of students in this study did not have a constant in-house father figure from whom to develop a healthy and realistic perception of manhood. College can be an important space to intellectually tackle the culture of manhood for both men and women. Therefore, educators should establish new views of cultural education as opportunities that also expose young adults to positive male figures in order to balance their cultural lives. Young children are not the only ones who need male mentors of color. Young adults need them too. And young men are not the only ones who benefit from male mentorship. Both men and women need healthy male mentoring. The focus on manhood in fields like education and sociology might need to be expanded beyond research on the number of men who are in prison, unemployed, or on drugs, along with the social structures that create these struggles, to also directly addressing the impact of their imprisonment, oppression, and drug addiction on the children that they leave behind. In some of my own work, I have also followed a traditional deficit-centered approach toward men of color. In past journal articles, I have sought to shed light on the larger historical context that has shaped the educational experiences of people of color—to illustrate that social exclusion has not "just happened upon" people of color—it has been a steady and intentional process. The factors that might affect why many young black men, for example, do not finish or even get to college are numerous and have been building for years. In my article "Mr. Nigger: The Challenges of Educating African American Males in America," I discuss several issues that have contributed to why black men in contemporary society might be called "mister" but are in many ways still treated with a niggardly regard. Some of these factors include America's racial past; community-based poverty, crime, and addiction; a failing pubic school system; shifts in the criminal justice system; dysfunctional family structures; and media/pop culture's impact on self-concept.[1] This is necessary work, and these problems must be acknowledged. But in taking this approach, I contributed another article with a long list of problems and a short focus on solutions, potential, and possibility. Admittedly, my past work has in some sense been focused on pathology—has contributed to a base of literature that identified the symptoms and diagnosed the problem, rather than focusing on prescribing or testing an innovation to transform the overall health of our students. This goodness is the essence of culture. And so culture should be our focus.

University practitioners might create more opportunities to discuss issues of fatherhood and provide more cultural programs that intentionally provide opportunities for students of color to develop relationships with men of color. This educational space cannot be dominated by "experts" and "scholars." We need more everyday fathers, single men, community leaders, and spiritual leaders engaged on the college campus as experts on their own experience. Finally, a space for critical dialogue on family must leverage students as knowledge producers. It must include opportunities for students to discuss their personal experiences rather than sitting idly as audience members.

The Interior

Undoubtedly, the cultural education discussion must start with the world the student knows. This world is strongly tied to family bonds. Inside the cultural house, students rest on the comforting cushions of mommies, mamas, and mom-moms. They come to understand how to navigate the outside world through the religious and artistic values taught inside the home. And it is in the home that they develop their first understanding of the importance of education. The strong impact and importance of families to students of color reveals that the university should do more to include families of color into the college experience. Beyond addressing the absence of men in students' lives, we must also wrestle with the presence of the entire family. There are so many benefits of including the family. More actively involving families might help to dispel the "myth" of the college experience among family members and also help them to feel more comfortable and able to give support. This is particularly important for families of first-generation students. Additionally, greater involvement of parents in college life might help to communicate an institutional value for the overall role that family plays in a student's life. These students revealed their parents and grandparents to be more than family—they were also teachers. Colleges might also benefit from looking at parents in a different light. They might invite family members to facilitate workshops, serve as panelists, and lecture on campus—and not just the potential donors. They might veer off the beaten path of traditional academic programming (lectures, brown bags) and create family/community events like family dinners, community storytelling circles, or cultural "family vacations" that invite families to travel on cultural learning excursions and educational trips with their students. Whatever the shape this educational space might take, if we want to make our campus communities more cultural we must find creative ways to include rather than exclude families.

What the students in this study pointed out is the need to have their real home communities understand and support their college experience. As I reflected on this issue, I thought it almost shameful that many of the students that I have come to know very personally, whom I talk to daily, whom I regularly invite to my home for group dinners, whom I love like members of my own family—I do not even know their mothers' names. These women, who clearly have been among the most central figures in getting these students to college, are disconnected from the experience for the vast majority of their children's college career. I reflected on how diligently my colleagues work to get students to stop going home as often, to stop calling home, and to become completely immersed in their new campus community. College adjustment is undoubtedly important. However, could we possibly change our views of what healthy adjustment looks like? Could students possibly establish a "both home and campus" paradigm rather than being forced to adopt the "either family or college" philosophy? It seems that finding ways to merge these two worlds may help students to transition culturally into and out of college. For it is home where students will most often find themselves a few days after commencement, and it is with their families that they will experience the rest of their lives.

The Kitchen

Education as a space in the cultural home can be found in the kitchen. It is the life food that parents work hard to afford. It is the space where everyone belongs. People might belong there because they can smell the aroma from several rooms away and come to the kitchen to claim their plate. They might belong because they have a history of good cooks in their family so they feel at home in the kitchen. Or they may come to sit in the kitchen because they are aware that someone has worked hard to prepare the meal and they respectfully take their place at the table. Whatever the reason may be, everyone hangs out in the kitchen. What I took away from how students discussed education was that they do not doubt if they belong in college—so why do we constantly focus on convincing them of their place? Too often, our services originate from the intent of making students of color feel that they belong and that they have a right to be there. Perhaps we need to refocus the lens and begin to affirm what they already know—they belong there because they have a proud heritage of commitment to education, because their families worked hard for them to get there, or simply because they are the manifestation of their ancestors' dreams. Approaching service from a point of abundant reasons why college is their rightful inheritance, as opposed to a deficit focus that centers on everything working against them, may be helpful. This does not mean that practitioners should ignore educational obstacles in their services—some students do need transition centers, tutoring centers, and academic support centers. What I am suggesting is that in our conversations and interactions with students and in the focus of some of our programs, we balance the deficiencies with abundance and make students of color feel about their campus as they do their culture: "This is my home; of course I belong."

The Family Room

Religion, art, and land took the shape of the family room. Young adults want to see and understand these concepts as functional spaces of involvement. To them, these are not stuffy living rooms to be admired but never touched or spaces that are so formal that they serve no real daily function in the home.

These findings of the study imply that attendance at religious and cultural arts events should not be automatically assumed for students of color. Just because you plan a cultural program does not obligate students to be there. To put it plainly, students are not going to come to programs that suck or hold no relevance in their lives. In order to appeal to students, these programs should communicate their usefulness—the function that they will play in students' lives. This function may be to provide opportunities for fellowship, to creatively engage politics and social change, or to pass on tactics of survival (some of the core things that students actually value about culture). We must push ourselves to find innovative ways to bring theory to practice—to interpret how students define culture and what they value about it into campus cultural programs.

The Neighborhood

Understanding the value of community and extended networks to students of color is critical to establishing better educational practice. Students value the sense of being surrounded by love rather than having to seek it out. In general, students in this study valued feeling a sense of togetherness within any community—the school, neighborhood, or family. Opportunities for fellowship provided the means to demonstrate closeness. When researching university cultural centers, I found several statements about these centers being a "home away from home" or the staff feeling like "family" to the students.[2] Some do it well, and others still fall short. Cultural spaces on campus that can genuinely establish these ideals seem to be deeply appreciated by students. Similarly, cultural programs that provide opportunities for fellowship—for the community to connect—were also greatly valued. This finding supports previous research on the necessity to build up the cultural community on campus by establishing a critical mass within the student population, recruiting more faculty of color, and supporting more physical spaces that can provide a venue for cultural fellowship, as do our homelands and neighborhoods. Undoubtedly, those efforts are needed to retain students, but the outcomes of this study illustrate that these efforts also help students to have a culturally meaningful college experience. Through the interactions with peers, faculty, and staff of color, students do not merely stay in college; instead, they continue their cultural journey.

The Foundation: Cultural Efficacy

Many students wrote directly in their portraits how much they appreciated the opportunity to reflect on and discuss their culture. The space established through the study allowed them to understand their cultural experience more clearly. Ultimately, even this act of research and scholarship, which engaged students in reflective writing and dialogue about their experiences, helped to put students in a position to assume the role of cultural leader, whether in their family or community. Their comments suggested a need to incorporate more opportunities for cultural research, reflection, and story sharing by (not just about) college students of color as a form of cultural engagement. Many talked about how "valuable this opportunity" was to think about their family, their past, and their culture. Several pointed out that they were not sure what the real definition of culture was, but to them culture was about things like family, education, and struggle, and they preferred seeing culture in that way. Like an artist, as they described their culture, they took a step back, looked at it, and liked what they saw. Many expressed a deep desire, motivated by the process of reflection and dialogue, to play an active role in helping to sustain their cultural heritage. These statements that ended twenty of the self-portraits expressed a desire to pass it on, to keep it going, and to embrace the idea "It's my turn." I consider these statements to be evidence of cultural efficacy—a desire to take action in creating new cultural legacies or to play a role in maintaining the cultural legacies that they have inherited.

The contemporary young adult of color fits into what Swidler[3] describes as a "settled" cultural life. In settled lives, culture is often hidden by habit and normality. It often seems hard to see the cultural engagement of college students. Their cultural habits, skills, and styles may have become imperceptible even to them and difficult for them to articulate. According to Swidler, in settled periods, "ideology has both diversified, by being adapted to varied life circumstances, and gone underground, so pervading ordinary experiences as to blend imperceptibly" into everyday life.[4] The daily routine can sometimes overshadow culture. But just because young people live and experience culture differently does not make it dead. It has instead settled into their lives and blended into their personal background. Participants in this study articulated their culture as unique and different, but were initially hesitant to define what their culture was. As students of our society, they were plagued by internal pressure to recite a definition. Instead, I encouraged them to sketch a unique vision—to paint their own picture. When they met this challenge, the picture that they painted was abstract, difficult even for them to convert from theory to practice. Students voiced a need for cultural resources on campus but were not be able to point to a specific cultural ritual, tradition, or practice that they expected of the university. This seems to be the professional challenge of cultural practitioners in higher education—to be able to interpret the portrait that students paint of their culture into viable programs and resources that will both interest students and help them to develop. The charge of the cultural practitioner is to bring this imperceptible image of culture into focus on campus and to ensure that the beauty of the portrait is not overwhelmed by the shadows of department tradition, repetition, and stagnation. We have to ignite creativity and innovation in the field of higher education. Sir Ken Robinson[5] has advanced the notion that education actually educates the creativity out of people. We are taught to conform, to be robots engaged in repetitive actions, to not question, and to be quiet. I don't think students are the only victims. Our standards of practice, tendency to "benchmark" (copy) what others have done, "traditional" programs (that appeal to only the administrators who create them), and inability to brainstorm a structure or format for a program beyond a lecture, performance, retreat, dialogue group, or film showing illustrate that educators are also being drained of creativity. When I first graduated from college, I spent a year working in the field of public relations. I did not have a serious media-driven PR job. I had the fun and creative type of job that sent me all over the country planning events and coming up with idea after idea that would wow people and give them the time of their lives. As an Oscar Mayer Wienermobile driver (yes, I drove the hotdog), I was continuously challenged to find new and creative ways to make something as simple as a grill with a hotdog new and exciting. Later, as an event-marketing executive at Momentum, IMC, I recall that randomly throughout the day a whistle would be blown and everyone would stop what we were doing to go into the "brainstorm" room and come up with an outrageous event idea for the Coca-Cola Company (our primary client). These sessions were filled with energy and creative challenge. I am very thankful for those brief opportunities to work with energetic and creative thinkers and doers. Being constantly pushed to expand my innovative limits—to think differently, creatively, and in an outrageous manner—served me well during my years working in university cultural centers. Every cultural event that I planned turned to gold and excited students. We must get energized about the possibilities of doing things differently and blazing new paths.

Finally, students revealed that culture was authentic, honest, and real. It was most often about the process of negotiating oppression and ambition, race and ethnicity, ritual and purpose, discretion and disclosure. The full image of culture was revealed when family or community members were brave and bold enough to tell the true cultural story. Culture was about honest revelation—experiences that completely reveal true selves with all the positive attributes and negative shortcomings. To truly be a cultural group member or ally you must be willing to admit to your mistakes and shortcomings. As educators, we can learn a lot from this. We are not perfect, so why can we not take criticism or admit that our departments could do better? These students admitted to serious personal failures. They admitted to faults and areas in their lives that needed to be improved. If they could so honestly and bravely evaluate themselves, we must at least try to do better with honestly evaluating our professional performance and the work production of the departments that we lead. When was the last time that you faced your professional faults head-on as did these brave students? What programs on your campus need to be discarded? When was the last time you had a truly *new* idea? How do you push yourself every year to surpass your own expectations? This study illustrates that when you bare yourself as an act of genuine love and desire to be made better, the cultural community embraces you and takes hold of those shortcomings to help you transform them. That the cultural experience allowed members to be their full and honest selves was a critical piece of learning for me. Whether it was stories of mothers crying at the kitchen table, parents managing money poorly, or parental drug addiction, these stories illustrated that regardless of your shortcomings and in spite of your mistakes culture is a space in which you can still be loved.

Inspiring Cultural Leadership in Contemporary Young Adults

Exploring culturally influenced leadership means exploring the full spectrum of a leader's life experience. Pulling together the literature on leadership and culture with the lived insight and wisdom from cultural leaders and contemporary college students, we can conceptualize cultural leadership to include five key characteristics:

1. **An understanding of the cultural self.** Cultural leaders are constantly exploring and deepening their understanding of their cultural values, beliefs, and ideologies. Cultural leaders are reflective, wise, and holistic leaders who understand that the collective of their life experiences—in the classroom or on the block, in college or in church, through professional networks or through dysfunctional family trees—has made them who they are.

2. **A use of culture as a leadership tool.** Cultural leadership draws on things like the cultural arts, family and community fellowship, spirituality, and other creative forms of expression to create social change. Cultural leadership values the potential of culture to serve as a community education tool to teach politics of survival and to create a space for dialogue, discussion, action, and change.

3. **A value for serving.** Like the family, community, or village that grooms culture, cultural leadership is a selfless act. Cultural leaders understand that leadership is not about hierarchy, position, or top-down structures.

4. **A sense of community love and rootedness.** Cultural leaders are rooted in the community (to both the people and the land) in such a way that they do not feel like outsiders even if they are. Ultimately, this deep connection, commitment, and loyalty to a community is rooted in love. Cultural leaders are driven by an ethic of love—a love for people, a love for justice, and the hope for all people to experience not only equality (equality allows for basic needs to be accessed and met) but also, more importantly, a life filled with joy and love (which is a higher state of being).

5. **A critical lens.** Navigating the world when you are a part of an underrepresented cultural group often causes you to view that world a bit differently. The lived experience of underrepresented ethnic groups has taught us that important change is made when we turn a critical eye toward social norms, laws, values, and behaviors. We must embrace the art of questioning. Cultural leadership compels us to voice and act on our criticisms in an effort to make our world more inclusive, democratic, and free.

Practical Implications

There are several considerations for practice in order to either create a cultural leadership program or incorporate cultural study into educational experiences:

1. Include exercises for students to reflect on the leadership lessons learned from their communities and families. Invite families into the process as either participants or facilitators.
2. Thoughtfully incorporate the use of the cultural arts as a tool for students to engage leadership (social action through poetry, performance, folk art, music).
3. Expand the canon of who and what you teach. Stretch further than simply including the major and popular social leaders of color. Reach to also include more localized citizens and families. And critically explore the contemporary and historical social issues that have deeply impacted the lives of oppressed peoples.
4. Connect with community-based leaders in new and exciting ways. Truly embracing the opportunities present in public scholarship allows our "community work" to be local, regional, national, or global in nature. It also allows us to reframe our interactions with communities beyond a "service" orientation. For example, some universities sponsor leadership study immersions on American Indian Reservations. Also, inviting community-based scholars to facilitate workshops on campus, guest lecture in classes, or help to develop a sustainable and mutually beneficial partnership can add important cultural knowledge to a leadership education program. Finally, global opportunities to study, observe, and engage leadership can potentially be a life-changing experience for students.

This approach may indeed define what a "cultural environment" is for students of color. It may consist less of institutional public statements, presentations, or written documents on the college's "commitment" to culture. Creating a cultural environment may instead be about doing the hard work and taking the difficult action of unconditionally loving students, supporting students, and providing truly adequate resources and spaces where they can be themselves without judgment or being made to feel that they are asking for too much. Establishing a truly authentic and loving cultural environment on our campuses requires the *courage* to truly transform both the physical and philosophical architecture of higher education.

Epilogue

Art is a crucial part of my existence—as a woman, as an educator, and even as a researcher. Every piece of work that I produce is at some level poetic. And so, rather than write traditional field notes as I conducted this study, I crafted from my notes a spoken poem summarizing the insights that I gained from this research, which I share below:

Cultural Legacy
Toby S. Jenkins

We need some inspiration . . . some fire
We need a spark or revelation to ignite our desire
To want more, to do more, to be more for our families
To understand what it means to lay down a legacy
To cultivate and grow, to sculpt and to mold . . . skills in another soul
That helps them to go farther . . . to be the constant gardener . . .
of their values and ideologies
To help them to navigate the geography of their destiny
To help them determine what direction to travel . . .
How to steer on dirt road or on gravel
That's sometimes filled with glass and rocks
To understand that sometimes life might frighten and shock
but there's a sign up ahead
A familial compass that has led
you to this point, so don't disappoint
them by missing the point
of why you were put here
They taught you to drive, open eyes no fear . . .
Because of them you can now steer
your life forward. So just wait
That spirit will tell you what exit to take
That memory will help you know when to brake . . .

Your ancestors' hopes and dreams are at stake
We are their garden—
The rose that they grew through hardened
Soil . . . The flower that they nurtured and toiled for
They taught us how to garden
and now it's time to put on the gloves and grow more
and be more and do more for my family
I need . . . to plant the seed . . . of a love ethic so strong . . .
That later generations and after several duplications
Of my genes . . . the spirit that I originally put in it
lives on
I want to pass down values and leave clues
for distant nephews that are confused
About what to do with their life
I want to put together the pieces of the puzzle of life for my nieces
And give them skills and confidence that increases
Their opportunities in life
That demands them to make the most of their life . . .
That commands their attention to take their life seriously . . .
I just want them to succeed me
I don't want to go the extra mile . . .
I want to go so far I wind up in exile trying to love my child
Because that child is my heaven
My infinite life support—My grandchild will be my resurrection
She will forever allow my soul to give insight and wisdom
My family's actions are the true judgment on my soul
And if they can do right because of some wisdom I told . . .
if they can grow old
Being guided by the cultural values that I sewed
onto the fabric of my family's foundation
Then let that be my motivation to lay . . . down . . . a legacy

To all of the elders whose spirits were named in this study, I say thank you for laying down a legacy—the cultural foundation from which all of these stories were told.

Appendix

Research Methods

> Every portrait that is painted with feeling is a portrait of the artist, not the sitter. The sitter is merely an accident, the occasion. It is not he who is revealed by the painter; it is rather the painter, who, on the coloured canvas, reveals himself. The reason I will not exhibit this picture is that I am afraid that I have shown in it the secret of my soul. —**Oscar Wilde,** quoted in S. Lawrence-Lightfoot and J. Davis, *The Art of Portraiture*

Qualitative Inquiry

I used qualitative inquiry for this research study, as it offered an opportunity for deep examination of the multiple dimensions of a very complex human topic. My goal, which was to paint a holistic picture of the concept of culture as described by students, fits well with the qualitative process. D. Krathwohl describes qualitative methods as particularly beneficial when seeking to determine how to understand a phenomenon.[1] This methodology, then, is ideal in the study of a very complex concept about which there is either little knowledge or when existing knowledge is manifold and varied. R. E. Stake lists several advantages to the use of qualitative methods. They include the ability to humanize a problem, to help people or situations come to life, to allow the researcher to get inside of others' world view, and to assist in attaching emotion or real feeling to a phenomenon that makes the study of it more consistent with how it is actually experienced in life.[2] Stake notes that the intent is "not necessarily to map and conquer the world but to sophisticate the beholding of it."[3] Krathwohl further expands the benefits by establishing when qualitative inquiry is most appropriate. I present four of these instances, which are particularly important to this study:

1. When research must emphasize discovery rather than validation
2. When the focus is on the internal dynamics of a situation or problem rather than on its effect or product
3. When the interest lies in the diversity and unique qualities among people
4. When examples are needed to put "meat" on statistical "bones"[4]

The last instance is particularly meaningful to this study. Many studies have substantially shown the need for and benefit of expanding cultural resources on college campuses.[5] The question that remains is "Now what?" Now that we agree that campuses must commit to cultural resources, now that culturally focused departments, centers, institutes, and human resources are increasing in number, how do we approach this concept of culture? As Krathwohl explains: "Qualitative research is especially helpful when it provides us with someone's perceptions of a situation that permits us to understand his or her behavior. For example, much has been made of how so-called culturally deprived children see the world as hopeless. But when, through qualitative research, a study reveals in detail the hopes, fears, dreams, and nightmares of a few cases that general statement takes on new meaning."[6]

This explanation offers an important insight regarding the issue of cultural practice. It may not be enough to simply know that students desire cultural opportunities if this knowledge is not complemented with a deeper understanding of what "culture" actually means and looks like to students. The ability to clearly understand the concept of culture as it is understood by the students we serve may have significant impact on the level of student engagement with cultural opportunities on campus and the meaningful growth that they obtain as a result of this engagement. In this regard, culture should be replicated not on the basis of outside definitions or administrative opinions of culture that may hold no relevance or meaning to students, but on the portrait that students themselves draw of culture.

Of particular significance for my study is the use of *narrative* to gain a deeper sense of the lived experience that is so much a part of qualitative inquiry. In outlining the key components of qualitative inquiry, T. Schram stresses that voice is generally critical to qualitative inquiry. This includes both the voice of the subject and the voice of the researcher. According to Schram, "Inquiry, like fieldwork, is a human endeavor in which personal contact and straight talk can carry you further along than academic posturing and heaped jargon."[7] Therefore, value is placed on research presentation that is as personal, as approachable, and as human as the subjects studied.

Methodological Approaches

I used *phenomenology* as the methodological approach of this study. C. Marshall and G. Rossman define *phenomenology* as the study of lived experience and how people understand this experience. It assumes that there is an "essence" to shared experiences that can be articulated through narration.[8] As J. Creswell notes, "Researchers search for the essential, invariant structure (essence) or the central underlying meaning of the experience and emphasize the intentionality of consciousness where experiences contain both the outward appearances and inward consciousness based on memory, image, and meaning."[9] Therefore, for this study, culture involves much more than the outward appearance of ritual, tradition, and symbol; it also involves the meanings that people attach to these experiences, other influences, and the histories that surround them. To an observer, culture might seem to be one set of experiences. But in the minds of those being observed, it might also involve a host of other experiences. Phenomenology involves the process of reduction to uncover the possible meanings of these experiences. This process also involves accounting for researcher prejudice by bracketing the researcher's personal experiences and by including intuition and imagination in the process to paint a broad portrait of the experience.[10] Phenomenology, therefore, is a creative process that welcomes the depth and complexity of the human experience.

Storytelling and Voice. We learn to love stories at a very early age. Stories serve to teach moral lessons, share knowledge, and pass on values. They provide us with a context to better understand complex issues or broad concepts. Stories help us make sense of the meanings of life experiences. According to J. Banks-Wallace, storytelling, the interactive process of sharing stories, is a vehicle for preserving culture and passing it on to future generations. In some cases, stories can serve as touchstones that evoke shared memories and feelings between the storyteller and the listener.[11] As a touchstone experience, listening to another person's story may bring forth memories or feelings and help the listener to better contextualize and understand his or her own experience—what it is to be a black woman or a latino male in the United States or why culture holds such special meaning for a person. Its historical role in African/African American and Native American cultures has been most widely noted. In many traditional African cultures, storytelling was an important and necessary social practice, with the griot, or story keeper, held in high regard.[12] Even in contemporary African American literature, the work of Zora Neale Hurston is viewed as one of the foundations for African American literature.[13] The stories that Hurston collected in the South in the early 1930s offer a glimpse of the lives of African Americans and the culture that was created out of their lived experiences. These stories sustain legacies by providing verbal pictures of the past that put the present more clearly into focus.

> The technique of storytelling transcends race, class, generations, and other differences and allows people to communicate on common ground through a common story. Storytelling is universal. It has its roots in ancient African societies, and for centuries, people have used stories to entertain and educate as well as to instill values and inspire people to action. Describing storytelling as a new nontraditional approach to advocacy sounds strange, given its historical roots, but in modern times, with the advent of complicated electronic media communication methods, storytelling has become a lost art. Organizers often overlook the power of the spoken word and of shared experiences as a way of communicating and moving people to action.[14]

The recent media and public interest in the slave narrative archives through countless television specials, theatrical productions, and texts also points to the continued value of storytelling. As John Henrike Clarke stated, "The role of history to a people is that of mother to a child. It tells you who you are, what you are, where you have been and where you are going."[15] In a time when social and historical scholars question the authenticity of history and social studies texts and warn against the strong influence of mass media in shaping social knowledge, the stories derived from the community—from families, elders, and children—provide a very important opportunity to understand what culture means to people and what factors contribute to its persisting importance.[16] Tavis Smiley shares a quote by Catherine Conant that further explains: "Over the course of the last century, the American culture largely abandoned oral stories and a setting for a collective imaginative experience. Today the norm is for people to be passive viewers, responding to a medium that offers images that are contrived and manipulated to evoke specific responses. Audience imagination is not required but rather their willingness to accept universal images they are shown."[17]

Allowing students an opportunity to truly reflect on their experiences—to get at the root of their culture—is an important aid to self-understanding and rebellion against negative social ideas. Smiley points out that reflection plays a crucial role in community action and cultural sustainability. He describes reflection as "the deliberate process of taking your actions into account, examining them, learning from them, and then adjusting your future actions in accordance with the lessons learned."[18] This definition seems to underscore the very idea of culture as a tool kit of experiences, values, and lessons that serve to inform how daily life is approached. The reflection shared through stories helps to sustain a sense of self—a proof of existence and history. Therefore, people cling to the stories of the past as they would to a warm and beautiful robe—culture is both a valuable garment to be worn and admired by others and a functional cloak to provide protection against external forces.

J. Featherstone has noted the value of using storytelling to inform research. He explains both the richness and complexity of the information gained through story and the significant responsibility of the researcher.

> The telling of stories can be a profound form of scholarship moving serious study close to the frontiers of art in the capacity to express complex truth and moral context in intelligible ways. . . . The methodologies are inseparable from the vision. Historians have used narrative as a way in which to make sense of lives and institutions over time, but over years they have grown abashed by its lack of scientific rigor. Now, as we look for ways to explore context and describe the thick textures of lives over time in institutions with a history, we want to reckon with the author's own stance and commitment to the people being written about. Storytelling takes on a fresh importance.[19]

In this study, which relies heavily on the use of story, voice is the most crucial element of data collection, data analysis, and conclusion. It is the student voice that is collected, the student voice that is analyzed, and ultimately the student voice that gives form and definition to the concept of culture. In this regard, the final shape of culture is formed by the students' shared thoughts. This process allows student cultures to be defined on their own terms. This study provides a clearer understanding of how students conceptualize the broad idea of culture, which can then be more thoughtfully approached within educational practice.

Portraiture. Given the focus on culture and cultural narratives, this study also used portraiture as a methodology that extends the work of phenomenology. Portraiture combines science and art to paint a holistic picture of an experience or phenomenon. Sara Lawrence-Lightfoot and J. Davis, the creators of this method of inquiry, offer the following description: "Portraiture is a method of qualitative research that blurs the boundaries of aesthetics and empiricism in an effort to capture the complexity, dynamics, and subtlety of human experience and organizational life. Portraits seek to record and interpret the perspectives and experiences of the people they are studying, documenting their voices and their visions—their authority, knowledge, and wisdom."[20]

Portraiture shares in the traditions and values of phenomenology, but it expands the boundaries of phenomenology by combining "empirical and aesthetic description; in its focus on the convergence of narrative and analysis; in its goal of speaking to broader audiences beyond the academy; in its standard of authenticity rather than reliability and validity; and in its explicit recognition of the use of self as the primary research instrument for documenting and interpreting the perspectives and experiences of the people and the cultures being studied."[21] Innate in portraiture is the idea of boundary crossing. Through the science of portraiture, the researcher crosses personal boundaries to gain a more intimate understanding of participants. And through the art of portraiture, the researcher crosses creative boundaries to blend art and science through narrative portraits that share stories and convey meaning in ways that other traditional methods may not allow.[22] As an example of boundary crossing, Lawrence-Lightfoot and Davis offer W.E.B. Du Bois. If I consider Zora Neale Hurston to be the grandmother of story collecting, then Sara Lawrence-Lightfoot and Davis clearly view Du Bois as the grandfather of boundary-crossing research. "W.E.B. Du Bois was the quintessential boundary crosser. More than any other social scientist I can think of, in his work and in his life, Du Bois captured the interdisciplinary as he moved from social philosophy to empirical sociology to autobiography to political essays to poetry and literature to social activism. He invented a way of being, a point of view, a style of work that quite naturally, dynamically, organically integrated science, art, history, and activism."[23]

By living in the communities with the people about whom he wrote, Du Bois crossed personal boundaries that allowed him to better understand their experience. But also, in writing across academic boundaries, Du Bois, as a researcher, illustrated the various methods through which a concept can be understood. The value that portraiture places on this interdisciplinary approach to research in many ways is also a value for the holistic researcher, who is able to integrate all his or her personal and professional interests, talents, and modes of expression into the work. As a researcher, I am able to use portraiture to more fully present how I view and analyze the world, as an educator, artist, and activist. Moreover, portraiture sees imagination as a crucial skill that is needed to accurately "draw" cultures. Creative imagination is needed to provide a thick description that both interprets people's experiences and presents content in a manner that readers are able to understand and imagine. Portraitists are always seeking the responses "Oh, I get it" and "Oh, I see."[24]

By allowing the researcher to cross boundaries along lines of the art and science of his or her work, portraiture provides the ability to paint a more vivid, fuller, more accurate portrait of the whole. Lawrence-Lightfoot explains this phenomenon by sharing her personal experiences as an artist reexamining her earlier work. She describes the act of looking at a portrait as different from the act of looking into a mirror. A portrait is not a simple replica—it is a creative interpretation that projects the essence of the artist or the subject. Qualities of character and history, experience and memory are painted onto the canvas. This approach may be more in line with what it means to truly examine culture. It implies creation rather than copying—it is not something we can simply look at and duplicate; we must, instead, look into it and produce it. In this regard, Lawrence-Lightfoot's goal in establishing this methodology was to create a venue for creative and deep exploration. As she states, "I wanted the written pieces to convey the authority, wisdom, and perspective of the subjects, but I wanted them to feel—as I had felt—that the portrait did not look like them, but somehow managed to reveal their essence. I wanted them to experience the portraits as both familiar and exotic, so that in reading them they would be introduced to a perspective that they had not considered before."[25] Therefore, a portrait is not a stagnant description; it is a complex result of living and sharing. And the portrait should provide insight even to those who participate as subjects, for whom reading a portrait should be more than reading a biography; it should unveil patterns, meanings, purposes, and values that may have been separated by the rituals of daily life and are not easily sewn together by those who do not analyze life as a professional practice.

Setting and Context. Three sites were used in this study. The first school is a smaller campus of a large predominantly white university in the Northeast. The university as a whole has a student body of over 50,000. The campus houses 5,500 undergraduates and a little over 3,500 graduate students. The campus is located in an urban city. It is a campus that blends into the city landscape physically and culturally. The college sits in a predominantly African American community within a very culturally diverse city. City demographics establish the city as 53 percent black or African American, 26 percent white or Euro-American, and 14 percent from other racial groups. Among the three major racial groups, 29 percent of residents are Latino or Hispanic (from any race). Ninety percent of the student body comes from within the state. The university undergraduate student population is 53 percent female, and of the 5,500 students, 3,800 classify themselves as African American, Asian, Latino, or other. On this particular campus, white students constitute only 29 percent of the student population. Both on the campus and beyond, a high level of structural diversity exists.

The second school is located in a largely rural setting. The total university system has a student enrollment of a little over 80,000 students. This particular campus houses over 40,000 students. The major differences in the size of the student populations and in the location of both of the campuses allow for cross-analysis of both institution type (rural/urban) and size (small/large). Students of color constitute a little over 12 percent of the student population, or 5,300 students—a stark contrast to the other campus, where students of color make up about 70 percent of the student body. The university is located in a city with a similar majority-white demographic structure; the town is 90 percent white.

The third school is located in the metropolitan D.C. area. It has a total enrollment of 32,562, with about 20,000 undergraduates. The school has about 4,000 Asian students, 2,500 African American students, 2,500 Latino students, 130 indigenous students, and 15,000 white students. Thus, the overall racial composition is about 10,000 students of color and 15,000 white students—by and large a close number.

Participants. The university sites were selected on the basis of the existence of a culturally focused leadership development experience. All institutions offer a semester-long cultural leadership course in which students learn leadership development and explore the unique way that culture influences the leadership proxy. This study is less concerned with the actual experience of the course than with the groups of students who participated in the course. In order to ensure that student perceptions were not influenced by external definitions of culture, data collection took place prior to any formal discussions on culture. The cohort structure of both groups allowed initial group interviews and individual follow-up. Because these students met regularly, with the assistance of the program administrators, I was able to ensure 100 percent completion of the self-authored narratives.

A sample of 18 students of color participated in the original study; in the five years since its completion, more than 100 young adults came to participate in the larger study, bringing the total to 118 cultural self-portraits examined for this book. Students ranged from freshmen through seniors. The study included 30 white students; 20 Asian American students; 42 African American, West Indian, or African students and 26 Latino students.

Data Collection Procedures

The study included two phases of research. The first phase focused on the perceptions of the concept of culture and the role of cultural engagement in college. I conducted group interviews of students to determine how students defined culture and what structures they felt constituted their culture. The interview questions were semistructured to allow all group members to contribute and to feed off one another's responses. The second phase of research engaged students in writing a cultural self-portrait. The self-portrait is a written narrative of any length that shares students' cultural stories—what culture means to them, their family histories, influences and experiences that they believe impact their culture. They share this information by telling the personal stories of their lives, which results in a more in-depth and individual portrait of their cultural selves. I imposed no limit to or requirement for the length, in order to allow students the freedom to write intimately and freely.

Students had six weeks from the time of the interview to write their self-portraits independently. I encouraged them to include any other information that they perceived as relevant, including information that was not covered in the questions listed, photographs, and artifacts. The self-portraits provided a deeper view of the participants' cultural lives by allowing the students to explore the concept of culture through private, personal reflection and dialogue with their families. I encouraged the students to reflect on their family histories in order to articulate their culture in a way that may not have been possible during the interviews. Also, rather than provide students with an external definition of culture into which to fit their experiences, I asked them to take time to reflect deeply on their past experiences and histories, including but not limited to values, traditions, and rituals and to include such elements in their stories only if they saw fit. Students' broad experiences in life served as the larger story from which I could identify cultural themes, values, traditions, practices, and guiding ethics. Structuring the self-portrait in this way allowed both students with concrete ideas about culture and students with a less-clearly defined articulation of culture an opportunity to reflect on cultural experiences and concepts. These reflections, when analyzed, revealed student ideologies and definitions of culture in a contemporary America.

Notes

Introduction

1. Frye 2011, 2.
2. Maxwell 2007.
3. Bordas 2007, 9.
4. Montuori 2005, 374.
5. Ibid., 375.
6. Featherstone 1989, 377.
7. Barnes 1990; Delgado 1990; Banks-Wallace 2002; Ladson-Billings 1998; Ladson-Billings and Tate 1995.
8. Barnes 1990, 1864.
9. Delgado 1990.
10. Surhone, Timpledon, and Marseken 2010, 10.
11. Stanford 1996, 36.
12. Jenkins 2009a.

Chapter 1: There's No Place like Home

1. Gates 2007, 91.
2. Takaki 1994.
3. Woodson 1977.
4. hooks 1999.
5. Ibid., 71.
6. Ibid., 73.
7. Allen 1992, 87.
8. Bynoe 2004; Smiley 2006; Marable 2005; Powell 2006.
9. Du Bois 1903.
10. Ibid., 1.

11. Dalai Lama 1998, 1.
12. hooks 1999, 51.
13. Marable 2005, 43.
14. Jenkins 2003.
15. Patton 2006; Smiley 1998.
16. Gates 1995, ix.
17. Bowles 2006; Macleod 1995.
18. Perry and Ting 2002.
19. Ibid., 5.
20. Hurtado et al. 1998.
21. Yosso 2005.
22. O'Neill and Chatman 1999.
23. Ibid., 2.
24. Ibid., 3.
25. Garrod and Kilkenny 2007, 106.
26. Chavez and Guido-Dibrito 1999, 44.
27. hooks 1994.
28. Ogbu 1992.
29. Baxter-Magolda 1992.
30. Ibid.
31. Swidler 1986.
32. Ibid.
33. See Collins 1986.
34. Ibid., S22.
35. Bennett and Bennett 2004.
36. Ibid.
37. Karenga 2005.
38. Ibid.
39. Ibid.
40. Marable 1998, 43.

Chapter 2: A Half-Full Glass of Family Bonds

1. Chavez and Guido-Dibrito 1999.
2. Rock 1999.
3. Boyd and Allen 1995.
4. Schneider and Schneider 2001.
5. Ibid.
6. Boyd and Allen 1995, 25
7. Edelman 1989, 2–3.
8. Ibid.
9. Ibid., 16.
10. Boyd and Allen 1995.
11. McCall 1995.
12. Office of Minority Health, 2010.
13. Columbo et al. 2010, 27.
14. Pew Research Center 2011.

15. Ibid.
16. Chavez and Guido-Dibrito 1999.
17. Ibid.
18. Ibid., 140.
19. Smiley 2006.
20. Ibid., 6.
21. Patillo-McCoy 2000.
22. Ibid., 54.
23. Angelou 1994.
24. Ibid., 130.

Chapter 3: A Politic of Survival

1. Shakur 2003.
2. Edelman 1992.
3. Ibid., vii.

Chapter 4: Education, Culture, and Freedom

1. Jenkins 2009a.
2. Jehangir 2010.
3. Rodriquez 2001, 30.
4. Rodriguez 2001; Jenkins 2009a.
5. Jehangir 2010, 26.
6. Shockley 2008.
7. Rendon, Nora, and Jalomo 2004.
8. Hurtado 1996.
9. Rendon, Nora, and Jalomo 2008, 128.
10. Padilla and Perez 2003.
11. Ibid., 39.
12. Hoxie 1984.
13. Wright 1996, 87.
14. Lynn 2006, 110.
15. Campbell 2008.
16. Ibid., 9.
17. Penn Center Web site 2011.
18. Campbell 2008, 5.
19. Lynn 2006, 115.
20. See Delpit 2001; Stedman 1997; Tharp and Gallimore 1991.
21. See NCES 2004.
22. See Asante 2007.
23. Shockley 2008.
24. Gause 2008.
25. Freire 1970, 47.
26. Gause 2008.
27. Cody 2011.
28. Boyer 1997, 76–77.

29. Ibid., 64.
30. Jenkins and Walton 2005, 2006.
31. Jenkins and Walton 2006, 2.

Chapter 5: Art, Land, and Spirit

1. B. Robinson 1995–2008.
2. Curtis 2010.
3. Ibid.
4. Harvey 1999.
5. Ibid., 70.
6. Mitchell 2002, 51.
7. King 1963.
8. Ibid., 23.
9. hooks 2001, 72–73.
10. Dalai Lama, n.d.
11. Kessler 2000.
12. See Fowler 1981, 24 (cited in Kessler 2000).
13. Ibid., 59.
14. Rendon 2008, 2.
15. Santow 2008, 71.
16. Ibid., 73.
17. Jenkins 2011, 11.
18. Bachin 2008, 351.
19. Ibid, 352.
20. Tuan 1977. 149.
21. hooks 2009, 6.
22. Jenkins 2005.
23. Jenkins 2006.
24. Bythewood and Coker 2009.
25. Bynoe 2004, 20.
26. Ibid., 21.
27. Karenga, n.d.
28. "Def Poetry Jam on Tour" 2001.
29. Hughes, n.d.
30. McKay, n.d.
31. Dyson and Sohail 2009.
32. Collins 1986.
33. Jenkins 2006.
34. hooks 1994.
35. Ibid.
36. Ibid., 46.
37. Jenkins 2006, 2011.
38. Jenkins 2009a.
39. Collins 2000.
40. King 1968.
41. Ibid., 34.

Chapter 6: Cultural Heritage Still Matters

1. Nam 2001, xxxi.
2. Ibid.
3. Ibid., xxx.
4. Chavez and Guido-Dibrito 1999.
5. Ibid., 40.
6. Baghir-Zada 1999.
7. African Americans in the 20th Century. Available at www.courses.rochester.edu, p. 1.
8. Waters 2001.
9. Johnson and Smith 1998.
10. Waters 2001.
11. Ibid.
12. Ibid.

Chapter 7: The House That Struggle Built

1. Jenkins 2006.
2. Patton 2006.
3. Swidler 1986.
4. Ibid., 3.
5. K. Robinson 2010.

Appendix

1. Krathwohl 1998.
2. Stake 1995.
3. Ibid., 229.
4. Krathwohl 1998.
5. Hurtado 1996; Harper 2006; Milem and Hakuta 2000. See also Tierney 2002, 216; Allen 1992.
6. Krathwohl 1998, 231.
7. Schram 2003, 54.
8. Marshall and Rossman 1999.
9. Creswell 1998, 42.
10. Ibid.
11. Banks-Wallace 2002.
12. Ibid.
13. Gates 1989.
14. Smiley 2006, 74.
15. Quoted in Snipes and Bourne 1996.
16. hooks 1994.
17. Quoted in Smiley 2006, 75.
18. Ibid., 77.
19. Featherstone 1989, 377.
20. Lawrence-Lightfoot and Davis 1997, xv.

21. Ibid., 13.
22. Ibid.
23. Ibid., 7.
24. Ibid.
25. Ibid., 4.

References

Allen, W. 1992. "The Color of Success: African-American College Student Outcomes at Predominantly White and Historically Black Public Colleges and Universities." *Harvard Educational Review* 62 (1): 32–50.

Angelou, Maya. 1994. *The Complete Collected Poems of Maya Angelou.* New York: Random House.

Asante, M. 2007. *The Role of Afro-centricity.* Available at http://www.asante.net/articles/42/the-role-of-an-afrocentric-ideology/.

Bachin, Robin. 2008. "Mapping Out Spaces of Race Pride: The Social Geography of Leisure on the South Side of Chicago, 1900–1919." In *"We Shall Independent Be": African American Place Making and the Struggle to Claim Space in the United States*, ed. Angel David Nieves and Leslie M. Alexander, 351–367. Boulder: University of Colorado Press.

Baghir-Zadaís, R. 1999. "Positions of Ethnic Minorities in Contemporary Society." *Southwest Educational Development Laboratory* 4 (1): 13–38.

Banks-Wallace, J. 2002. "Talk That Talk: Storytelling and Analysis Rooted in African American Oral Tradition." *Qualitative Health Research* 12 (3): 410–426.

Barnes, R. 1990. "Race Consciousness: The Thematic Content of Racial Distinctiveness in Critical Race Scholarship." *Harvard Law Review* 103 (8): 91–94.

Baxter-Magolda, M. 1992. *Knowing and Reasoning in College: Gender Related Patterns in Student Intellectual Development.* San Francisco: Jossey-Bass.

Bennett, J. M., and M. J. Bennett. 2004. *Developing Intercultural Competence: A Reader.* Portland, OR: Intercultural Communication Institute.

Bordas, Juana. 2007. *Salsa, Soul, and Spirit: Leadership for a Multicultural Age.* San Francisco: Berrett-Koehler Publishers.

Bowles, W. 2006. *Cultural Capital.* Available at http://www.williambowles.info/mimo/refs/tece1ef.htm.

Boyd, H., and R. Allen. 1995. *Brotherman: The Odyssey of Black Men in America—An Anthology*. New York: One World Publishers.

Boyer, E. 1997. *Scholarship Reconsidered: Priorities of the Professoriate*. Stanford, CA: Carnegie Foundation for the Advancement of Teaching.

Bynoe, Y. 2004. *Stand and Deliver: Political Activism, Leadership, and Hip Hop Culture*. New York: Soft Skull Press.

Bythewood, R., and C. Coker. 2009. *Notorious*. Motion picture. Los Angeles: Twentieth Century Fox.

Campbell, E. 2008. *Gullah Cultural Legacies*. Self-published.

Chavez, A., and F. Guido-Dibrito. 1999. "Racial and Ethnic Identity and Development." *New Directions for Adult and Continuing Education* 84:10–32.

Cody, A. 2011. "Confronting the Inequality Juggernaut: A Q&A with Jonathan Kozol." Available at http://blogs.edweek.org/teachers/living-in-dialogue/2011/07/time_to_get_off_our_knees_why.html.

Collins, P. H. 1986. "Learning from the Outsider Within: The Sociological Significance of Black Feminist Thought." *Social Problems* 33 (6): S14–S32.

———. 2000. *Black Feminist Thought*. New York: Routledge.

Columbo, G., R. Cullen, and B. Lisle. 2010. *Rereading America: Cultural Context for Critical Thinking and Writing*. New York: Bedford–St. Martin's Press.

Creswell, J. 1998. *Qualitative Inquiry and Research Design: Choosing among Five Traditions*. Thousand Oaks, CA: Sage Publications.

Curtis, E. 2010. "Five Myths about Mosques in America." *Washington Post*, August 10.

Dalai Lama. 1998. *The Art of Happiness: A Handbook for Living*. London: Hodder Press.

———. n.d. "The Paradox of Our Age." http://tumblr.com/tagged/the-paradox-of-our-age.

"Def Poetry Jam on Tour." 2001. Available at http://www.defpoetryjamontour.com/newsday_01.html.

Delgado, R. 1990. "When a Story Is Just a Story: Does Voice Really Matter?" *Virginia Law Review* 76 (1): 95–111.

Delpit, L. 2001. "Education in a Multicultural Society: Our Future's Greatest Challenge." In *Exploring Socio-cultural Themes in Education*, 2nd edition, ed. J. H. Strouse, 203–211. Upper Saddle River, NJ: Merrill Prentice-Hall.

Du Bois, W.E.B. 1903. "The Talented Tenth." *The Negro Problem: A Series of Articles by Representative Negroes of To-day*. Available at http://www.yale.edu/glc/archive/1148.htm.

Dyson, M., and D. Sohail. 2009. *Born to Use Mics*. New York: Civitas Books.

Edelman, M. 1989. *Families in Peril*. Cambridge, MA: Harvard University Press.

———. 1992. *The Measure of Our Success*. New York: HarperCollins.

Featherstone, J. 1989. "Balm in Gilead." *Harvard Educational Review* 59:367–378.

Fowler, J. 1981. *Stages of Faith: The Psychology of Human Development and the Quest for Meaning*. San Francisco: Harper and Row.

Freire, P. 1970. *Pedagogy of the Oppressed*. New York: Herder and Herder.

Frye, M. 2011. "Oppression." *Feminist Reading Group*. Available at http://feministtheoryreadinggroup.wordpress.com/2010/11/23/marilyn-frye-the-politics-of-reality-oppression/.

Garrod, A., and R. Kilkenny. 2007. *Balancing Two Worlds: Asian American College Students Tell Their Life Stories.* Ithaca, NY: Cornell University Press.

Gates, H. 1989. "Introduction: Narration and Cultural Memory in African American Tradition." In *Talk That Talk: An Anthology of African American Storytelling,* ed. L. Goss and M. Barnes, 15–19. New York: Simon and Schuster/Touchstone.

———. 1995. *Colored People: A Memoir.* New York: First Vintage Books.

———. 2007. *Finding Oprah's Roots: Finding Your Own.* New York: Crown Publishing Group.

Gause, C. P. 2008. *Integration Matters: Navigating Identity, Culture and Resistance.* New York: Peter Lang.

Gordon, D. 1993. "Worlds of Consequence: Feminist Ethnography as Social Action." *Critique of Anthropology* 13 (4): 429–443.

Harper, S. R. 2006. *Black Male Students at Public Flagship Universities in the U.S.: Status, Trends, and Implications for Policy and Practice.* Washington, DC: Joint Center for Political and Economic Studies.

Harvey, A. 1999. *Son of Man: The Mythical Path to Christ.* New York: Tarcher Press.

hooks, b. 1994. *Teaching to Transgress.* London: Routledge.

———. 1999. *Salvation: Black People and Love.* New York: Harper Perennial.

———. 2001. *All about Love: New Visions.* New York: HarperCollins.

———. 2009. *Belonging: A Culture of Place.* New York: Routledge.

Hoxie, F. 1984. *A Final Promise: The Campaign to Assimilate the Indians, 1880–1920.* Lincoln: University of Nebraska Press.

Hughes, L. n.d. "Let America Be America." Available at http://www.americanpoems. com/poets/Langston-Hughes/2385.

Hurtado, S. 1996. *How Diversity Affects Teaching and Learning.* Educational Record. Washington, DC: American Council on Education.

Hurtado, S., J. F. Milem, A. Clayton-Perderson, and W. A. Allen. 1998. "Enhancing Campus Climates for Racial/Ethnic Diversity: Educational Policy and Practice." *Review of Higher Education* 21 (3): 279–302.

Jehangir, R. 2010. *Higher Education and First Generation Students: Cultivating Community, Voice and Place for the New Majority.* New York: Palgrave Macmillan.

Jenkins, T. 2003. "The Color of Service." *About Campus Magazine* (May–June): 30–31.

———. 2005. "The Definition of a 'Soldier.'" Available at Glossmagazineonline.com.

———. 2006. "Mr. Nigger: The Challenges of Educating African American Males in American Society." *Journal of Black Studies* 37 (1): 127–155.

———. 2008. "The Five Point Plan: A Practical Framework for University Cultural Practice." *About Campus Magazine, College Student Educators International* 13 (2): 25–28.

———. 2009a. "A Portrait of Culture in Contemporary America." *NASPA Journal* 46 (2): 131–162.

———. 2009b. "A Seat at the Table I Set: Beyond Social Justice Allies." *About Campus Magazine, College Student Educators International* 14 (5): 27–29.

———. 2011a. "A Beautiful Mind: Black Male Intellectual Identity and Hip-Hop Culture." *Journal of Black Studies* 42, no. 8 (November): 1231–1251.

———. 2011b. "The Culture of the Kitchen: Recipes for Transformative Education within the African American Cultural Experience." *About Campus* 16, no. 2 (May/June): 11–19.

Jenkins, T., and C. Walton. 2005. "Setting the Stage for Character Development through Culturally Specific Advising Practices." *Journal of College and Character* 2 (2): 1–6.

——. 2006. "The Tri-sector Model of Cultural Practice: A Framework for Implementing Culture on Campus." In *Campus Commons: Building Inclusive Multicultural Communities through College Unions and Student Activities*, ed. Shaun R. Harper, 87–101. Bloomington, IN: ACUI Press.

Johnson, C., and P. Smith. 1998. *Africans in America: America's Journey through Slavery*. WGBH Series Research Team. New York: Harcourt Brace.

Karenga, M. 2005. *Kwanzaa: A Celebration of Family, Community and Culture*. Commemorative Edition. Los Angeles: University of Sankore Press.

——. n.d. "African Centered Education." Available at http://www.black-collegian.com/african/karenga.shtml.

Kessler, R. 2000. *The Soul of Education*. Alexandria, VA: Association of Supervision and Curriculum Development.

King, M. L., Jr. 1963. *Strength to Love*. Atlanta: First Fortress Press.

——. 1968. *Where Do We Go from Here: Chaos or Community?* Boston: Beacon Press.

Krathwohl, D. 1998. *Methods of Education and Social Science Research*. Long Grove, IL: Waveland Press.

Ladson-Billings, G. 1998. "Just What Is Critical Race Theory and What Is It Doing in a Nice Field like Education?" *Qualitative Studies in Education* 11 (1): 7–24.

Ladson-Billings, G., and W. Tate. 1995. "Toward a Critical Race Theory of Education." *Teachers College Record* 97 (1): 48–68.

Lawrence-Lightfoot, S., and J. Davis. 1997. *The Art and Science of Portraiture*. San Francisco: Jossey-Bass.

Lynn, M. 2006. "Race, Culture, and the Education of African Americans." *Educational Theory* 56 (1): 107–119.

Macleod, J. 1995. "Ain't No Making It: Aspirations and Attainment in a Low Income Neighborhood." *Social Reproduction in Theoretical Perspective*. Boulder, CO: Westview Press.

Marable, M. 1998. *Black Leadership*. New York: Columbia University Press.

——. 2005. "Black Culture Centers: Politics of Survival and Identity." In *Living Black History: Resurrecting the African American Intellectual Tradition*, ed. F. Hord, 41–53. Chicago: Third World Press.

Marshall, C., and G. Rossman. 1999. *Designing Qualitative Research*. Thousand Oaks, CA: Sage Publications.

Maxwell, J. 2007. "Position Leaders Destined to Disappoint." Available at http://www.businessweek.com/careers/content/jul2007/ca20070712_286277.htm.

McCall, N. 1995. *Makes Me Wanna Holler: A Young Black Man in America*. New York: Vintage Press.

McKay, C. n.d. "Outcast." Available at http://rinabcana.com/pocmofthcday/indcx.php/category/claude-mckay/.

Milem, J., and K. Hakuta. 2000. "The Benefits of Racial and Ethnic Diversity in Higher Education." In *Minorities in Higher Education 1999–2000: Seventeenth Annual Status Report*, ed. D. J. Wilds, 39–103. Washington, DC: American Council on Education.

Mitchell, S. 2002. *Bhagavad Gita: A New Translation*. New York: Three Rivers Press.

Mohanty, C. T. 2003. *Feminism without Borders: Decolonizing Theory, Practicing Solidarity*. Durham, NC: Duke University Press.

Montuori, A. 2005. "Literature Review as Creative Inquiry: Reframing Scholarship as a Creative Process." *Journal of Transformative Education* 1. Available at 1-000 DOI: 10.1177/1541344605279381.

Nam, Vickie. 2001. *Yell-Oh Girls*. New York: HarperCollins.

NCES. 2004. "The Condition of Education 2004." Available at http://nces.ed.gov/pubs2004/2004076.pdf.

Nieves, A., and L. Alexander, eds. 2008."*We Shall Independent Be*": African American Place Making and the Struggle to Claim Space in the United States. Boulder: University of Colorado Press.

Office of Minority Health. 2010. *The African American Profile*. Available at minorityhealth.hhs.gov/templates/browse.aspx?lvl=2&lvlID=51.

Ogbu, J. 1992. "Understanding Cultural Diversity and Learning." *Educational Researcher* 21 (8): 5–14.

O'Neill, S., and C. Chatman. 1999. "Social Construction of Racial and Ethnic Identity among African American and White Adolescents." Ann Arbor, MI: Gender and Achievement Research Program, University of Michigan.

Padilla, A., and W. Perez. 2003. "Acculturation, Social Identity, and Social Cognition: A New Perspective." *Hispanic Journal of Behavioral Sciences* 25 (1): 35–55.

Patillo-McCoy, M. 2000. *Black Picket Fences: Privilege and Peril among the Black Middle Class*. Chicago: University of Chicago Press.

Patton, L. D. 2006. "The Voice of Reason: A Qualitative Examination of Black Student Perceptions of Black Culture Centers. *Journal of College Student Development* 47 (6): 628–644.

Penn Center Web site. 2011. Available at http://www.penncenter.com/.

Perry, A., and M. Ting. 2002. "Historical Vestiges of Discrimination in UM's Greek System." *Connections: Newsletter of the Consortium on Race, Class, and Gender Education*.

Pew Research Center. 2011. "Social and Demographic Trends" Wealth Gaps Rise to Historic Highs between Whites, Blacks, and Hispanics." Available at http://pewsocialtrends.org/2011/07/26/wealth-gaps-rise-to-record-highs-between-whites-blacks-hispanics.

Powell, K. 2006. *Open Letters to America: Essays by Kevin Powell*. New York: Soft Skull Press.

Reinharz, S. 1992. *Feminist Methods in Social Research*. New York: Oxford University Press.

Rendón, L. 2008. *Sentipensante: Sensing/Thinking Pedagogy*. Sterling, VA: Stylus Press.

Rendón, L., A. Nora, and R. Jalomo. 2004. "Theoretical Considerations in the Study of Minority Student Retention in Higher Education." In *Reworking the Student Departure Puzzle*, ed. J. M. Braxton, 5–25. Nashville, TN: Vanderbilt University Press.

Robinson, B. A. 1995–2008. "Beliefs of Native Americans, from the Arctic to the Southwest." Available at http://www.religioustolerance.org/nataspir3.htm.

Robinson, Ken. 2010. *Out of Our Minds: Learning to Be Creative*. Mankato, MN: Capstone Press.

Rock, C., producer. 1999. *Bigger and Blacker*. Motion picture. HBO.

Rodriguez, S. 2001. *Giants among Us: First Generation College Graduates Who Live Activist Lives*. Nashville, TN: Vanderbilt University Press.

Santow, M. 2008. "Self-Determination, Race, Space, and Chicago's Woodlawn Organization in the 1960s." In *"We Shall Independent Be": African American Place Making and the Struggle to Claim Space in the United States*, ed. A. D. Nieves and L. M. Alexander, 71–82. Boulder, CO: University of Colorado Press.

Schneider, D., and C. Schneider. 2001. *Slavery in America: From Colonial Times to the Civil War*. New York: Checkmark Books.

Schram, T. 2003. *Conceptualizing Qualitative Fieldwork Methods for Fieldwork in Education and Social Science*. Upper Saddle River, NJ: Merrill Prentice Hall.

Shakur, Tupac. *The Resurrection*. Documentary. MTV Networks and Amaru Entertainment, 2003.

Shockley, K. G. 2008. "Afrocentric Education Leadership: Theory and Practice." *International Journal of Education Policy and Leadership* 3 (3): 10–17.

Smiley, T. 2006. *The Covenant with Black America*. Chicago: Third World Press.

Snipes, Wesley, and S. C. Bourne. 1996. *A Great and Mighty Walk*. Motion picture. U.S. Cinema Guild.

Stake, R. E. 1995. *The Art of Case Study Research*. Thousand Oaks, CA: Sage Publications.

Stanford, M. 1996. "Hegemony." *New Perspective* 2 (3): 32–48.

Stedman, L. 1997. "International Achievement Differences: An Assessment of a New Perspective." *Educational Researcher* 26 (3): 4–15. Available at DOI: 10.3102/0013189X026003004.

Surhone, L., M. Timpledon, and S. Marseken. 2010. *Transnational Feminism*. Beau Bassin: Betascript Publishing.

Swidler, A. 1986. "Culture in Action: Symbols and Strategies." *American Sociological Review* 51:273–286.

Takaki, R. 1994. *A Different Mirror: A History of Multicultural America*. Boston: Back Bay Books.

Tharp, R., and R. Gallimore. 1991. *The Instructional Conversation: Teaching and Learning in Social Activity*. Research Report 2. Santa Cruz, CA: National Center for Research on Cultural Diversity and Second Language Learning, University of California.

Tierney, W. G. 2002. "Power, Identity, and the Dilemma of College Student Departure." In *Reworking the Student Departure Puzzle*, ed. J. M. Braxton, 120–143. Nashville, TN: Vanderbilt Issues in Higher Education.

Tuan, Yi-Fu. 1977. *Space and Place: The Perspective of Experience*. Minneapolis: University of Minnesota Press.

Waters, Mary C. 2001. *Black Identities: West Indian Immigrant Dreams and American Realities*. Paperback edition. New York: Russell Sage Foundation and Harvard University Press.

Woodson, C. G. 1977. *The Mis-education of the Negro*. New York: Associated Publishers.

Wright, B. 1996. "The 'Untameable Savage Spirit': American Indians in Colonial Colleges." In *Racial and Ethnic Diversity in Higher Education*, ed. C. Turner, M. Garcia, A. Nora, and L. Rendón, 84–97. Boston: ASHE Reader Series/Simon and Schuster.

Yosso, T. 2005. "Whose Culture Has Capital? A Critical Race Theory Discussion of Community Cultural Wealth." *Race, Ethnicity, and Education* 8 (1): 69–91.

Index

Toby S. Jenkins is Assistant Professor of Higher Education and Integrative Studies at George Mason University.